China's State Enterprises

"Li and Cheong have written a very important and highly readable book. The conventional wisdom about SOEs, like most Western writing on China, sees the latter through a Western prism. The result: it has got China wrong for almost four decades. In contrast, they ground their nuanced argument in Chinese reality rather than Western assumption. They show that the differences between state and private enterprises are blurred and the intrinsic role SOEs have played in China's transformation."

—Martin Jacques, *Author of the global best-seller* When China Rules the World: the End of the Western World and the Birth of a New Global Order

Ran Li • Kee Cheok Cheong

China's State Enterprises

Changing Role in a Rapidly Transforming Economy

palgrave
macmillan

Ran Li
Institute of China Studies
University of Malaya
Kuala Lumpur, Malaysia

Kee Cheok Cheong
Institute of China Studies
University of Malaya
Kuala Lumpur, Malaysia

ISBN 978-981-13-0175-9 ISBN 978-981-13-0176-6 (eBook)
https://doi.org/10.1007/978-981-13-0176-6

Library of Congress Control Number: 2018943396

Cover illustration: © travel images / Alamy Stock Photo
Cover design by Tom Howey

Printed on acid-free paper

This Palgrave Macmillan imprint is published by the registered company Springer Nature Singapore Pte Ltd.
The registered company address is: 152 Beach Road, #21-01/04 Gateway East, Singapore 189721, Singapore

Preface

The year 2018 marks the 40th anniversary of China's "Reform and Opening-up" policy launched by Chairman Deng Xiaoping. This opening up is striking not only because it represented a complete reversal of the policy of isolation and "self-reliance" implemented during Mao Zedong's nearly three decades of rule, but equally because it seized the imagination of China's observers, especially Western, with the promise of a China that will embrace democracy and surrender to the dictates of market economics.

Forty years on, China has indeed opened its economy to competition, and new reforms of state enterprises have just been announced. However, rather than letting the market rule the economic transactions, China has taken, to use Robert Wade's words for the title of his book, to "governing the market". Far from retreating, the state has thrown its weight behind its enterprises, enabling some to become world leaders in their respective areas of business. China has learned capitalism well, but is practicing state-led capitalism. As for embracing democracy, there has been scant evidence of convergence to Western norms. Yet, this alternative model that challenges the very core of "mainstream" political and economic governance has produced over three decades of spectacular and uninterrupted economic growth, earning China the reputation of "economic powerhouse".

How can this apparent paradox be explained? This book, about China's state enterprises, key institutions of the state that, given their importance, undoubtedly figure prominently in the country's economic growth, attempts to offer an explanation. Expanded and updated from a PhD thesis written by the first author, it takes a revisionist view, arguing that much of the criticism leveled against the China "model" is based on mistaken premises, particularly that Western assumptions of the role of the state and its enterprises are universally applicable and hence relevant to China. Arising from these assumptions are, first, the clear separation between state and civil society and second, that state enterprises are necessarily inefficient by virtue of ownership.

The book challenges these assumptions and views. It does this by integrating Chinese history into the narrative, emphasizing, in particular, the antiquity of the Chinese state which well predates the concept of nation state, now used to characterize all states, and the very notion of democracy itself. This does not mean that the Chinese reject foreign concepts. But historians have long recognized, much more than economists today, that China has always looked primarily to its long history for lessons as guides for action, adapting and assimilating foreign concepts to fit the Chinese condition. It also draws upon Chinese history to argue against the assumption of a clear state-society divide arguing that given the importance of "Guanxi" (relationships) this divide is less important than often assumed. It highlights the Chinese state's shift towards owning fully only enterprises considered strategic, controlling others through equity or through relationships with enterprise leaders, and allowing the remainder to be privatized or liquidated. And it cites alternative Western theories that support a larger role for the state than that envisaged by neoliberal arguments. Recognizing that even these cannot fully reflect the Chinese context, it argues for acknowledging China as a historical and/or civilization state.

These themes are brought into sharper focus via case studies of a 100% state-owned bank, the history of which explains China's insistence on ownership of major financial institutions, and of a state-owned enterprise that was gradually transformed by state-enterprise reforms into a state-controlled but market-oriented enterprise. Such an enterprise-level (bottom-up) view is seldom written about.

Updating and expanding the state enterprise story is important for several reasons. First, being current is very important given the rapidly shifting landscape of China's enterprise reforms. That these continue to be enacted over a 40-year period testifies to the gradualist approach adopted since 1978 but more importantly attests to the attention the Chinese state continues to confer upon its enterprises. Second, the "Going Out" Strategy and especially the Belt and Road Initiative clearly point to the state's reform efforts being directed to strengthen the state enterprise sector rather than diminish its role. This role consists increasingly of serving the country's strategic interests, both of technological and know-how acquisition and of expanding global influence, a role few if any other state enterprise in the world is called upon to perform.

Readers of this book will notice a Malaysian slant in the narrative. This is partly because both authors are currently based in Malaysia but also because as a node in China's Maritime Silk Road and a founding member of ASEAN, Malaysia can serve as a regional base for Chinese enterprises as they expand in the ASEAN region. Thus, both case studies of state enterprises have internationalized their operations to Malaysia. China's future plans to leverage its state enterprises in this region, as well as the response of Southeast Asians to China's growing role, will be an interesting subject for future research.

In writing this book, we acknowledge with much gratitude Professors Edmund Terence Gomez and Danny Wong Tze Ken who motivated us to turn the thesis into a book project. An intellectual debt is also owed to Martin Jacques whose writings and expressed views are consonant with ours in this volume. We also acknowledge Professor Rajah Rasiah who provided valuable advice during the first author's PhD study, as well as Professor Dwight H. Perkins who was very supportive to this book. To our many colleagues at the Institute of China Studies, University of Malaya, we acknowledge their contributions through the many discussions we had with them. We are also grateful to an anonymous reviewer of our manuscript appointed by the publisher.

Kuala Lumpur, Malaysia — Ran Li
Kuala Lumpur, Malaysia — Kee Cheok Cheong

Contents

About the Authors

Ran Li is a research fellow at Institute of China Studies, University of Malaya. She obtained her doctoral degree in economics from the University of Malaya in 2014. She has been studying the Chinese state and state enterprises, and other research areas like development economics, urban economics, and Chinese outward investment. Her specialization is in the transformation of China's state enterprises, state enterprise system, and China's political-economic system, and her current areas of research include China's global strategy and China-Malaysia economic relations. Her previous writings have appeared in a number of international journals such as *China: An International Journal*, *Engineering Economics*, *Cities*, *International Journal of China Studies*, and *Journal of Contemporary Asia*.

Kee Cheok Cheong is currently a senior research fellow at the Institute of China Studies, University of Malaya. A graduate of the University of Malaya, he obtained his PhD from the London School of Economics. He has held the positions of dean at the Faculty of Economics and Administration, University of Malaya, and senior economist at the World Bank, Washington, DC, for which he continues to consult after he left. Since his return, he has co-authored two books and book chapters, and his published work includes over 40 papers in academic journals. His research interests include economic development, transition economies particularly China and Vietnam, international economic relations, education and human capital, and economic history, specifically relating to the Chinese overseas.

Abbreviations

ABC	Agricultural Bank of China
AFC	Asian Financial Crisis
AIIB	Asia Infrastructure Investment Bank
AMCs	Assets Management Companies
APEC	Asia-Pacific Economic Cooperation
ASEAN	Association of Southeast Asian Nations
BOC	Bank of China
BoCom	Bank of Communications
BRI	Belt and Road Initiative
CAMCE	China CAMC Engineering Co. Ltd.
CBRC	China Banking Regulatory Commission
CCB	China Construction Bank
CCCC	China Communications Construction Company
CDB	China Development Bank
CEB	China Everbright Bank
CEO	Chief Executive Officer
CIRC	China Insurance Regulatory Commission
CSCEC	China State Construction Engineering Corporation
CSRC	China Securities Regulatory Commission
FDI	Foreign Direct Investment
GATS	General Agreement on Trade in Services
GFC	Global Financial Crisis
HKSCCNL	Hong Kong Securities Clearing Company Nominees Limited
HKSE	Hong Kong Stock Exchange

HSBC	Hong Kong and Shanghai Banking Corporation
ICBC	Industrial and Commercial Bank of China
ICT	Information and Communication Technology
IPO	Initial Public Offering
LLL	Linkage-Leverage-Learning
M&A	Mergers and Acquisitions
NPLs	Non-Performing Loans
OECD	Organisation for Economic Co-operation and Development
OFDI	Outward Foreign Direct Investment
PBC	People's Bank of China
PCBC	People's Construction Bank of China
PCT	Patent Cooperation Treaty
PRC	People's Republic of China
PwC	PricewaterhouseCoopers
R&D	Research and Development
SABCSF	Sino-American-British Currency Stabilization Fund
SAFE	State Administration of Foreign Exchange
SASAC	State-owned Assets Supervision and Administration Commission
SETC	State Economic and Trade Commission
SEZs	Special Economic Zones
SRC	Soviet Republic of China
SSE	Shanghai Stock Exchange
TNCs	Transnational Corporations
TVEs	Township and Village Enterprises
VASs	Value-Added Services
WIPO	World Intellectual Property Organization
WTO	World Trade Organization

List of Figures

List of Tables

CHAPTER 1

Introduction

1.1 The Chinese State and Economic Growth

Over a century after its eclipse, China has arrived again at global center stage,[1] drawing increasing attention from economists, political scientists, international relations experts, other scholars, and observers. This attention derives in large measure from the fact that not only has China achieved impressive economic growth hitherto unmatched in magnitude and duration but also it has done so under a political system and using strategies which are quite different from those adopted by most other countries. Chinese economic growth is built on a political system that has collapsed in many other countries including the Soviet Union. Its economic policies also differ from what most other countries implement. The dominant institutional framework is what the Chinese leadership calls "socialism with Chinese characteristics" which keeps the Chinese Communist Party in the central role. But the reality is that China has a mixed economy in which the state has a major guiding role but with detailed economic decisions being to a large extent decentralized to lower level government.

China's emergence as an economic power has brought increased scrutiny of the manner of its rise. That this rise has relied on state power and is at variance with the approach favored and followed by advanced countries has led to criticism of the state and its institutions over which it exercises authority through ownership or control. Criticism leveled at the Chinese state takes two forms. The first is that its political order of authoritarian rule is unsustainable and will ultimately be overtaken by forces for

R. Li, K. C. Cheong, *China's State Enterprises*,
https://doi.org/10.1007/978-981-13-0176-6_1

democratization. Because the dominant political system in the world is democratic government in its various forms, many believe China must converge to this norm. Thus, Pei (2006) notes:

> if current trends continue, China's political system is more likely to experience decay than democracy … the very policies that the party adopted … are compounding the political and social ills that threaten its long-term survival.

The second is that authoritarianism cannot coexist with a true market economy. Hence, efforts to graft Western institutions onto an authoritarian structure also will not succeed. So commentators think that the Chinese political system must collapse, and even market reform under this system cannot work. For instance, Chang (2010) concluded that "China cannot make much progress toward (the rule of law), at least as long as the Communist Party is around." The second criticism, by extension, challenges the efficacy of China's numerous state enterprises, which have historically played a major role in the economy, and they need to be reformed through privatization or liquidation (Lal, 2006).[2]

Yet China's experience since the late 1970s has defied these predictions. It has achieved rapid economic growth for over three decades, through a model of growth that, though not quite approaching that of the developmental state, can nevertheless be described as state-led, or, at a minimum, state-guided. Unlike the rest of the world, China follows state-led growth, not private sector growth. State enterprises are at the heart of this model.

Given China's strategy, state enterprises remain major players in the economy. Already the largest enterprises in their respective sectors, they are growing larger. Szamosszegi and Kyle (2011) noted that "the observable state sector, which consists of state enterprises and the enterprises they directly control, accounts for approximately 40 percent of the Chinese output under reasonable assumptions."

For the above reasons, China's state enterprises have continued to occupy a central position in discussions of the role of the state. Despite their declining numbers and shares of industrial output and exports, these enterprises have remained major players in the economy. They are central to China's state-led growth strategy, but they have also been accused of holding the economy back. In reality, China's state enterprises have been going through many changes, and the state enterprise of today bears little resemblance to that in the 1990s.

1.2 State Enterprises as Central Institutions

Ever since the foundation of the People's Republic of China, state enterprises have been key instruments of the state's control of economic activities. Also, for as long as they have existed, these enterprises have been criticized as producing lower levels of output than non-state enterprises, and at lower levels of productivity. Allegations of waste and corruption have also been leveled at state enterprises, whose managers, many political appointees, have been found to have diverted enterprise funds for personal gain.[3] A wealth of empirical studies, to be detailed in Chap. 2, confirms the negative economic impact of Chinese state enterprise operations. This raises the question of why the Chinese state continues to allocate to these enterprises such a major role.

Before this question is answered, critics of China's state enterprises need to deal with one uncomfortable fact. As Table 1.1 shows, despite the perverse impact of these enterprises and the commanding heights they occupy in the economy, China's spectacular economic growth has remained unabated until after 2010. If these impacts were indeed material, is it then expected that growth rates would be even higher had these enterprises been privatized or closed? There is also scant correlation between economic growth and state enterprise reforms instituted. At least at the aggregate level, therefore, the perverse impact of state enterprises cannot be detected.

Table 1.1 China's economic growth and major state enterprise reform measures

Year	*GDP growth rate (%)*	*State enterprise reform*
1978	11.7	Enlarging operational autonomies; Linking profits of SEs to employees' benefits
1984	15.2	Separation of ownership rights and control rights; Manager/contract responsibility system
1993	13.9	Setting up modern enterprise system
1995	10.9	Grasping the large (state enterprises), letting go the small
1997	9.2	Helping loss-making ones get out of the difficulties
1999	7.7	Mixed ownership reform
2002	9.1	Supervision system for state-owned assets
2013	7.8	Putting forward overall objectives of state enterprise reform

Sources: GDP growth from World Bank database; reform details from Chap. 3

Coming to the question of China's state enterprise role, both Western theory and China-specific factors can be adduced as supporting arguments. As will be elaborated in Chap. 2, a number of Western theories argue for a sizable role of the state in mixed and market economies. And in the Western theory of public enterprises itself, state enterprises have to play both an economic and social role for which the trade-off is efficiency. Thus noted Baumol (1984: 14): "where circumstances are such that the profit motive drives firms to behave in a manner that conflicts with the social interest, inefficiency and indolence may become a virtue."

In the specific context of China, it must be remembered that prior to economic liberalization in 1978, these state enterprises were vital to the Chinese economy, accounting for about 80% of national gross domestic product (GDP), but also providing employment and a social safety net ("the iron rice bowl")[4] for the workforce, and hence ensuring social stability (Wang & Li, 2010: 5). Thus, China began reforms with a pervasive state enterprise sector performing both economic and social functions. With its gradualist approach, China's reforms of the state sector, even if aimed at shrinking this sector, would take time to unfold.

In addition, Li (2008), drawing from Minsky's (1986: Chapter 4) argument that a large government sector was vital for a capitalist market economy to maintain macroeconomic stability and avoid deep recessions, argued that the Chinese state-owned enterprise sector must be sufficiently large to be able to manage and implement very substantial public sector investment projects that accounted for about 50% of the total capital formation.

If we move away from purely economic arguments, an explanation can be found from political economy. Economics has never been the only reason for these enterprises' existence. As Hsu (2014) noted, the enterprises have also been central to the government's political economy: control over essential economic institutions is part and parcel of Communist Party control over the state apparatus. While economic liberalization was part of this political economy, it was motivated as much by the conferment of legitimacy to the Party leadership after the decade of the disastrous Cultural Revolution (1966–1976) (Lin, 1999) as by the (as yet unknown) perceived benefits of liberalization. This is why these enterprises have continued to exist despite the national leadership's strategy of moving toward a "socialist market economy". The caution with which reforms were enacted, exemplified by the gradualist approach, can then be explained by the fact that the same leaders who espoused liberalization were also those who participated in the design of the planning system, with socialism the dominant philosophy.

Finally, state enterprise reform, detailed in Chap. 3, has produced a continuum of state control through ownership and governance that makes it hard to delineate where state control ends and non-state control begins. Within this continuum are enterprises in which the state cannot claim majority ownership but nevertheless controls. In this organizational sense, the state is embedded in China's business community. It is for this reason that this book has avoided the use of the traditional term "state-owned enterprises", opting instead for the softer "state enterprises".

1.3 Why Study State Enterprises?

Beyond their sheer size and importance, the above discussion should lead to a number of issues that require examination, where scant work has been undertaken, or reexamination, and where the China context may necessitate rethinking conventional wisdoms. This is less about whether earlier work had been erroneous, but rather about the continuously changing landscape engendered by reforms necessitating frequent updating and reexamination.

Clearly the most important debate around China's state enterprises revolves around ownership and governance. Proponents of privatization railed against bloated state ownership, while China's leadership has come to value control over ownership, as Chap. 3 reveals. The place to begin discussion of this issue is to clarify the extent of state control through ownership and governance of enterprises. This is no easy task.

Although there was no shortage of literature on China's state enterprises, characterizing today's state enterprises still faces several major challenges due to their complexity as a result of successive rounds of reform. The defining distinction between state and private enterprises based on ownership encounters, for a country as decentralized as China, problems of clarifying which part and level of the state is the owner. How much state ownership exists is also hard to tell since some state enterprises are not directly owned by the state, but may be owned by an enterprise not with complete state ownership but under state control, or by multiple such enterprises. And in terms of governance, problems like which part of governance state power extends to, how much state involvement is in operations, how much does the state figure in providing a tilted playground for state enterprises, or what and how many state's strategies to follow also need to be solved. It also does not help that each level of government—central, provincial, and municipal/local—has its own state enterprises, render the notion of "state" much less clear than is the case in other countries. Therefore, specific state-control modes of China's state enterprises need to be examined.

A second issue relates to the roles China's state enterprises are and should be playing. Those who suggest that China's state enterprises should be privatized to prevent them from using their monopoly position to dominate markets while turning in below-average performances implicitly deny a non-commercial role for these enterprises. However, as later chapters show, China's state enterprises, already relieved of their social safety net responsibilities, are still required to pursue and fulfill both commercial and non-commercial responsibilities and obligations. Therefore, it is important to revisit their roles in light of functions like supporting the Chinese economy when called upon by the leadership, spurring technology innovation to strengthen Chinese international competiveness, helping the state overcome crises, and operationalizing the state strategy of "Going Out".[5]

The first and second issues lead to the third—how does ownership/control and the roles state enterprises play affect their performance? Making this determination requires definition of ownership/control as well as identification of enterprise roles. Despite quantification giving the appearance of precision, existing literature poses numerous problems, including whether non-state enterprises are synonymous with private enterprises, as is often assumed. Non-commercial roles of state enterprises have also often been ignored in assessing performance. Even if they have not, an important question is whether these other roles can be as easily quantified as rates of return on investment and therefore aggregated to yield an overall measure of performance.

1.4 Lines of Enquiry

The issues stated above raise several important questions, each question begetting a corresponding study objective, which may be further subdivided into sub-objectives.

The first question is: after state enterprise reform, what are the roles and characteristics of state enterprises in terms of ownership structure and governance mechanism (state-control mode)? How are these roles different from those of state enterprises envisaged in mainstream public enterprise theories (agency theory, property rights theory, public choice theory, and neoliberalism) as described in Chap. 2?

This requires understanding the dynamics of change as seen by how the state enterprise has evolved in line with state enterprise reform policies. This evolution can be shown to affect performance and to lead to further reforms. It also requires appreciation of how the state asserts control through ownership and governance. This role depends on the form of ownership (state-owned, state-holding, and state joint-stock) while governance is expressed through, for instance, hiring practices, incentives for performance, transparency of reporting, bureaucrats or professional hires, reporting channels, state involvement in decision-making, and the extent of state support and preferential policies.

The second question is what roles do China's state enterprises as key instruments of the state play to drive the growth in the economy, and how different are these roles from those envisaged by mainstream public enterprise theories (agency theory, property rights theory, public choice theory, and neoliberalism)? To what extent and how do state enterprises represent the state at the macro level, for instance in major events like China's World Trade Organization (WTO) admission and the 2008 Global Financial Crisis (GFC)? How successful have they been in this role? And are there trade-offs in meeting various state objectives? For instance, how does the profitability objective conflict with the objective of social protection?

The third line of enquiry is to relate the above issues of ownership structure and governance mechanism to performance by asking how do state enterprises perform in terms of profitability, competition, and innovation, and also how well does this performance accord with existing mainstream public enterprise theories. Specifically, do state enterprises make profits or losses as measured by standard profitability indicators like net profit margin, return on assets, and return on equity? To what extent does China's state enterprise face competition from other state enterprises, and non-state enterprises (private and foreign) in their markets? And do China's state enterprises engage in innovation, and is such innovation comparable to that undertaken by private enterprises?

1.5 Discourse Methodology

Despite the popularity of quantitative methods in analyzing state enterprise performance, the approach used in this book to elucidate the issues sketched above is qualitative. Apart from limitations like changing circumstances and the large number and types of state enterprises rendering generalization of findings, quantitative methods' strongest suite, difficult, qualitative approaches[6] have their own appeal, and naturally also weaknesses.

Thus, the qualitative research approach makes for a better understanding of the complex rationale, through identification, description, and interpretation. Its underlying principles are also helpful to this book's objectives and credibility. The first is its appreciation of the importance of context—that behavior is influenced by the physical, socio-cultural, and psychological environment—as the basis for naturalistic inquiry. The second principle is that behavior goes beyond what is observed by the investigator. Subjective meanings and perceptions of the subject are equally critical, and it is the researcher's responsibility to access these (Schmid, 1981).

Of the many methods of qualitative research, four are particularly relevant for the envisaged analysis. The first is historical research, defined as the systematic and objective location, evaluation, and synthesis of evidence in order to establish facts and draw conclusions about the traces that past events left behind (Gardner, 2006). The objective of historical research is to find out solutions to current problems which have their roots in the past, and to use the past to predict the future or to test theories and hypotheses about the past.

The historical approach has particular relevance for China. The Chinese have always relied on learning from the past; to them, the past has never been a foreign country. Thus Chinese leaders and their advisers today are looking not only at the globalizing world outside but also inward to the Chinese past for ideas to help them think about the future (Wang, 2014). Hence, referring to Chinese history provides lessons for the Chinese state of today. China cannot blindly copy what other countries have done but has to refer to its history to make decisions. This method for achieving better understanding of present policies, practices, problems, and institutions through past events is adopted in Chap. 3 which discusses the history of the Chinese state and in Chap. 4 in relation to China's banking sector.

The second approach is the case study which explores retrospectively or prospectively in depth facts and developments around a person, group, or event. This method is most appropriate in situations where it is impossible to separate the phenomenon from its context, in other words, it studies complex phenomena within their contexts.

In the context of this research, determining the extent of state ownership is important for understanding the role of the state in China's state enterprises. However, as already indicated, the state's ownership was also hard to grasp since the ownership forms were diverse. In terms of the state's control over a state enterprise, it is even harder to capture. The control methods included intervention in day-to-day operations, presence on the board of directors, preferential treatment, and so on. Given such complexity, it is doubtful whether comprehensive analysis is possible. The alternative approach of examining the above questions through the lens of specific cases is more feasible if not better.

This method for understanding complex issues is used in Chap. 5 with the banking sector as a brief study and Chap. 6 with ZTE Corporation in the context of state enterprise reform. In Chap. 5, a study of the banking sector is undertaken to see how the Chinese government has tried to improve the efficiency of the banking sector while at the same time ensuring that it follows and supports the government's strategies/policies. This case is embedded in the historical approach described earlier, and illustrates the complementary application of both approaches. Also, in Chap. 6, this study would use a case—ZTE Corporation—to verify the success of the state-control mode. ZTE Corporation, transformed by China's state enterprise reform, followed the state's strategies to restructure and what alternative reform measures it adopted. Its ownership structure was complex while state ownership was decreasing to an inconspicuous level.

These two methods are supported by a third, ethnography, which is designed to explore the cultural phenomena from the research's observation of the society from the point of view of the subject of the study (Hobbs, 2006; Sanjek, 1996). This study uses ethnography as a supporting research method because of its belief in the importance of culture in shaping Chinese institutions, beliefs, and behavior. This method is reflected in Chap. 4 by the history of the Chinese state, stressing the role played by Confucianism. Confucianism dates back over two millennia and it is the abiding cultural-political ideology for the entire history of imperial China as the basis of the view of the state. Despite the official repudiation of Confucianism by the leadership led by Mao Zedong in the earlier years of the People's Republic, a value system heavily influenced by Confucianism remains intact while the philosophy itself has reemerged to be endorsed by the current leadership, with the establishment of Confucius Institutes worldwide the most obvious manifestations of this endorsement (Paradise, 2009).

The fourth, also a supporting methodology, is phenomenology which investigates significant phenomena and their impact on those affected (Marton, 1986). In the present context, China's accession to the WTO and the onset of the 2008 GFC are major events that shaped the nature of the Chinese banking system, as discussed in Chap. 5. The initiatives taken by China, the establishment of the Asia Infrastructure Investment Bank (AIIB) and the massive Belt and Road Initiative (BRI) announced in 2013, discussed in Chap. 6, can also be said to support deployment of this methodology.

1.6 Structure of This Book

This book is structured as follows. This chapter has introduced readers to China's rise or more correctly reemergence that has invited much debate centered around a model that is best characterized as state-led. In this model, state enterprises are vital instruments of government control. The need to study these enterprises as well as suggested lines of enquiry to pursue are discussed in this chapter, together with the methodological approaches adopted. This discussion is situated in the context of (still ongoing) state enterprise reform that has been implemented over several decades. This broad discussion provides the setting and rationale for later chapters to explore different dimensions of what has become, thanks to many rounds of reforms, one of the most complex institutions in China today.

In the next chapter, Chinese state enterprises are set in their theoretical context which provides the foundation on which the bulk of judgments on Chinese state enterprises are based. It acknowledges that much has been written about China's state enterprises but finds little agreement on how they have performed, or even what they are. A major reason for this lack of a coherent view is that these enterprises have gone through several phases of reform, so that their nature and role have changed over time. An equally important reason is differences in perspectives. Most studies have been framed by Western theories of, and applicable to, public enterprise, so that conclusions were drawn and assessments were made assuming these theories hold. These theories are based on the market economy as the functioning environment and the nation state as the political-institutional frame. This chapter deals with both mainstream and alternative theoretical perspectives applied to Chinese state enterprises and provides empirical evidence of their performance. Mainstream theories discussed are agency theory, property rights, public choice, and neoliberalism. Alternative theories discussed are Minsky's financial instability hypothesis, economic embeddedness, market socialism, and the developmental state. To this has been added reference to China as a civilization state, one in which the entire civilization is located. This characterization speaks to the importance of historical factors in explaining the state's attitude toward state enterprises and the latter's response to the state. The chapter ends with a critique on the use of alternative perspectives to assess China's state enterprises.

Beginning with a review of the history of state enterprise reform, Chap. 3 examines China's state enterprise performance that speaks to their relationship with economic growth and distribution. It shows the impact of reform on performance, with a clear trade-off between market and non-market outcomes. The starting point of this chapter is the much-repeated criticism of Chinese state enterprises as a drag on the economy and the equally popular solution of privatization and/or liquidation. The assumptions on which this view is founded are first the superiority of private sector performance and a clear distinction between public and private enterprise. Framing the discussion in a historical context, this chapter takes issue with these assumptions, arguing that the Chinese state has a much larger role than that envisaged by the nation state concept and that the state and civil society are not mutually exclusive. It is also a reminder that state enterprise reform, described in some detail in this chapter, should not be viewed as primarily vindicating arguments of the need to privatize these enterprises but rather as efforts to streamline their operations to better serve the state. The chapter's recounting of state enterprise reforms ends with typologies of state enterprises today. Evidence of reform impact also shows that these reforms have strengthened governance and performance, while divestiture and consolidation have produced fewer but larger and stronger state enterprises. However the link between these enterprises and economic growth is not easily established from empirical work. That between state enterprise reform and income distribution has been perverse is clear as state enterprises abandon their social protection role (Fig. 1.1).

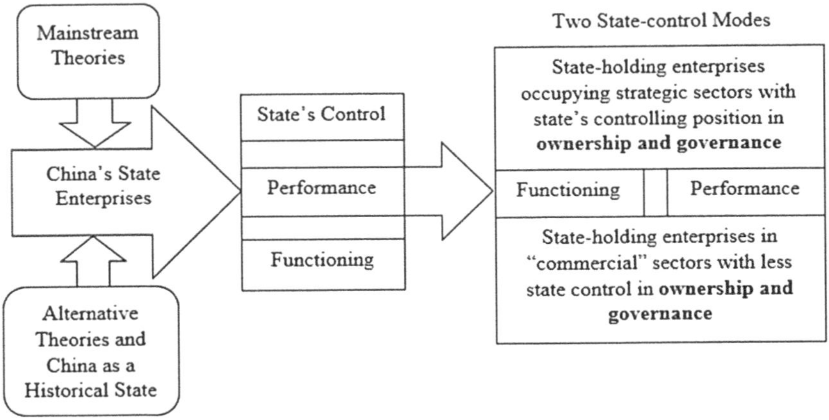

Fig. 1.1 Analytical framework for Chaps. 3, 4, 5. Source: The authors

Chapter 4 focuses on a strategic industry—China's banking sector. Through historical lenses, it explains why despite the rise of non-state banking the state retains full ownership of the largest banks. It also illustrates the argument made in Chap. 2 about the relevance of history in China's policy calculus. It also illustrates the macroeconomic role of state enterprises surveyed in Chap. 3. China's banking sector is considered a strategic sector and its five state banks are the largest by asset ownership in China, and since the onset of the GFC impacted Western global banks, among the largest in the world. Its designation as a strategic sector coincides with a slower pace of reforms compared with those for other state enterprises. The reasons for this divergence are historical, being rooted in China's unhappy experience during the early years of its modern banking history. This history, dating from the Qing Dynasty, is charted in a section of this chapter. This is followed by a review of how China's banking sector responded to the state's policies to reform the sector through strengthening efficiency and governance. These reforms have brought about China's banking sector today. An area of particular relevance is the link between state control and ownership/governance in state-holding commercial banks. Major policy initiatives and external circumstances impact the performance of China's state-holding banks. The major initiatives reviewed are China's entry into the WTO in 2001 and the state's decision to expand its global role at around the same time. The external development discussed is the onset of the GFC in late 2008. Section 4.5 offers some concluding remarks about this sector.

Chapter 5 then analyzes another major type of state enterprise—"commercial" state enterprises—through a case study of an electronics enterprise. Chapter 2 has provided an account of the many layers of state enterprise reform that have produced a complex web of enterprises with varying degrees of state participation through ownership or control. This account raises important questions as to what "state enterprise" means in the Chinese context. Do the nature and characteristics of these enterprises conform to those of stereotype state enterprises understood in mainstream Western literature on this subject? Just as important, how have Chinese state enterprise reforms impacted these enterprises' performance? While answers can be found at the macroeconomic level, deep insights into how these reforms shaped the operations of enterprises can only be gleaned through examining such changes—representing the impact of reforms and response to them—at the enterprise level. A major state enterprise in the electronics sector, ZTE Corporation, is chosen for analysis. This chapter traces how state enterprise reform progressively yielded a reduction of state ownership but not necessarily with the loss of state control, shows how this control was exercised lightly, and how pursuit of and/or compliance with state strategies have benefited the enterprise. The operations of the enterprise also speak specifically to how issues like agency costs are handled in the context of Chinese enterprises and generally to areas of divergence between Chinese governance and governance as commonly understood.

Chapter 6 traces the next phase of the role of state enterprises as they support China's strategy of gaining greater international recognition, hampered so far by the existing international economic order orchestrated by the US after the Second World War. Since liberalization in 1978, China has earned a formidable reputation as a destination for foreign direct investment (FDI). This began to change during the turn of the century when the Chinese government announced its "Going Out" strategy encouraging Chinese enterprises to expand overseas. Factors driving this internationalization included the government's objective of playing a larger role in international affairs as well as strengthening the international competitiveness of Chinese enterprises. Not surprisingly, state enterprises were the first to respond to the government's call. This chapter describes the process of "Going Out" and the twin objectives of state enterprises in doing so—to support the government's strategy of extending its influence and to seek markets. The former role is exemplified by China's outward FDI (OFDI) in Africa. The latter is illustrated by again using ZTE's internationalizing its operations in Malaysia as an example of state enterprises pursuing a market-seeking objective. The chapter also distinguishes between two types of state enterprises, financial and non-financial, both of which are integral to the government's internationalization efforts. The penultimate section of this chapter deals with the massive BRI launched by China in 2013. This exercise, prompted as much by strategic as by economic considerations, is expected to see a much larger role for both state and non-state enterprises. This chapter concludes with thoughts on this arguably unique role for state enterprises not found in those of other countries. How to measure this unprecedented role will also speak to how state enterprises should be assessed.

This final chapter draws together the many strands that course through the prior discussion of state enterprises. These strands set the Chinese situation apart from the prevalent critiques of the Chinese state and its enterprises. First, the prominence of the state in society has deep historical and cultural roots. Second, Chinese state enterprises are not all state-owned; many are state controlled, this control being exercised formally through a complex web and layers of ownership, and informally through government influence on enterprise CEOs. Third, the distinction between state and non-state enterprises is nowhere as sharp as Western theories suggest. Fourth, because many state enterprises are listed on stock exchanges, they operate according to commercial principles and are profitable, contradicting prevailing arguments to the contrary. Finally, state enterprises play an important role in the government's internationalization efforts. Taken together, these points suggest that the use of Western theory to assess China's state enterprises fails both on account of flawed assumptions (state-private dichotomy) and characterization (profit and efficiency as criteria of performance). Indeed, the Chinese state enterprise has no parallel in Western theory or practice. This is not to argue that this enterprise is superior to its Western counterpart. But any assessment should be grounded on what its role actually is, not what critics think it should be.

Notes

1. Based on gross domestic product (GDP) by the World Bank, China was the second largest country in the world. The average annual GDP growth rate was 9.26% in five years from 2008 to 2012 (The World Bank, 2012).

2. In Gordon Chang's book *The Coming Collapse of China* (Chang, 2001), Chapter 3 was titled "State Enterprises Are Dying" and Chapter 7 "The State Attacks the Private Sector".
3. Hsu (2014) reported on fraud uncovered in 11 state enterprises by the National Audit Office, together with 35 cases of bribery and embezzlement in 2014.
4. The "iron rice bowl" (铁饭碗) is a Chinese term that refers to guaranteed job security which state enterprises used to offer.
5. The "Going Out" (走出去) strategy, announced in 1999, was a strategy to have Chinese enterprises investing overseas and internationalizing their operations.
6. Kirk and Miller (1988) suggested a working definition of qualitative research that reflects these two principles. They defined it as "a particular tradition in social science that fundamentally depends on watching people in their own territory and interacting with them in their own language, on their own terms".

References

Baumol, W.J. (1984). Towards a theory of public enterprise. *Atlantic Economic Journal 12*(1): 13–19.

Chang, G.G. (2001). *The Coming Collapse of China*. London: Arrow Arrow.

Chang, G.G. (2010). China's economy to reach $ 123 trillion? *Forbes*. Retrieved from http://www.forbes.com/2010/01/07/china-economy-robert-fogel-opinions-columnists-gordon-g-chang.html

Gardner, P. (2006). *Historical analysis: The SAGE Dictionary of social research methods*. London, England: SAGE Publications, Ltd.

Hobbs, D. (2006). Ethnography. *The Sage dictionary of social research methods (S. 101–102)*. London: Sage.

Hsu, S. (2014). China's changing state-owned enterprise landscape. *The Diplomat*, June 25. Retrieved from http://thediplomat.com/2014/06/chinas-changing-state-owned-enterprise-landscape/

Kirk, J., & Miller, M.L. (1988). Reliability and validity in qualitative research. *International Journal of Qualitative Studies in Education*, 1(1).

Lal, D. (2006). A proposal to privatize Chinese enterprises and end financial repression. *The Cato Journal, 26*(2), 275–286.

Li, M. (2008). *Three essays on China's state-owned enterprises: Towards an alternative to privatization*. Amherst: University of Massachusetts.

Lin, J.Y. (1999). Policy burdens, soft budget constraint and state enterprise reform in China. Working paper. Retrieved from http://repository.ust.hk/ir/Record/1783.1-1818

Marton, F. (1986). Phenomenography—A research approach to investigating different understandings of reality. *Journal of Thought, 21*(2), 28–49.
Minsky, H.P. (1986). Stabilizing an unstable economy. New Haven and London: Yale University Press.
Paradise, J.F. (2009). China and international harmony: The role of Confucius Institutes in bolstering Beijing's soft power. *Asian Survey, 49*(4), 647–669.
Pei, M. (2006). The dark side of China's rise. *Foreign Policy, 153* (March/April), 32–40.
Sanjek, R. (1996). Ethnography. In A. Barnard & J. Spencer (Eds.), *Encyclopedia of social and cultural anthropology*. London and New York: Routledge.
Schmid, H. (1981). Qualitative research and occupational therapy. *The American Journal of Occupational Therapy, 35*(2), 105–106.
Szamosszegi, A., & Kyle, C. (2011). An analysis of state-owned enterprises and state capitalism in China. Capital Trade, Incorporated for US-China Economic and Security Review Commission. Retrieved from https://www.uscc.gov/sites/default/files/Research/10_26_11_CapitalTradeSOEStudy.pdf
The World Bank (2012). The World Bank database for China. Retrieved from http://data.worldbank.org/country/china
Wang, G. (2014). *Another China cycle: Committed to reform*. Singapore: World Scientific.
Wang, C., & Li, L. (2010). *State-owned enterprise reform in China*. Beijing: Peking University, mimeo.

CHAPTER 2

China's State Enterprises—Theories and Evidence

Good government consists in the ruler being a ruler, the minister being a minister, the father being a father, and the son being a son (Confucius, Lunyu *12.11).*

2.1 Introduction

Much has been written about China's state enterprises. But there is little agreement on how they have performed, or even what they are. A major reason for this lack of a coherent view is that these enterprises have gone through several phases of reform. As the economic landscape for these enterprises shifts with each phase of reform, the nature of critiques and assessment of their performance also change. Another factor is differences in perception. By and large, most studies have been framed by Western theories of, and applicable to, public enterprise, so that conclusions were drawn and assessments were made assuming these theories hold. These theories are based on the market economy as the functioning environment and the nation state as the political-institutional frame.

When it came to empirical studies, there has been no dearth of work to support the above theories. Findings from this empirical work have also shown considerable consistency despite the fact that successive reforms have changed the operating environment for these enterprises, and state enterprises have responded differently to each reform, and to different reforms. The march of time has also seen state enterprises respond to

R. Li, K. C. Cheong, *China's State Enterprises*,
https://doi.org/10.1007/978-981-13-0176-6_2

external circumstances. For instance, the onset of the Global Financial Crisis in 2008 had seen state financial institutions shoulder the responsibility for keeping economic growth intact. There is no unanimity of views, however. Chapter 3 will document findings that do not lend support to mainstream theories. Perhaps this lack of agreement stems from the fact that in spatial terms many studies cover specific subsectors rather than the entire state enterprise sector. Given the size of China's state enterprise sector, few studies have been able to claim more than partial coverage whether in geographical or institutional terms.

Alternative theories, although less commonly cited but also framed in a market or mixed economy, and placing greater emphasis on the role of the state, can lay some claim to have relevance for China's state enterprises. Because modern China's starting point was central planning and the Chinese state predates by millennia the nation state, the applicability of each theory can be brought into question. To the extent that the concept of state itself in China and the West may not fully coincide, understanding the former is vital in any discussion of Chinese state enterprises. Recognizing the Chinese state's antiquity and uniqueness, historians have referred to China as being a "historical state".

This chapter has four sections. The next section presents mainstream Western theories on public enterprises, highlighting their implications for state enterprise performance. The theories discussed are agency theory, property rights theory, public choice theory, and neoliberalism. Corresponding to these theories, Sect. 2.3 gives an account of extant empirical work that generally lends support to these theories. This body of work—theory and evidence—can be referred to, however imperfectly, as "conventional wisdom". This chapter also reminds the reader that this conventional wisdom is subject to challenge, although the former's proponents, by making the same judgments over time, are clearly unfazed by this challenge. Section 2.4 looks at alternative theories—of Minsky's financial instability hypothesis, economic embeddedness, market socialism, and the developmental state—that provide no less cogent arguments than mainstream theories that are applicable to the Chinese situation. But they suffer the same limitations as mainstream theories in their use of the nation state premise. In Sect. 2.5, we introduce the concept of historical state and apply it to China. We argue that it is this state that should frame discussions of China's state enterprises. Section 2.6 draws some tentative conclusions from this broad review.

2.2 Mainstream Theories on Public Enterprises

Scholars writing on the underperformance of public enterprises, in this case in China, typically cite theory to support their findings. The textbook treatment of these enterprises is that they are less efficient than private enterprises on account of one or more of the following reasons: the need to meet both economic and social objectives, management by bureaucrats lacking professional experience, lack of accountability engendered by soft budget constraints, and inability to respond quickly as conditions change.[1]

However, Sikorski (1993) argued: "There is no general theory of public enterprise, and the miscellany of separate theorizations on the subject has created a conceptual quagmire." Similarly, Baumol (1984: 15) pointed out that the existence of public goods did not in and of itself justify the establishment of public enterprises. He went on to argue that there is not even unanimity of views that private enterprises perform better (Baumol, 1984: 14). Yet what Sikorski calls "separate theorizations" does point to and is used to justify findings of the superiority of private enterprises over public. And it is on the basis of these theorizations that Chinese state enterprises are criticized and the case is made for their privatization or closure. While this chapter does not intend to add to this general debate, it does need to clarify what might be the bases of widespread criticism of Chinese state enterprises. To do that, identification of what these theorizations are is needed. Major examples, briefly described here, are agency theory, property rights theory, public choice theory, and neoliberalism.

2.2.1 Agency Theory

Put forward by Jensen and Meckling (1976), agency theory argues that there are likely to be conflicts between the principal (owner) and the agent (manager) since their respective interests diverge (Bebchuk & Fried, 2004). If the agent becomes also the principal of an enterprise, such conflicts would disappear, given the coincidence of interests (Dharwadkar, George, & Brandes, 2000). This can also be explained through the relationship between the provider and the user of enterprise resources. As the principal, the provider is the owner of those enterprise resources. The manager who puts these enterprise resources to use is the agent. If the manager is the owner of these enterprise resources, he/she would work hard for his/her own interests in both capacities. Thus, there would be no agency problem. However, if the manager is not the owner of enterprise resources but their custodian, a function for which he/she is remunerated, any motivation to maximize returns from the use of resources may be subordinated to that of maximizing his/her own remuneration. The likelihood of this occurring gives rise to three "agency" costs: monitoring costs, bonding costs, and residual losses. Monitoring costs refer to costs that external shareholders have to incur in monitoring the manager's behavior. Bonding costs are costs that arise from the manager spending time and effort in acquiring the principal's trust instead of in maximizing returns to the firm. Residual losses refer to other costs resulting from interest conflicts between the principal and the agent.

Applied to state enterprises, if state ownership is transferred to private hands, the objective of that state enterprise would be redirected to serve private owners. Although the principal-agent problem would not entirely disappear, the divergence of interests between owner and manager would be narrowed in that both are directed at monetary benefits so that agency costs would be reduced. It is on the basis of this argument that private sector enterprises are considered more efficient than state enterprises (Estrin & Pérotin, 1991).

2.2.2 Property Rights Theory

Property rights theory is an important area of institutional economics and traces its origins to a number of scholars. For the present discussion, property rights determine how the property or asset is used and owned (Alchian, 1987). The property can be used by individuals, associations, or governments (Guerin, 2003). Property rights theory argues that the more direct and strengthened are the rights to the property, the better it would be used (Alchian & Demsetz, 1973). In other words, property rights enable the principal to exercise his/her rights to realize the optimal utilization of the property. These rights include ownership right, possession right, control right, use right, earnings right, and disposition right. As long as the property boundary is clear, there is no transaction cost. The efficiency of resource allocation was decided by the distinctiveness of the property boundary (Coase, 1937, 1959, 1960; Stigler, 1971).

In an enterprise, the relationship between the principal and the agent can also be considered as a contract transaction. Therefore, property rights within the enterprise affect the efficiency of that enterprise. The principal has ownership rights over his/her enterprise, and therefore the incentive to improve the efficiency of that enterprise that would generate better returns and increase its value. But state ownership has no locus for the benefits of ownership and hence no incentives because the state is an institution with many actors. In other words, the boundary of property rights is not clear with state ownership. If state ownership is transferred to private hands, the latter would exercise their rights to realize maximized profits on their acquisitions (Alchian & Demsetz, 1972; Demsetz, 1967).

2.2.3 *Public Choice Theory*

Public choice theory seeks to explain, by the use of economic tools, how decisions are made by the state through its key actors. In making these decisions, the theory adopts the assumption from economics in which individuals are motivated by self-interest. It therefore argues that state actors' individual interests are given priority over public interests (Buchanan, 1954; Buchanan & Tullock, 1962). Public interests would not be pursued by the representatives of the state, and the state's objectives would not be pursued by bureaucrats. Bureaucrats, being state employees, have security of tenure, with little downside risks should things go wrong with the enterprises they manage. And while bureaucrats are accountable to the people of the state, voters have neither the incentive nor the knowledge to monitor bureaucrats' actions (Downs, 1957).

In this situation, state-appointed managers would impose on state enterprises' goals that help them acquire political influence which undermines efficiency. The inefficiency of state enterprises is thus an outcome of public choice theory. Contrast this with private entities that would focus on their own interests to make the enterprise better. Thus, like the theories before it, changing ownership from state to private would dispense with political intervention and incentivize the search for efficiency.

2.2.4 *Neoliberalism*

Although the concept of neoliberalism has somewhat different meanings when used by different scholars and over time, it is commonly understood both by its proponents and critics, to champion the preeminence of the free market that resonates with the nineteenth-century ideas of laissez faire and economic liberalism. It supports economic liberalization, free trade and open markets, privatization and deregulation of state activities, and fiscal austerity. The role of the state is to be kept at a minimum (Boas & Gans-Morse, 2009). There has to be no restrictions on the freedom of movement for capital, labor, goods, and services. As succinctly put in the report "The World Bank and the State" written by the Bretton Woods Project (Bretton Woods Project, 2000: 5):

> Market competition … best defines and serves the "public interest", because individuals can best express their choices through the market; individual freedom and prosperity are maximized as funds are allocated efficiently, people can purchase what they want at prices determined according to supply and demand, and wealth generated by private effort "trickles down" to the benefit of all.

Under neoliberalism, there is no room for state enterprises since private enterprises are the most efficient in an environment of liberalized trade and open markets. While recognizing the existence of public goods, neoliberals emphasize the role of the private sector in determining economic priorities in production and distribution (Harvey, 2005; Shearmur, 1992). The development of pro-corporate political policies by the state would also restrict the public sector's role (Chomsky, 1999). However, with interventions by the state that distort the functioning of the market, the state enterprise cannot be run efficiently. Hence, according to this theory, state enterprises should be privatized.

These theories all point to the cost of having the state-run enterprises. While not necessarily related to one another, they provide, at least superficially, justification for why Chinese state enterprises perform poorly in both absolute terms and relative to their private sector counterparts. Indeed, as shown below, these theories have been used, explicitly or implicitly, as blanket criticism of the Chinese state sector as a whole, without too much regard for the variation in performance of individual state enterprises, and without acknowledging the impact of successive rounds of reform (see, e.g. Wildau, 2016).

2.3 Empirical Studies Supporting Mainstream Theories

A great deal of empirical research has been done on China's state enterprises. A large body of evidence supports the predictions of mainstream Western theories, a smaller body refutes them, while yet others are inconclusive. In some ways, as the state enterprise sector has been undergoing reform, comparing studies of different time periods may not be fully valid.

It is also true that a few studies have examined how state enterprises have changed over time. The studies in this section have findings that support mainstream public enterprise theories. Findings that do not support mainstream public enterprise theories will be discussed in Chap. 3. In reviewing these findings, context must be borne in mind—at any particular point in time, certain state enterprise reforms have been announced or are being implemented. These reforms are also not entirely driven by domestic agendas—major international events, such as the 1997–1999 Asian Financial Crisis, China's efforts to join the WTO that ended successfully in 2001, and the onset of the 2008 Global Financial Crisis, also intervene to drive reforms. These developments, both domestic and external, are therefore woven into the following narrative.

In the early years of state enterprise reform, when the state transferred responsibilities in output decision-making to China's state enterprises and the profit retention rate was raised, managers were paid more bonuses, hired more workers, and invested for the enterprise. As a result, increased autonomies led to higher productivity (Groves, Hong, McMillan, & Naughton, 1994). However, as state enterprise managers were selected and supervised by government bureaucrats, managers faced the agency problem of conflicting incentives—maximizing enterprise returns versus advancing their individual prospects for political goodwill and/or promotion. Soft budget constraints facing state enterprises only made agency problems worse since managers see little penalty in underperformance (Bai & Wang, 1998). As for the enterprises from the newly emergent non-state sector, namely, township and village enterprises (TVEs), their efforts to meet local governments' goals of increasing government revenues, rural employment, and incomes while being simultaneously market competitive were largely undermined by employment and local public goods supply quotas that distorted the market signals they received. As a result, their performance was not comparable to that of genuine private enterprises in terms of efficiency (Jin & Qian, 1998).

Also in these earlier reform years, empirical analysis of China's state enterprises showed the firms' profitability positively related to legal person shares but negatively related to state shares. And labor productivity also correlated negatively with the proportion of state shares in a state enterprise. These results suggested the inefficiency of state ownership (Xu & Wang, 1999). Till 1996, China's state enterprises were in a serious crisis in terms of their poor performance. The root of this crisis was their high agency cost that stemmed from collusion among state agencies (local officials and state enterprise managers) and a flawed managerial incentive scheme, which led to the inefficiency of and mounting losses for state enterprises. A better managerial incentive scheme for state enterprises managers and less political intervention and informational asymmetry were proposed as were better monitoring of state enterprise performance (Mi & Wang, 2000).

Another cross-country empirical analysis of 29 provinces, municipalities, and autonomous regions during 1978–1989 came to the conclusion that private and semi-private enterprises contributed to China's economic growth; in contrast, China's state enterprises damaged growth (Chen & Feng, 2000). Lack of autonomy and unclear property rights were said to have contributed to the poor performance, but reform measures to solve this inefficiency taken up to that time were not sufficiently bold (Sha & Lin, 2001).

Other areas in which state enterprises underperformed were also highlighted by some studies. That China's state enterprises' environmental performance (pollution control performance) was worse than that of private enterprises and foreign enterprises was the conclusion of the survey of China's 1000 industrial enterprises of three provinces and based on enterprise-level information in 1999 (Wang & Jin, 2002). Through investigating a sample of state enterprises during 1980–1994, in terms of state enterprises' financing sources for fixed investment, it was found that bank finance was linked more to profitability than direct government transfers, since getting bank finance enabled state enterprise managers to take greater risks (Cull & Xu, 2003).

Studies of poor state enterprise performance led to calls for China to privatize state enterprises to maintain and accelerate economic development. To achieve successful privatization, transfers of technologies by the state were encouraged (Ding & Motwani, 2001). Through evaluating 634 listed state enterprises that were privatized during 1994–1998, Sun & Tong (2003) concluded that earning ability, real sales, and workers' productivity improved, foreign ownership had limited impact on performance, while state ownership negatively affected the performance of those enterprises. By examining the Chief Executive Officer's (CEO's) compensation of China's state enterprises during the 1980s, Mengistae and Xu (2004) found that compensation was less sensitive to enterprise performance, but more sensitive to managerial return. In socialist and transition economies with serious informational asymmetry, policy burdens from the state would result in moral hazard for state enterprise managers and soft budget constraint problems, which led to state enterprises' low efficiency. State control of state enterprise managers was also found to result in the inefficiency of state enterprises (Lin & Li, 2004).

Along with profound ownership changes in China's state enterprises since 1979, management of state enterprises was also transformed from centrally planned into new forms, with variations across ownership forms and localities. But reform of state enterprises took time because of historical legacies, organizational inertia, and continued government interference (Hassard, Morris, & Sheehan, 2004). Corporate financing choices and dividend distribution decisions were impacted by the extent of political interference, managerial entrenchment, and institutional control. The political cost approach suggested a better governance structure in China's state enterprise reform with less state involvements (Su, 2005).

Based on a sample of 5284 partially privatized state enterprises in China during 1991–2001, a study by Wei, Xie, and Zhang (2005) examined if firm value was affected by ownership structure, and found state shares were negatively correlated with firm value while foreign share ownership was positively related to firm value. Among China's listed enterprises, different types of controlling shareholders had different uses of incentive pay. If the controlling shareholder was a state agency, performance-related pay was not used. If the controlling shareholder was a private block holder or state enterprise, the CEO's pay was related to the increase in shareholders' wealth or increase in profitability. But the effectiveness of the incentive system was low since CEO's pay-performance sensitivity was low (Firth, Fung, & Rui, 2006).

In another study using a panel data of 165 rural and urban enterprises in Nanjing city and its environs, privatization policies were adopted for the weakest unban enterprises, and private ownership contributed to improvements in productivity and profitability (Dong, Putterman, & Unel, 2006). With the state continuing to control China's state enterprises even after the privatization and listing in the stock market, it was found that economic efficiency and financial performance were not improved much (Chen, Firth, & Rui, 2006). The long-term managerial incentive problem and the management selection problem arose from the fact that managers of state enterprises were selected by bureaucrats rather than by entrepreneurs. On this basis, Zhang (2006) concluded that these built-in problems of state ownership could not be overcome no matter what governance reform was instituted for state enterprises except by privatization. By examining how much a sample of 461 publicly listed manufacturing enterprises' corporate governance practices affected their productive efficiency during 1999–2002, conclusions were drawn that state ownership and state legal person ownership negatively affected efficiency because of political interference.

Although less frequent as state enterprise reform continued after 2000, the negative findings for state enterprises continued to surface. For instance, it was found that state banks in China were less cost-efficient and profit-efficient than joint-stock banks (Ariff & Can, 2008). Foreign banks were also found to be more efficient than the big-four state-holding Chinese banks. Even minority foreign ownership within big-four state-holding Chinese banks had a significant positive effect on the performance in terms of efficiency (Berger, Hasan, & Zhou, 2009). The big-four state-holding commercial banks had the worst performance in terms of profitability, efficiency, and asset quality compared with private and foreign banks in China. However, foreign acquisition or public listing could be the positive factor to improve their performance (Lin & Zhang, 2009). A joint-stock structure was verified to be more profitable for Chinese banks compared to state ownership (Jiang, Yao, & Zhang, 2009).

Another study found that the privatization of China's state enterprises resulted in higher sales, labor productivity, and profitability, the last because of decreases of the managerial expenses in relation to sales. The impact of privatization was more sustainable when state ownership was reduced from majority to minority in an enterprise (Bai, Lu, & Tao, 2009). The greater the transfer of state control through ownership and governance to private hands, the more efficiencies were achieved (Lin, Ma, & Su, 2009).

When controlling shares were transferred from the state to private owners, the performance was improved significantly in a sample of 127 Chinese listed enterprises. The authors of this study Huang and Wang (2011) suggested that the Chinese state should continue to reduce its controlling ownership to enhance operating efficiency and profitability. The central government's control was also found to have a significantly negative influence on the performance of privatized state enterprises, casting doubt on the government strategy of retaining control while reducing ownership (Yang, 2012).

Criticism of state enterprise performance heated up again after state banks were called upon to advance credit as part of China's 4 trillion stimulus plan to combat the Global Financial Crisis. Li (2013) argued that this increased risks associated with non-performing loans (NPLs).

Under the Basel Accords III, the refinancing of banks was aimed at banks meeting the specified capital adequacy ratio. Because of lower interest margins, banks would exaggerate the size of their balance sheets to keep profits (Li, 2013). In a separate development, President Xi Jinping's campaign to combat corruption has exposed this problem in state enterprises, with it getting increasingly serious (Zhu, 2014). Again, government intervention through political incentives and the uncertainty of executive appointment was alleged to damage the performance of state enterprises. Abandoning the administrative selection system of the state enterprise executives was considered key to improving efficiency and speeding up compensation reform (Wang & Wei, 2014). State enterprise monopoly was once again said to have negatively impacted performance (Du, Tian, Zhang, & Li, 2014). Reducing the policy burdens of state enterprises was suggested as a way to improve the performance. One of the measurements was to reduce redundant staff (Chen & Tang, 2014).

Criticism of state banks has also been predicated upon the argument that as bank management of China was appointed by the government, with little managerial expertise and ineffective incentive schemes, it was hard for them to maximize shareholders' interests. Diversification in loans, deposits, assets, and geography were associated with worse performance and lower efficiency. But foreign ownership could play a mitigating role in the diseconomies of diversification (Berger, Hasan, & Zhou, 2010).

One role of state enterprises that has been mostly forgotten with liberalization in 1978 is as a social safety net for the millions of their employees. This role, as well as that of nation-building, was played primarily by these enterprises from the founding of the People's Republic in 1949 to at least a decade after liberalization (Fan & Hope, 2013: 2) Under President Hu Jintao and Premier Wen Jiabao, the Chinese leadership gave top priority to building a "harmonious society"[2] which implied reducing income and regional disparities. This call was in response to the fact that the faster the economic growth, the greater the income disparities and the lower the possibility of achieving social justice by income redistribution. Hence, although greater economic efficiency could be realized by privatization, it was at the expense of social justice.

But culpability for greater inequality cannot be pinned on privatization alone. To the extent that state enterprise reforms were designed to strengthen enterprise performance, government control through ownership and governance of the key industrial sectors and maintenance of monopolies over sectors which were profitable, wealth flowed to the state and the people became poorer. Moreover, due to the state monopoly in these sectors, the private sector had to struggle even as it was asked to play an increasing role in China's economy (Zheng & Chen, 2007). When an attempt was made to find out if corporate ownership was related to enterprises' equity risk (measured as the volatility of enterprises' stock returns) and stock returns, it emerged that state ownership led to higher stock volatility and lower stock returns (Zou & Adams, 2008). State ownership increased agency conflicts because of diverse incentives of bureaucrats and state agencies in the process of maximizing the firm value.

Dominant as these negative views of Chinese state enterprises are, they are not overwhelmingly accepted, even in Western intellectual circles. Those opposed to the assumption of the supremacy of free markets implicit in public enterprise theories argue for a much more prominent role of the state. This contrarian view is premised both on mainstream economic theories and on theories other than those discussed above. We look at these theories next.

2.4 In Defense of State Enterprises—Alternative Theories Integrating the Role of the State

Even within the framework of mainstream theories, there are situations when state enterprises have a role to play. Baumol (1984: 14–17) discussed the situation of "moral hazard" in which complete reliance on market forces can lead to perverse outcomes opposite of what is intended. He argued that "most if not all of the generally accepted tasks of the public sector share this attribute, at least to some degree." There is also the case of a natural monopoly where high fixed costs render it inefficient to have more than one producer of a good or service. In this instance, government ownership of this monopoly prevents a private enterprise from using its monopoly power to charge exorbitant prices.

Further, while the above theories underpin negative views of state enterprises, they are not the only theories that speak to the role of the state. Alternative Western theories give much greater prominence to the state's role. In the context of China, with its long history of state governance of the economy, might these theories have greater relevance to the Chinese case than the theories cited earlier? In this section, we discuss four such theories.

2.4.1 Minsky's Financial Instability Hypothesis

Hyman Minsky, whose work rose to prominence only posthumously with the onset of the Global Financial Crisis, argued that in capitalist economies, financial markets are inherently unstable, contradicting Malkiel and Fama's (1970) efficient market hypothesis which dominated thinking in the latter half of the twentieth century and which underpinned the so-called Great Moderation[3] that saw reduced business cycle fluctuations from the 1980s onwards. He rejected the notion that markets self-regulate. Instead Minsky (1986: 7) argued:

> Economic systems are not natural systems. An economy is a social organization created either through legislation or by an evolutionary process of intervention and innovation. Policy can change both the details and the overall character of the economy, and ... actual economic processes depend on economic and social institutions.

These remarks led to his advocacy of a government big enough (his reference to "Big Government") to deal effectively with the challenge of boom-bust cycles and kick-start stalled economies.

Minsky's views have clear appeal in defending China's state control of the banking sector and its use to deal with the adverse impact of the Global Financial Crisis. Yet again, to the extent that the Minsky hypothesis is set within a fully capitalist system, its relevance to China's partially marketized system is at best partial.

2.4.2 Economic Embeddedness

A number of scholars argue that the human economy is always embedded in society. Economic historian Karl Polanyi was credited with creating this term (Polanyi, 1944, 1957). He was of the view that in non-market societies there are no pure economic institutions and economic activities are deeply "embedded" in non-economic institutions. In market societies, rationalization of economic activities has facilitated "disembeddedness" from society. Moving beyond Polanyi, Granovetter (1985) argued that even in market societies, the rationality assumption in neoclassical economics produced an "undersocialized account" of human behavior. Even if the state made no direct economic intervention, its policies affect society, including economic transactions conducted therein. This means that any economic activity is influenced not just by economic factors and actors but also by non-economic institutions (Plattner, 1989). Thus, the economy is not autonomous as it is assumed in economic theory, but subordinated to politics, religion, and social relations. The state as a key institution of society is central to this embeddedness.

Although embeddedness is more in line with the role of the state in China, there are also important differences. First, as will be explained later, Polanyi and others had premised their arguments on a concept of a state defined as a "nation state", but the Chinese state has existed well before this concept became reality in Europe. The nature of the Chinese state has evolved, learning from its own history, but also absorbing Western state concepts. Second, Chinese society views the state as occupying the top tier of an orderly hierarchical society, not separate from it.

2.4.3 Market Socialism

Market socialism, sometimes broadly labeled a "mixed economy", is based on the notion that a socialist state would own the means of production but the prices of commodities are determined by the free market for equilibrating markets (Buchanan, 1985; Gregory & Stuart, 2004). A socialist state would play a guiding role in adjusting market-determined prices to facilitate market transactions that produce equitable allocation of resources. Because a pure market economy takes no account of distribution, the state has to step in to own, control, and manage the means of production, leaving free market forces to drive efficiency and competitiveness. The state also intervenes in setting some prices, ensuring that prices of goods and services sold to the lower income groups are not beyond their reach, and goods and services sold by them fetch a decent return. Prices of other goods and services are market-determined (Lange, 1936, 1937; Le Grand & Estrin, 1989).

China is referred to officially as a socialist market economy; since the beginning of economic transformation launched by Deng Xiaoping in 1978, many market decisions have been transferred to non-state actors. Deng himself preferred to call his creation "socialism with Chinese characteristics". It was defined as "a multi-ownership-oriented basic market economic system, with the public ownership in the dominance" (People.cn, 1984, 2007). And as Deng noted in his 1984 speech cited earlier, "the socialist sector is the mainstay of our economy". When China began its reform, it felt that it could combine socialism with elements of the market economy. The socialist mode of production had to be adapted to incorporate capitalist techniques to thrive (Bremmer, 2009; The Economist, 2012). The Chinese state has a major influence both on the amount and the nature of investment in China, particularly in infrastructure and in the selection of key sectors for development, as well as in human capital formation and in the direction of scientific and technological research (Tisdell, 2009). When state ownership was becoming less and less important in China, the means of production were owned less and less by the state. Except for strategic state enterprises in which prices were mainly determined by the state, other state enterprises had varying degrees of state ownership and market-determined prices. Nevertheless, the state has retained control over major state enterprises. Thus, the free market pricing system had not fully been adopted in China.

While the market socialism model appears a good fit for the Chinese experience, this similarity is more superficial than substantive. For one thing, China's reform began from a situation of central planning, whereas market socialism assumed that the underlying economic system is a free market one. It is also tempting to believe that if two parties start reform at either end of the market spectrum, they will have systems that meet along this spectrum. In fact, as China's experience shows, there is no such convergence. China's model of transition, combining a strong state economic presence with a thriving non-state sector, has no equivalent in the world. Vietnam, which likewise adopted a gradualist approach to reform, is the closest, but in Vietnam, the private sector has yet to develop to be able to compete with state enterprises.

2.4.4 Developmental State

A developmental state is a state that follows a state-designed development path. Given this, it legitimizes state intervention in policy formulation and implementation which is favored over a liberal open market (Leftwich, 1994). First used by Chalmers Johnson (1982) to characterize the development model in Japan, the developmental state is conceptually positioned between a liberal open economy and a centrally planned model. In countries pursuing the developmental state model, the state follows a state-designed development path. The state has a major role in guiding the private sector through proactive industrial policy (Wade, 1990; Woo-Cumings, 1999). In Japan, the government is represented on the boards of the country's conglomerates, the *keiretsu*. Through this means, the institutional foundations of Japanese industrial policies were supervised and coordinated by Japan's bureaucratic elites. The Japanese government was thus able to ensure that its objectives were met by the private sector (Johnson, 1982). Among other countries, Korea comes closest to following this model.

China's model of development also relies heavily on a proactive state role. In that sense, it embodies elements of the developmental state model (Leftwich, 1995). What is different for China is that while Japan and Korea intervene in the market to promote private sector enterprises (The Economist, 1997), the Chinese state supports its own enterprises to promote growth—the so-called state-led model (Yip, 2012). Yip contrasted the Chinese model with the neoliberal model by characterizing the former as "the state controls the capital" and the latter as "capital controlling the state", a clear reference to state capture by capitalist vested interests. Underlying this assumption is the Chinese understanding, as stated earlier, that the state and civil society are not mutually exclusive but the state is part of society, and to which the people look to in promoting growth and development.

Although more sympathetic to the role of the Chinese state, these theories remain limited in their applicability by their being grounded in the concept of the nation state. But as already indicated, the Chinese state is indigenously evolved over a long period of time. China's unification was attributed to Qin state's annexation by conquest six other states in 221 BC.[4] This was nearly two millennia before the concept of nation state emerged in Europe.[5]

2.5 China as a Historical State

Scholars, mainly historians, have argued that China, while adapting to new circumstances, always looks back to its own long history in seeking solutions to problems and challenges. Wang (2014) described how the May 4th Movement of 1919 became a reference point for subsequent movements and reforms. This is because the Chinese state has existed for over two millennia, predating the conceptualization and emergence of the now dominant nation state. Although bearing a close resemblance to a nation state, and despite transitions from imperial rule through republicanism, Leninism and to the "market socialism" of today, all within a century, the modern Chinese state is the outcome of centuries of evolution. Kuhn (2002) argued that this state has been "shaped decisively by the flow of its internal history", although external models of governance have left their mark. Nevertheless, the Chinese state remains more the product of its own history than of foreign influences. Wang Gungwu, a leading China scholar and historian, shares this view. He notes (Wang, 2013: 21):

> No country can really begin only with the modern. China has its own heritage that serves as valuable social capital ... Each country's past experiences remain embedded in how its people think and act in the present.

And in making a comparison between the "modern nation state" and the "ancient Chinese state", Niu (2012: 17) concluded that "though modern China has been totally involved in the modern world system, it has never escaped the unconscious or inertial power of its own history."

What are the salient characteristics of this indigenously evolved state? First, its prime objectives are defense of the realm and guardianship of its civilization and its people, including economic modernization and society transformation (Jacques, 2011; Shambaugh, 2000). These objectives, together with the need to modernize post-Qing Dynasty China, give the state a far larger role than that of a nation state. Pye (1992) famously writes that China is a civilization pretending to be a state. Jacques (2011) and Hsiung (2012) refer to China as a civilization state, wherein lies the entire civilization (Hsiung, 2012; Jacques, 2011). Zhang (2012) goes further to characterize the country as a "civilizational" state, which combines the essential qualities of a civilization state with features of the modern nation state. This role is reinforced by China's modern history, in which the chaos that reigned just after the establishment of the 1911 republic could only be solved by strong leadership backed by the apparatus of state (Zhou, 2010).

Second, the relationship between the state and Chinese society is much closer than in Western societies. Indeed, the state is at the apex of an orderly hierarchy in which layers of society make up the rest of the pyramid. This hierarchy is expressed in the remark by Confucius in his Confucian Analects (论语) shown at the beginning of this chapter. Not only is there no mutual exclusivity between state and society, the state, a product of and deriving its strength from Confucian thinking for much of China's history, is very much part of society, deriving its authority from its missions above (Li, 1997). This thinking of the existence of an orderly hierarchy is reflected in the use of Chinese terms. For instance, the parent-child hierarchy relating to the state and citizenry is shown by the reference to officials as "parental officials" (Fumuguan父母官). Another example of hierarchy with the state above the family as its building block can be found even today when a nation is referred to as "nation-family" (Guojia 国家). Indeed, Wang (2013) argues that this concept of hierarchy also applies to China's relationship with its neighbors and poses a barrier to the Chinese adoption of the Western concept of nation state.

That the Chinese state, viewed in its historical context, is materially different from what the West believes to be the Western norm for a modern state should lead us, first, to question the belief that China's future depends on its convergence to Western norms of state and governance. The assimilation of new concepts of state governance is not necessarily a wholesale endorsement of these concepts but rather responses to adapt to a changing world, and consistent with what China has done throughout history. The Chinese state remains, to borrow from Kissinger "singularly Chinese, defined by its long history and cultural identity" (Kissinger, 2011).

Last, China's missions for its state imply a role that goes well beyond what is expected of a nation state. Quite the opposite of what critics of the pervasive influence of the Chinese government believe, MacFarquhar and Fairbank (1987) noted the small size of the Chinese state in relation to its considerable mandate. And whatever reforms China is implementing, they are not to diminish state control, only to consolidate and strengthen the competitiveness of state enterprises (Wei, 2015). Not surprisingly, given the lens through which the Chinese state has been viewed, this understanding has eluded many commentators (see, for instance, The Economist, 2015). Hence, from a historical perspective, neither the size of the state sector nor the Chinese model of state-led growth, also referred to as state capitalism, should surprise. These salient features must be borne in mind as we examine the magnitude and role of state enterprises.

2.6 Conclusion: A Critique of Existing Mainstream Literature

This review of theories and empirical work raises important questions about the objectivity of extant research on China's state enterprises. First, mainstream Western models have been extensively applied explicitly as well as implicitly to China's state enterprise sector to justify findings as predicted by these models and to argue against state involvements in state enterprises. Empirical findings, especially in the early years of reform, have overwhelming found state enterprises to be inefficient. But such work has been based on assumptions that do not fully reflect or apply to the Chinese situation. In addition, state enterprises as instruments of state policy, a very important role in China as its economic heft grows, have not been taken into account. That trade-offs exist in the pursuit of often conflicting objectives has been all but forgotten. Also largely ignored have been other Western theories that allow for a much larger role for the state.

Second, since reform has transformed these enterprises over time, the conclusions that studies reach should change with the implementation of sequential reforms. Studies that cover the early days of reform would have failed to reflect the impact of subsequent reform. Studies using more recent data would not have captured the non-commercial role these enterprises had originally to play. And any time series analysis that includes major reform changes would, through the process of averaging, capture neither the situation before nor the situation after these changes. No matter which time period is chosen, the relevance of the results obtained can be called into question. And this does not even include questions of coverage—state control through ownership and governance varies across the tens of thousands of state enterprises at national, provincial, and local levels.

Third, in reviewing the transition process of China's state enterprises, it should first be noted that the state's control in state enterprises varies. From enterprise to enterprise, the nature of China's state enterprises undergoes transformation continuously. The challenge is how to capture the latest changes. China's state enterprises represent a new complex ownership and governance form, requiring clarification of the extent of state's involvement. This means that cross-section studies capture not a homogenous group of enterprises but a large variety of enterprises in various states of transformation and with varying degrees of state ownership. How ownership power is exercised also varies from enterprise to enterprise. Like time series analyses, the generalizability of findings from these studies would thus be compromised. Further, given the limitations of both time series and cross-sectional data applied to state enterprises in China, the use of panel data only compounds these limitations.

Fourth, the Chinese state may have other objectives for state enterprises not highlighted in Western theories. The focus on efficiency and profitability obscures an important role of state enterprises to take on positive externalities, chief among them being the provision of a social safety net for workers. So the role of state enterprise in much of the current discussion is not complete. To be fair, the internalization of externalities is very much a part of mainstream economic theory of the role of government. It is this preoccupation with efficiency, perhaps abetted by neoliberalism, which is to blame. And as already indicated and will be elaborated in Chap. 6, Chinese state enterprises are also called upon to fulfill strategic objectives of the state.

Perhaps, the most important conclusion to emerge from this chapter is that given the complexity of China's state enterprises, multi-firm or sectorial analysis, even if yielding important findings, must be complemented by in-depth studies of major enterprises, with the choice of enterprises made to cover different enterprise types. There is little to be gained by attempting comprehensive coverage. This brings us back to the challenging task of classification of state enterprises. Nevertheless, a good starting point is the official classification into three broad types—strategic/central enterprises wholly owned by the state, state-holding enterprises in which the government is the majority or largest single shareholder, and state joint-stock enterprises over which the state exercises no control. This is the approach adopted in this book.

Notes

1. Other reasons have been stated to be excessive political influence, bureaucratic culture, corruption, and capture by vested interests.
2. This call to revive an ancient Confucian philosophy was made in the 6th Plenary State Session of the 16th Central Committee of the Communist Party of China in 2006. This call emanated from the recognition that rapid economic growth had brought with it worsening income inequality and social justice (The Central People's Government of the People's Republic of China, 2009).
3. The term "Great Moderation" was used by Stock and Watson (2003).
4. Ying Zheng (嬴政), king of Qin, became Emperor Qin Shi Huang (秦始皇, First Emperor of Qin) upon unification (Bodde, 1987).
5. There is no agreement about when nation states emerged. Peck (2011: 3) dated its emergence to Europe in sixteenth and seventeenth centuries.

References

Alchian, A.A. (1987). Property rights. In J. Eatwell, M. Milgate, & P. Newma (Eds.), *The new Palgrave: Dictionary of ecconomics (First Edition)* (pp. 1031–1034). London: Palgrave Macmillan.

Alchian, A.A., & Demsetz, H. (1972). Production, information costs, and economic organization. *The American Economic Review, 62*(5), 777–795.

Alchian, A.A., & Demsetz, H. (1973). The property right paradigm. *The Journal of Economic History, 33*(01), 16–27.

Ariff, M., & Can, L. (2008). Cost and profit efficiency of Chinese banks: A non-parametric analysis. *China Economic Review, 19*(2), 260–273.

Bai, C., & Wang, Y. (1998). Bureaucratic control and the soft budget constraint. *Journal of Comparative Economics, 26*(1), 41–61.

Bai, C., Lu, J., & Tao, Z. (2009). How does privatization work in China? *Journal of Comparative Economics, 37*(3), 453–470.

Baumol, W.J. (1984). Toward a theory of public enterprise. *Atlantic Economic Journal, 12*, 13–19.

Boas, T.C., & Gans-Morse, J. (2009). Neoliberalism: From new liberal philosophy to anti-liberal slogan. *Studies in Comparative International Development, 44*(2), 137–161.

Bebchuk, L.A., & Fried, J.M. (2004). *Pay without performance: The unfulfilled promise of executive compensation*. Cambridge, MA: Harvard University Press.

Berger, A.N., Hasan, I., & Zhou, M.M. (2009). Bank ownership and efficiency in China: What will happen in the world's largest nation? *Journal of Banking & Finance, 33*(1), 113–130.

Berger, A.N., Hasan, I., & Zhou, M. (2010). The effects of focus versus diversification on bank performance: Evidence from Chinese banks. *Journal of Banking & Finance, 34*(7), 1417–1435.

Bodde, D. (1987). The state and empire of Qin. In D. Twitchett, & M. Loewe (Eds.). *The cambridge history of China, Volume 1: The Ch'in and Han Empires, 221 BC-AD 220* (pp. 20–103). Cambridge, UK: Cambridge University Press.

Bremmer, I. (2009). State capitalism comes of age: The end of the free market? *Foreign Affairs, 88*(3), 40–55.

Bretton Woods Project. (2000). The World Bank and the State: A Recipe for Change? London.

Buchanan, J.M. (1954). Social choice, democracy, and free markets. *Journal of Political Economy*, 62(2), 114–123.

Buchanan, A.E. (1985). *Ethics, efficiency, and the market*. Lanham, Maryland: Rowman & Littlefield Publishers.

Buchanan, J.M., & Tullock, G. (1962). *The calculus of consent: Logical foundations of constitutional democracy*. Ann Arbor, US: University of Michigan Press.

Chen, B., & Feng, Y. (2000). Determinants of economic growth in China: Private enterprise, education, and openness. *China Economic Review, 11*(1), 1–15.

Chen, G., Firth, M., & Rui, O. (2006). Have China's enterprise reforms led to improved efficiency and profitability? *Emerging Markets Review, 7*(1), 82–109.

Chen, L., & Tang, Y. (2014). If partial privatization of state enterprises can reduce their policy burdens. *Research on Economics and Management, 2014*(7).

Chomsky, N. (1999). *Profit over people: Neoliberalism and global order*. New York: Seven Stories Press.

Coase, R.H. (1937). The nature of the firm. *Economica, 4*(16), 386–405.

Coase, R.H. (1959). The Federal Communications Commission. *Journal of Law and Economics, 2*, 1–40.
Coase, R.H. (1960). The problem of social cost. *Journal of Law and Economics, 3*, 1–44.
Cull, R., & Xu, L.C. (2003). Who gets credit? The behavior of bureaucrats and state banks in allocating credit to Chinese state-owned enterprises. *Journal of Development Economics, 71*(2), 533–559.
Demsetz, H. (1967). Toward a theory of property rights. *The American Economic Review, 57*(2), 347–359.
Dharwadkar, B., George, G., & Brandes, P. (2000). Privatization in emerging economies: An agency theory perspective. *Academy of Management Review, 25*(3), 650–669.
Ding, J., & Motwani, J. (2001). Transfer of technology: A critical element in China's privatization process. *International Journal of Technology Management, 21*(5-6), 453–462.
Dong, X., Putterman, L., & Unel, B. (2006). Privatization and firm performance: A comparison between rural and urban enterprises in China. *Journal of Comparative Economics, 34*(3), 608–633.
Downs, A. (1957). *An Economic Theory of Democracy.* New York: Harper.
Du, X., Tian, Y., Zhang, G., & Li, L. (2014). Relationship between monopoly expansion of state enterprise and its performance - evidence study based on financial data of listed companies in China. *Technology Economics, 33*(6).
Estrin, S., & Pérotin, V. (1991). Does ownership always matter? *International Journal of Industrial Organization, 9*(1), 55–72.
Malkiel, B.G. and Fama, E.F. (1970). Efficient capital markets: A review of theory and empirical work. *The Journal of Finance, 25*(2), 383–417.
Fan, G. & Hope, N.C. (2013). The role of state-owned enterprises in the Chinese economy. Retrieved from https://www.chinausfocus.com/2022/wp-content/uploads/Part+02-Chapter+16.pdf
Firth, M., Fung, P.M.Y., & Rui, O.M. (2006). Corporate performance and CEO compensation in China. *Journal of Corporate Finance, 12*(4), 693–714.
Granovetter, M. (1985). Economic action and social structure: The problem of embeddedness. *American Journal of Sociology 91*(3), 481–510.
Gregory, P.R., & Stuart, R.C. (2004). *Comparing economic systems in the Twenty-first century.* Houghton Mifflin.
Groves, T., Hong, Y., McMillan, J., & Naughton, B. (1994). Autonomy and incentives in Chinese state enterprises. *The Quarterly Journal of Economics, 109*(1), 183–209.
Guerin, K. (2003). Property rights and environmental policy: A New Zealand perspective. New Zealand Treasury.
Harvey, D. (2005). *A brief history of neoliberalism.* Oxford University Press.

Hassard, J., Morris, J., & Sheehan, J. (2004). The "third way": The future of work and organization in a "corporatized" Chinese economy. *International Journal of Human Resource Management, 15*(2), 314–330.

Hsiung, J.C. (2012). *China into its second rise: Myths, puzzles, paradoxes, and challenge to theory.* World Scientific.

Huang, Z., & Wang, K. (2011). Ultimate privatization and change in firm performance: Evidence from China. *China Economic Review, 22*(1), 121–132.

Jacques, M. (2011). How China will change the way we think: The case of the state. Retrieved from http://www.transatlanticacademy.org/publications/how-china-will-change-way-we-thinkthe-case-state

Jensen, M.C., & Meckling, W.H. (1976). Theory of the firm: Managerial behavior, agency costs and ownership structure. *Journal of Financial Economics, 3*(4), 305–360.

Jiang, C., Yao, S., & Zhang, Z. (2009). The effects of governance changes on bank efficiency in China: A stochastic distance function approach. *China Economic Review, 20*(4), 717–731.

Jin, H., & Qian, Y. (1998). Public versus private ownership of firms: Evidence from rural China. *The Quarterly Journal of Economics, 113*(3), 773–808.

Johnson, C. (1982). *MITI and the Japanese miracle: The growth of industrial policy: 1925-1975.* Stanford University Press.

Kissinger, H. (2011). *On China.* Penguin Canada.

Kuhn, P.A. (2002). *Origins of the modern Chinese state.* Stanford University Press.

The Economist (1997). China adopts the chaebol. Retrieved from http://www.economist.com/node/90635

The Economist (2012). The rise of state capitalism. Retrieved from http://www.economist.com/node/21543160

The Economist (2015). A whimper, not a bang. September 19. Retrieved from http://www.economist.com/news/business/21665065-chinas-plan-reform-its-troubled-state-firms-fails-impress-whimper-not-bang

The Central People's Government of the People's Republic of China (2009). The footprint - 2006: The construction of a harmonious society. Retrieved from http://www.gov.cn/jrzg/2009-10/15/content_1440408.htm

Tisdell, C. (2009). *Economic reform and openness in China: China's development policies in the last 30 years.* School of Economics, University of Queensland.

Lange, O. (1936). On the economic theory of socialism: Part one. *The Review of Economic Studies, 4*(1), 53–71.

Lange, O. (1937). On the economic theory of socialism: Part two. *The Review of Economic Studies, 4*(2), 123–142.

Le Grand, J., & Estrin, S. (1989). *Market socialism.* Clarendon Press.

Leftwich, A. (1994). *The developmental state.* Department of Politics, University of York.

Leftwich, A. (1995). Bringing politics back in: Towards a model of the developmental state. *The Journal of Development Studies, 31*(3), 400–427.
Li, C. (1997). Confucian value and democratic value. *The Journal of Value Inquiry, 31*, 183–193.
Li, H. (2013). China's banking sector's NPLs are coming. Retrieved from http://finance.qq.com/zt2013/focus/yhyhz.htm?pgv_ref=aio2012&ptlang=2052
Lin, C., Ma, Y., & Su, D. (2009). Corporate governance and firm efficiency: Evidence from China's publicly listed firms. *Managerial and Decision Economics, 30*(3), 193–209.
Lin, X., & Zhang, Y. (2009). Bank ownership reform and bank performance in China. *Journal of Banking & Finance, 33*(1), 20–29.
Lin, Y., & Li, Z. (2004). Policy burden, moral hazard and soft budget constraint. *Economic Research Journal* (2).
MacFarquhar, R., & Fairbank, J.K. (Eds.). (1987). The cambridge history of China, Volume 14: The People's Republic, Part 1: The emergence of revolutionary China, 1949–1965. Cambridge, UK: Cambridge University Press.
Mengistae, T., & Xu, L. (2004). Agency theory and executive compensation: The case of Chinese state-owned enterprises. *Journal of Labor Economics, 22*(3), 615–637.
Mi, Z., & Wang, X. (2000). Agency cost and the crisis of China's SOE. *China Economic Review, 11*(3), 297–317.
Minsky, H.P. (1986). *Stabilizing an Unstable Economy*. Yale: Yale University Press.
Niu, G. (2012). Globalization and the transformation of the Chinese state: Comparing modern nation state and the ancient Chinese state. *Ritsumei Studies in Language and Culture, 23*(4): 17–29.
People.cn (1984). Building a socialism with a specifically Chinese character. Retrieved from http://en.people.cn/dengxp/vol3/text/c1220.html
People.cn (2007). Socialism with Chinese characteristics. Retrieved from http://en.people.cn/90002/92169/92211/6275043.html
Pick, A.C. (2011). The nation state: An essay. Retrieved from http://www.thenationstate.co.uk/TheNationState.pdf
Plattner, S. (1989). *Economic anthropology*. Stanford University Press.
Polanyi, K. (1944). *The great transformation: the political and economic origins of our time*. New York: Rineheart and Co.
Polanyi, K. (1957). The economy as instituted process. In M. Granovetter & R. Swedberg (Eds.), *The sociology of economic life*. Boulder, US: Westview Press.
Pye, L.W. (1992). *The spirit of Chinese politics*. Cambridge, US: Harvard University Press.
Sha, K., & Lin, S. (2001). Reforming China's construction state-owned enterprises. *Building Research and Information, 29*(4), 270–276.
Shambaugh, D. (2000). *The modern Chinese state*. Cambridge, UK: Cambridge University Press.

Shearmur, J. (1992). In defense of neoliberalism. *Journal of Democracy, 3*(3), 75–81.

Sikorski, D. (1993). A General Critique of the Theory on Public Enterprise: Part I. *International Journal of Public Sector Management, 6*(2).

Stigler, G.J. (1971). The theory of economic regulation. *The Bell Journal of Economics and Management Science, 2*(1), 3–21.

Stock, J. & Watson, M. (2003). Has the business cycle changed and why? In M. Gertler & K. Rogoff (Eds.), *NBER Macroeconomics Annual 2002*, Volume 17 (pp. 159–218). Cambridge, MA: MIT Press.

Su, D. (2005). Corporate finance and state enterprise reform in China. *China Economic Review, 16*(2), 118–148.

Sun, Q., & Tong, W.H.S. (2003). China share issue privatization: the extent of its success. *Journal of Financial Economics, 70*(2), 183–222.

Wade, R. (1990). *Governing the market: Economic theory and the role of government in East Asian industrialization*. Princeton University Press.

Wang, G. (2013) *Renewal: The Chinese state and the new global history*. Hong Kong: Chinese University Press.

Wang, G. (2014). *Another China cycle: Committed to reform*. Singapore: World Scientific.

Wang, H., & Jin, Y. (2002). *Industrial ownership and environmental performance: evidence from China*. The World Bank: Policy Research Working Paper. Development Research Group.

Wang, X., & Wei, J. (2014). The reason of China's state enterprises executive compensation control and its impact on performance - based on the principal "inequality aversion" model. *Journal of Beijing Technology and Business University (Social Science), 2014*(1).

Wei, L. (2015). China unveils overhaul of bloated state sector. *Wall Street Journal*, September 13. Retrieved from http://www.wsj.com/articles/china-to-allow-state-owned-enterprises-to-sell-shares-to-public-1442138335

Wei, Z., Xie, F., & Zhang, S. (2005). Ownership structure and firm value in China's privatized firms: 1991–2001. *Journal of Financial and Quantitative Analysis, 40*(1), 87–108.

Wildau, G. (2016). China's state-owned zombie economy. *Financial Times*, March 1. Retrieved from https://www.ft.com/content/253d7eb0-ca6c-11e5-84df-70594b99fc47

Woo-Cumings, M. (1999). *The developmental state*. New York: Cornell University Press.

Yang, M. (2012). Analysis of the factors influencing corporate performance variance after the privatization share issue of Chinese state enterprises. *Economic Survey, 2012*(1).

Yip, K.W. (2012). *The uniqueness of China's development model: 1842–2049*. Singapore: World Scientific Publishing Company.

Xu, X., & Wang, Y. (1999). Ownership structure and corporate governance in Chinese stock companies. *China Economic Review, 10*(1), 75–98.

Zhang, J. (2006). The total assets of China's banking sector are nearly 40 trillion yuan. *Xinhua News*. Retrieved from http://news.xinhuanet.com/newscenter/2006-05/25/content_4600765.htm

Zhang, W. (2012). *The China wave: Rise of a civilizational state*. World Scientific.

Zheng, Y., & Chen, M. (2007). *China's recent state-owned enterprise reform and its social consequences*. Briefing Series-Issue 23. China Policy Institute. The University of Nottingham.

Zhou, G. (2010). In search of a new China: State, society and the fate of modern China. Retrieved from http://ucsdmodernchinesehistory.wordpress.com/2010/03/27/841/

Zhu, C. (2014). Constructive thinking of anticorrosive mechanism for state enterprises. *People's Tribune, 2014*(11).

Zou, H., & Adams, M. B. (2008). Corporate ownership, equity risk and returns in the People's Republic of China. *Journal of International Business Studies, 39*(7), 1149–1168.

CHAPTER 3

State Enterprises, Economic Growth, and Distribution

Zi Gong asked about government. The Master said, "Enough food, enough weapons and the confidence of the people."
子贡问政。子曰:"足食,足兵,民信之矣。"
(Confucian Analects, 12: 7).
The duke Jing of Qi asked the Master about government. The Master replied, "Let the king rule, the minister govern, the father parent, the son obey."
齐景公问政于孔子。孔子对曰:"君君,臣臣,父父,子子"。
(Confucian Analects, 12: 11).

3.1 Introduction

In earlier chapters, two themes have been surfaced by critics of China's development model. One (Chap. 1) is the unsustainability of the country's existing political order, a one-party state led by the Communist Party, of which Chang (2010) and Pei (2006) are major exponents.[1] The premise of statements of this genre therefore is that China does not embrace democracy, specifically Western-style democracy, and liberal market economics. The second (Chap. 2) argues that China's state enterprise sector is a drag on the economy and needs to be reformed through privatization or liquidation (Kwan, 2010; Lal, 2006), and that these state enterprises would not have survived had it not been for the government's role in tilting the playing field in their favor.

R. Li, K. C. Cheong, *China's State Enterprises*,
https://doi.org/10.1007/978-981-13-0176-6_3

This chapter deals with the second theme. In countering the mainstream commentary on Chinese state enterprises, it presents an alternative view of Chinese state enterprises, arguing that these state enterprises are part and parcel of the role of the state that has been historically at variance with that of most other nation states. It delves deeper into the discussion beyond the arena of economics that economic studies of the Chinese state and its state enterprises largely neglect. The argument is made here that direct application of Western theories relating to state enterprises with their built-in assumptions is therefore a flawed approach.

Lacking a national data set and with limited sector-wide statistics, this chapter, like the previous, bases its analysis on empirical work undertaken by numerous researchers. The discussion is therefore anecdotal and subjected to the same limitations this body of work is saddled with. Since empirical research deals with specific aspects or particular geographic areas, any macroeconomic implications drawn are necessarily tentative.

In the next section, the Chinese state is placed in its historical context as a basis for a more balanced assessment of its state enterprises. This is consistent with the perspective of China being a historical state. Section 3.3 then surveys the history of state enterprise reform that emerges from this historical context. Section 3.4 reviews the role of state enterprises within the framework of the Chinese state. Sections 3.5 and 3.6 examine, at the sectoral and macroeconomic levels, the possible links between the state enterprise sector and China's economic growth and income/wealth distribution, followed by the conclusion in Sect. 3.6.

3.2 Understanding State Enterprises—The Chinese State in Historical Context

In economic terms, the dominant Western view of the role of the state is that of an internalizer of externalities and a provider of public goods. In support of this view, a range of theories—public choice, agency, organization, and property rights—also seek to explain the differences between state and private enterprise performance (Chap. 2). Their conclusion, that private enterprises perform better than state enterprises, speaks of the importance of ownership, and is premised upon the clear distinction between state and private sector activity, or, more broadly, between state and civil society.

Since state enterprises are institutions of the state, their role depends on the larger role of the state. There is now increasing recognition that for China, the latter role is at variance with the role of the state envisaged by Western economists for at least two reasons, both of which have historical and cultural roots (Hsiung, 2012; Jacques, 2009; Zhang, 2012). First, the modern Chinese state has been largely shaped by its long history rather than by principles that underpin the prevailing nation states, the history of which is much more recent. Despite transitions from millennia of imperial rule through republicanism, Leninism and to "market socialism" today, the Chinese state has endured being "shaped decisively by the flow of its internal history" (Hsiung, 2012; Kuhn, 2002) rather than by external models of governance, which were, however, eventually absorbed and adapted to fit the role played by the indigenously developed Chinese state.

Regardless of the influences that impact the Chinese state, continuity and perpetuation are ensured by its enduring missions, which, as stated by Jacques (2011) and Shambaugh (2000), are defense of the realm and guardianship of its civilization and its people, a role that necessitates economic modernization and social transformation. The second mission in the guardianship of its civilization gives China its distinctiveness—in the state lies the entire civilization, leading Jacques and Zhang to call it a "civilization state" which is distinct from a nation state.[2]

The dominant role of the state in China is not hard to understand from a historical perspective. For thousands of years, China was under imperial rule, it being accepted by Chinese society that the emperor as the Son of Heaven and the father of the people has absolute authority to rule under the Mandate of Heaven. This mandate was derived not from laws or rules but from moral authority. As already indicated, this authority was further embedded by the state's and society's embrace of Confucianism. Confucian philosophy held that there existed a natural order in the universe and that this order should be reflected in human relations, including that between the emperor and his subjects.

This moral authority was exercised through officials, referred to as "Fumuguan" (parental officials). The state played its role by engaging in public works that enhanced or guaranteed the welfare of subjects, the Great Wall of China and the Grand Canal being outstanding examples (Parker, 1908). An even better example is the state's role in taming the Yellow River over the last four millennia. This river, seen as the cradle of Chinese civilization, has been both a source of sustenance and of immense destruction. Connell (2013) noted:

> The productivity made possible by the Yellow River has provided the economic surpluses that have supported brilliant civilizations in the region since the second millennium BCE, but its periodic breakouts and changes in direction as it threads across more than five thousand kilometers of western and northern China have caused some of the worst disasters in recorded history.

Modern Chinese history is also conducive to the growth of a strong state. Zhou (2010) argues that there was a need for a strong state in post-Qing dynasty China as the country attempted to maintain social stability and modernize rapidly, following the example of Japan's Meiji era. An alternative explanation for China's current brand of market socialism being a variant of modern capitalism focuses on the country's recent history as it makes the transition from a command economy (Gabriele & Schettino, 2012). Gabriele, a proponent of this explication, argues that China's recent history makes for an important state role. Although rife with faults, China's market socialism may evolve into a more sophisticated form with no diminution in the size of the state. Thus, history has produced a role for the Chinese state that goes well beyond the mandate of the nation state, which is legalistic and political. This is well recognized by Western historians and political scientists, if not by economists (Kuhn, 2002; Shambaugh, 2000; Wong, 1997).

Second, the concept of state and civil society as being mutually exclusive—regarded largely as the norm of Western societies—has also been challenged by some scholars for being inapplicable to China (Huang, 2008; Wakeman, 1993). These scholars view the relationship between the state and civil society in China as non-mutually exclusive—that is, the state, albeit a large discrete part of it, is very much a part of society and works closely rather than in competition with the civil society. Thus, the debate about the appropriate size of the government is immaterial for China.

Historians have recognized that Confucianism, which dates back over two millennia and was the abiding cultural-political ideology for the entire history of imperial China, forms the basis of the Chinese view of the state. The resilience of Confucianism is demonstrated by the fact that it is experiencing a revival under the current regime in the form of Confucius Institutes.[3] According to Confucius, the state is rooted in the Chinese civilization and constitutes the highest hierarchy in the social order, below which are the family and the individual.[4] Li (1997) argues that the values of a hierarchical paternalistic system are not necessarily compatible with the Western notions of democracy, which stress the exercise of personal rights. Instead of equal rights entitlement as protection for the weak, Confucianism relies on "Ren" (仁), an attribute loosely translated as benevolence, imposing limitations on the stronger ones. Thus, this explains why liberal democracy as understood in the West is alien to China for much of its history. While this is also true even for many Western European countries, the dominance of Confucianism as the accepted code of conduct in China's society throughout its history sets the country apart from other countries. The "Keju" (科举) system of examinations is based on Confucian principles for professional advancement in government service, and the state was the primary source of employment and career progression, thereby ensuring the state's preeminence in Chinese society.[5]

The dominance of Confucianism in Chinese politics and society notwithstanding, it is not the only philosophy that was important in China's history. Legalism (Fajia (法家)), which gained preeminence during the time of Shi Huangdi and also during later parts of Chinese history, was, in its emphasis on rules and institutions rather than relationships, antithetical to Confucianism (Zhou, 2011). Yet not only did it not challenge imperial rule, it advocated absolute power for the ruler and was associated with harsh authoritarian rule by the state (Fu, 1996). In addition, it is materially different from Western concepts of the rule of law in that its argument advocating the observance of law is to ensure fidelity to the monarch (He, 2011). It is thus true that the objective of fidelity to the monarch and hence the state remained preeminent in Chinese society.

Those who know of the existence of a Western-style civil society in China acknowledged that Chinese civil society is either different from that in the West, or that it is small in presence. Thus, Goldman (2000) noted that diverse views and activities that sought to influence state decision-making in the early twentieth-century China were shaped chiefly by "Chinese collectivist views" rather than by individual rights. "Political rights", Goldman (2000) added, "were seen, as they are today in China, not as individual or group claims against the state so much as a limited arena of legitimate interests within the state". In the same year Goldman's article was published, Zhou (2000) wrote that Chinese society was both fragmented and restricted by the Chinese state, consumed by the need to maintain social stability while undertaking rapid modernization.

This characterization of the Chinese state has three implications, all of which are significant to the discussion of its role and institutions.

First, the assimilation of new concepts of state governance should not necessarily be seen as a wholesale embrace of these concepts but as responses needed to fulfill its missions in a world in which these concepts have gained ascendancy. This means that the belief that China's future depends on its convergence to Western norms of state and governance is misplaced. As Huang (2008) noted, "China's present cannot be, and China's future should not be, equated simply with the modern Western path of capitalism, liberal democracy, and the nation-state." Second, China's missions for its state go well beyond the mandate of the Western nation state, and hence define for it a far larger role. From a historical perspective, the Chinese model of state-led growth, also referred to as state capitalism, is therefore not surprising. Finally, the nature and attitude of Chinese society are such that the distinction between the Chinese state and its civil society is nowhere as sharp as Western theories of public enterprise assume it to be. In other words, Chinese societies look to the state for their welfare much more than societies in the West.

This understanding of the Chinese state has several implications for its state enterprises and ongoing reforms. First, state enterprises are core institutions of the Chinese state and their streamlining through reform should not be understood as representing a desire to reduce their importance. Instead, the reforms should be seen through the objective of making them more effective in their support of government strategies and policies. Second, state enterprise reform should be seen in its historical context of assimilating what are considered best practices of modern Western state enterprises into an endogenously evolved system and not as efforts primarily to converge to Western norms with respect to state enterprises. These reforms are elaborated in the next section.

3.3 State Enterprise Reform: A History of Major Transformations

China's state enterprises have been key instruments of state control of the country's economic activities. Over the last decades, they have been transformed to enterprises having varying degrees of control through ownership and governance by the state. Before 1978, the state controlled the whole economy but the lack of incentives resulted in most state sectors performing poorly.

Recognizing this early on in December 1978, the government started in a phased manner, in the spirit of Deng Xiaoping's "feeling the stones to cross a river", both governance and ownership reform of state enterprises. Governance reform began with enlarging operational autonomies to provide adequate incentives to managers—through increasing autonomy for managers to set prices and wages, hiring and firing employees, and investing and profit retention. Profits or losses of state enterprises were linked to employees' benefits and managers were allowed to share part of profits, in order to arouse the enthusiasm of state enterprises and incentivize employees.

In the 1980s, mounting state enterprise losses caused the state to transfer funds as loans instead of grants. In 1983, tax reform enabled the state to obtain fiscal revenues from the state enterprises by "taxes replacing profits turn-in". Organizational reforms were also initiated. Managerial positions in state enterprises were urged to be delinked from government hierarchical positions. The year 1984 saw the dissociation of state enterprises from the government and the separation of ownership rights and control rights. Specific measures like manager/contract responsibility system were introduced. In terms of supervision, the Administrative Bureau of State-owned Assets was established directly under the State Council in 1988 to strengthen the management of state-owned assets. In 1993, to develop the bond and stock financing in China's newly established capital market state enterprises were required to corporatize. But corporatization was to spell the end of the "iron rice bowl" for state enterprise employees because such costs had to be taken off the books of state enterprises if they were to be attractive to investors in the stock exchanges. Thus, the "modern enterprise system" was established while company laws were also promulgated that marked the beginning of the end for these enterprises' social welfare role.

The need to protect state enterprises that were considered strategic by the state was manifested through a major reform in 1995, when a policy called "grasping the large (state enterprises), letting go the small" was launched to have the state retain ownership/control of the largest state enterprises while smaller state enterprises were allowed to be merged, acquired, liquidated, and so on. Only about 1000 were treated as large and owned by the state. State enterprises that the government retained were in strategic sectors considered crucial to the country's national and economic security, and included financial, mining, steel, telecommunications, transportation, utilities, oil, and military-related production enterprises. In supporting these large state enterprises, the government also sought to create large state enterprise groups that are competitive in the international market.

During the 1990s, continued operating losses of state enterprises caused so much non-performing loans (NPLs) that in 1997 a three-year plan of reform was initiated to have state enterprises set up the modern enterprise system and assist loss-making state enterprises to get out of the difficulties. State commercial banks were enlisted to deal with their NPLs, while four specialized financial assets management companies were set up to implement debt-for-equity swaps for affected key state enterprises in difficulties.

State enterprises also came under the purview of the State-owned Assets Supervision and Administration Commission (SASAC) established in 2003. The report of the 16th National Congress of the Communist Party of China in 2002 required the central, provincial, and municipal governments to set up management institutions for state-owned assets. The establishment of central and local SASACs unified the management of state-owned employees, operations, and assets of state enterprises.

Simultaneously, ownership reform proceeded. In 1986, the state introduced the joint-stock system to state enterprises. The pilot project of the joint-stock system was put forward as early as 1986, but it was only adopted for a few large and medium state enterprises. In 1992, the State Council promulgated 11 regulations that broadened the coverage of the joint-stock system.

From 1993, the state enterprises were urged to raise finance in bond and stock markets. In 1995, in the spirit of "letting go the small", the ownership forms of medium and small state enterprises were restructured through channels such as reorganizing, merging, joint venture, partnership, sale, and liquidation. In 1999, the 4th Plenary State Session of the 15th Central Committee of the Communist Party of China proposed large and medium state enterprises to become joint-stock enterprises through public listing, joint venture, and cross holdings. But the key ("strategic") state enterprises had to be controlled by the government in terms of ownership.

Successively, in order to make state enterprises serve the public better and become independent business entities, the 3rd Plenary State Session of the 16th Central Committee of the Communist Party of China in 2003 encouraged the large state enterprises under SASACs to absorb foreign and social capital through public listing in capital markets.

To maintain government control, the "split-share system", introduced in 1990, became an institutional feature in China (Cooper, 2008: 53). Under this system, shares in listed state enterprises were separated into tradable shares and non-tradable shares. The state and legal persons[6] were holders of non-tradable shares which could not be traded in the stock market. By contrast, tradable shares were public shares that could be traded in the two stock exchanges and owned by institutional and individual shareholders. The latter had weaker bargaining power.

This unequal power caused conflict between the two types of shareholders. In 2005, the China Securities Regulatory Commission launched the pilot project of split-share reform. A compromise was struck whereby holders of tradable shares obtained additional shares from non-tradable shareholders, subject to a minimum state share proportion for state enterprises. This process was implemented gradually so as not to destabilize the stock markets brought about by the increase in the number of shares that could be traded in the stock markets. Nevertheless, the tradable shares became valued by the market and the original problem of non-tradable shares was progressively overcome (Dong & Zhang, 2008). With these institutional arrangements in place, the trend toward more tradable shares accelerated, so that by 2014, only a tenth of state enterprise shares were non-tradable (Table 3.1).

Table 3.1 Tradable and non-tradable shares in China's share markets (2004–2014)

Year	*Total issued shares (Billion)*	*Tradable shares (Billion)*	*% of shares tradable*
2004	714.94	257.71	36.05
2005	762.95	291.48	38.20
2006	1489.76	563.78	37.84
2007	2241.69	1033.15	46.09
2008	2452.29	1257.89	51.29
2009	2616.29	1975.95	75.52
2010	3318.44	2564.2	77.27
2011	3609.55	2885.03	79.93
2012	3839.50	3133.96	81.62
2013	4056.91	3674.42	90.57
2014	4361.01	3910.43	89.67

Source: China Securities Regulatory Commission (2015). Securities market yearly data. Retrieved from http://www.csrc.gov.cn/pub/newsite/sjtj/zqscyb/

Since November 2013, the 3rd Plenary State Session of the 18th Central Committee of the Communist Party of China put forward the overall objective of deepening state enterprise reform. In March 2014, President Xi Jinping pointed out that state enterprises should not be weakened, but needed instead to be strengthened (The Central People's Government of the People's Republic of China, 2015a).

Since the China's economic growth deceleration (its so-called new normal economy) (Zhang & Chen, 2017), supply-side structural reforms had been announced in November 10, 2015 (People.com.cn, 2015). As the "visible hand" to manage the economy on behalf of the Chinese state, state enterprises underwent further reform to strengthen economic growth qualitatively. First, as the hard core of the economy, China's state enterprises through mergers and regrouping were to improve their competitiveness and performance, which would provide long-term motivation for economic growth. Second, the profitability of state enterprises was most worrying among all enterprises, and had suffered the most from serious excess capacity; thus state enterprises would be the key undertaker to reduce excess capacity (e.g. in steel and coal production) (Wallstreetcn.com, 2015).

In September 13, 2015, the State Council put forward "Instructions on Deepening the Reform of State Enterprises" to achieve the above objectives by the year 2020 (Fig. 3.1). First, "mixed ownership reform", through welcoming non-state participation, actually strengthened the control of the state. And in the corporatization process of state enterprises,

Fig. 3.1 Main objectives of state enterprise reform by 2020. Source: The authors

a sound corporate governance structure and a perfect marketization mechanism needed to be better emphasized. Further, in order to create greater separation between the government and the state enterprises, the authorization management system of state-owned assets was divided into three hierarchies: the government, state-owned capital investment, and operation companies and state enterprises. Third, to optimize the distribution and structure of the state enterprise sector, as well as for them to play a leading role, the central government urged state enterprises to restructure and merge into conglomerates. Last, in order to consolidate the political core role of Communist Party, strengthening the core position of the Party Committee[7] in the corporate governance structure of state enterprises was urged (The Central People's Government of the People's Republic of China, 2015b).

The SASAC, Ministry of Finance of the People's Republic of China, and National Development and Reform Commission issued "the State Council of the People's Republic of China's Guidance on Deepening the Reform of State Enterprises". In order to push forward the reform in accordance of state enterprises in different function definition and classification, state enterprises were divided into two big categories: for-profit state enterprises and state enterprises dedicated to public welfare. The former category was further subdivided into (1) those engaged in full competition industries and areas; and (2) those engaged in activities related to national security, at national economy lifeline industries and areas, or undertaking major social projects. State enterprises dedicated to public welfare are to take care of the livelihood of the people, serve the society, and provide public products and services (The Ministry of Finance of the People's Republic of China, 2015).

For for-profit state enterprises whose main business at full competition industries and areas, corporate system reform,[8] joint-stock system reform,[9] and mixed ownership reform[10] were to be adopted, thus the ownership structure was diversified to include state-holding or state joint-stock. Supervision is stressed, but management autonomy had also to be ensured, for example, by adopting the professional manager system.

For for-profit state enterprises whose main business is related to national security, at national economy lifeline industries and areas, or undertaking major social projects, they should be state-owned or state-holding. Supervision should be adopted to ensure those serve national major strategies and macro-control policies.

State enterprises dedicated to public welfare must be wholly state-owned and fully controlled, but non-state entities could take part in their operations through purchasing services, franchise, or functioning as an entrusted agency.

In 2016, during the State Enterprise Party Construction Work Conference, Xi stressed the need to unswervingly adhere to the Communist Party's leadership of state enterprises, use the party organization's leadership and political core role in state enterprises, and ensure that the state policies be followed and significant deployments be carried out in state enterprises (Xinhuanet, 2016).

The Central Economic Work Conference in December 2016 also sent a strong signal that the mixed ownership reform briefly described above was an important breakthrough to the reform of state enterprises. The first batch of mixed ownership reform pilot projects had been carried out in seven areas, namely, electric power, oil, gas, railway, civil aviation, telecommunication, and the military industry. Non-state investors' capital was also welcome. The year 2017 was announced as the year of mix-ownership reform (The State-owned Assets Supervision and Administration, 2017). This gesture is to improve the efficiency of state enterprises, but it does not mean the central government loosens the grip of thoses enterprises.

To summarize, the roadmap of China's state enterprise reform is shown in Fig. 3.2. China's state enterprises have traveled a long and uneven road, but the journey continues.

This account makes it clear that the corporate reform of state enterprises has been transformative. On the one hand, the state conducted governance reform to streamline its control. On the other hand, ownership reform was conducted simultaneously through directly transferring a part of state ownership to the public (private, foreign). Mixed ownership forms of state enterprises have also emerged with the state, state legal persons (state enterprise), other legal persons (other enterprises), and natural persons (individuals) as owners.

The above reforms have produced what official sources refer to as three types of state enterprises today, only one of which fits the public enterprise stereotype in mainstream Western economics. According to the National Bureau of Statistics of the People's Republic of China (The National Bureau of Statistics of the People's Republic of China, 2009), state enterprises are classified as follows. The first type consists of enterprises wholly owned by the state only—referred to as "state-owned enterprises"—that refers to wholly state-owned enterprises, wholly state-owned companies, and state joint-run enterprises. The second type, referred to as

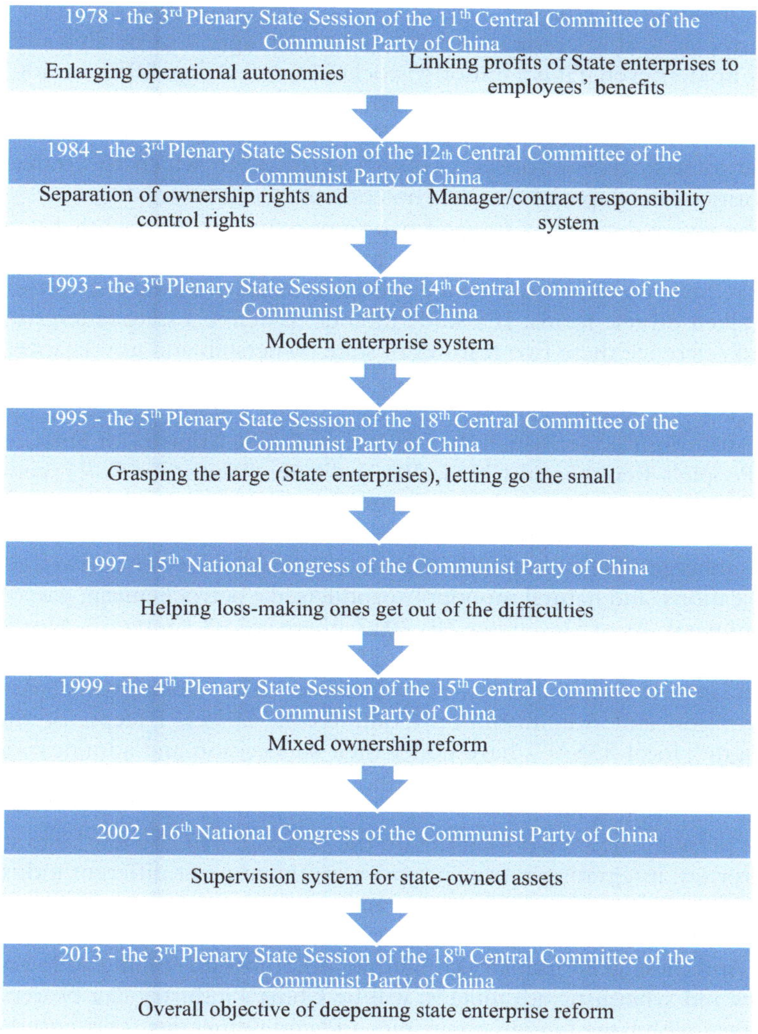

Fig. 3.2 The roadmap of China's state enterprise reform. Source: The authors

"state-holding enterprises", are those enterprises in which the state has majority ownership (more than 50%), or has the highest ownership among stock holders even if it is a minority stockholder (less than 50%), or not the highest but where the state exercises control through the agreement to make sure the state has de facto control. The third type, referred to as "state joint-stock enterprises", consists of those in which the state has minority ownership and exercises no control.

The above definitions stressed two important dimensions, that is, the state's ownership and control of the enterprise. However, after state enterprise reform, the state's ownership and governance of a state enterprise has also taken diverse forms. If a study intends to define a state enterprise, it has to reference these two features of state ownership and governance.

Even officially, however, the above is not the only classification of state enterprises. The government also classifies state enterprises according to the institutions under which they functioned (The Ministry of Finance of the People's Republic of China, 2013). Firstly, "Yangqi" (央企) (central enterprises) are controlled and supervised by the central government through SASAC. "Yangqi" have operations in strategic industries producing public goods like national defense, power grids, water and telecommunications, and natural monopoly products like petrochemical, gas, coal, and mineral. As of December 29, 2017, there are 98 "Yangqi". Most are 100% state-owned. The subsidiaries of "Yangqi" were classified as primary, secondary, tertiary, and lower subsidiary (The State-owned Assets Supervision and Administration Commission, 2017). Except for those "Yangqi", local SASACs have under their supervision and administration local state enterprises, which are under local governments (provincial, municipal, county, etc.).

At present, the state is focusing on the development of a few large state enterprises, integrating those enterprises in the same or different industry into "giants" in the form of mergers and acquisitions (M&A). That is why the total number of "Yangqi" is reducing but their share of total output is not. And these giant industry conglomerates, through reaping scale economies and synergistic advantages, will be China's industry flag bearers to compete with large foreign companies and conglomerates. Through these means, state enterprise conglomerates would enhance their competitiveness in the global economy. In addition, the merger of state enterprise in the same industry is also aimed at reducing wasteful competition among those in the same industry while improving their efficiency.

Secondly, the other strategic sector—that of financial institutions—is supervised by the People's Bank of China (PBC), the China Banking

Regulatory Commission (CBRC), the China Securities Regulatory Commission (CSRC), the China Insurance Regulatory Commission (CIRC), and the State Administration of Foreign Exchange (SAFE). We discuss this sector at greater length in Chap. 4.

Lastly, a group of state enterprises is supervised by departments under the State Council like tobacco, gold, radio and television, culture, publishing, and other industries. What are called "social service organizations" are under this category. They are engaged in education, technology, health, culture, and so on, and were set up by the state to provide social welfare to the citizenry and funded by state assets. According to regulations from the State Council, a social service organization could not be defined as a non-governmental organization or non-profit organization. First, it was not just initiated but also supervised by government institutions. Second, it could set up for-profit organizations based on Corporate Law (The State Council of the People's Republic of China, 2004).

Notably, there are uncounted state enterprises not supervised by any three above categories of departments under the State Council. For example, ZTE Corporation in Chap. 5 is a state-holding enterprise, but not controlled and supervised by any above government departments. Those are categorized as for-profit state enterprises engaged in full competition industries and areas and they are called "commercial" state enterprises in this book.

In addition, for-profit state enterprises engaged in activities related to national security, at national economy lifeline industries and areas, or undertaking major social projects are so-called strategic state enterprises in strategic industries (including the banking sector or financial institutions in this book). The above last group "social service organizations" is to be equivalent to state enterprises dedicated to public welfare.

Figure 3.3 shows the sequence of state enterprise reforms. As with China's entire transition from central planning to the market, this reform proceeded through a process of trial and error, in line with the central government's intention to incorporate the private sector according to the objective of constructing a socialist market economy. In this process, many problems were encountered so that one state enterprise reform called for further reform. At the same time, given the importance of state enterprises, the impact of reform on these enterprises also determined not only the pace but more importantly the success or failure of China's economic transition.

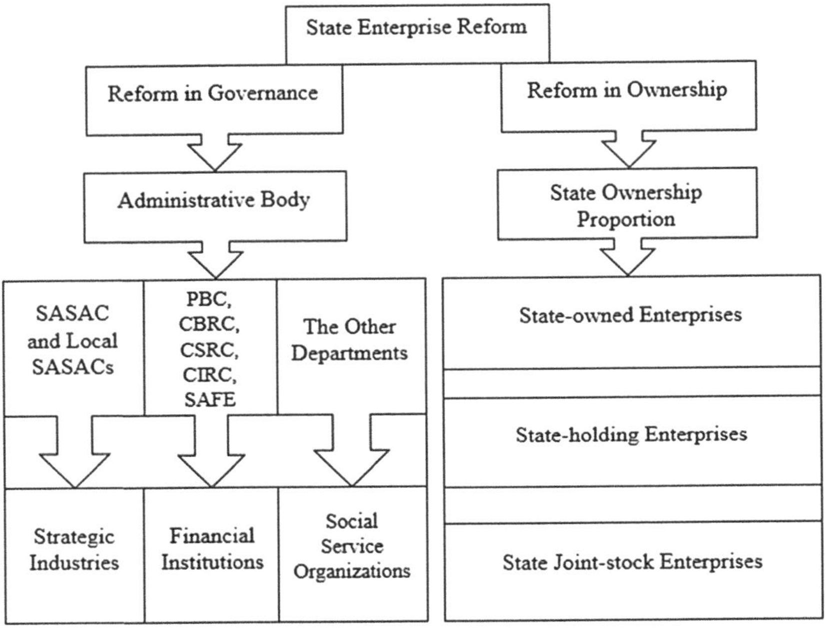

Fig. 3.3 The sequence of state enterprise reform. Source: The authors

3.4 Characterizing China's State Enterprises: Ownership, Governance, and Performance

As key institutions of the Chinese state, state enterprises are central to the discussion of the state's role. Although there has been a decline in the state enterprises' contribution in terms of the number of enterprises, industrial output, and exports, they remain major players in the economy while their presence is increasingly felt on the global stage. Table 3.2 reports statistics of industrial state enterprises that are wholly owned and majority-owned by the government. These figures understate the government's corporate ownership in this sector because enterprises in which the government is a minority shareholder are excluded. Worth noting is the fact that while the number of state enterprises in 2009 was reduced to just under one-eighth of that in 2000, their share in output and employment has only been halved and fallen to two-fifths respectively, suggesting that these enterprises have become larger over time. Data from the second national economic

Table 3.2 Selected statistics of Chinese industrial state enterprises (2000–2009)[a]

Year	*No. of state enterprises as % of all state enterprises*	*State enterprise output as % of total output*	*State enterprise employment as % of total employment*
2000	32.8	47.3	53.9
2001	27.3	44.4	49.2
2002	22.6	40.8	43.9
2003	17.5	37.5	37.6
2004	12.9 (2.0)[b]	35.2 (15.3)	29.8 (13.7)
2005	10.1	33.3	27.2
2006	8.3 (5.3)	31.2 (14.9)	24.5 (15.1)
2007	6.1 (3.4)	29.5 (13.7)	22.1 (12.9)
2008	5.0 (2.6)	28.4 (13.1)	20.3 (11.4)
2009	4.7 (2.5)	26.7 (12.5)	20.4 (11.1)

Source: China Statistical Yearbook, 2000–2009

[a]Includes state enterprises which are wholly or majority-owned by the state only. Enterprises in which the state has minority ownership are excluded

[b]Includes state enterprises wholly owned by the state only (with only one single-large stockholder that is the state)

census, conducted in 2008, confirmed this development. State enterprises in the industrial and service sectors held RMB 63 trillion out of RMB 208 trillion, or 30% of total assets, which translate into about 13.4 times the size of non-state enterprises in terms of average assets.[11] The decline in the proportion of wholly owned state enterprises is less than that of majority-owned enterprises.

The rich historical discourse on China's state and state-civil society relations seems to have completely evaded the economic debate on Chinese state enterprises. Thus, viewed through the Western economic lens, Chinese state enterprises have been characterized as "technologically inefficient", "moribund", or "very poor relative to the non-state sector", which are stereotyped traits of weaknesses of Western state enterprises (Broadman, 1999; Mai & Perkins, 1997). The state enterprises are therefore blamed for increasing economic vulnerability, damaging the private sector, and retarding the country's long-term economic growth. As for the commentary on the state, the debate over state enterprises is framed in terms of private versus government ownership, with privatization the ultimate goal in reform.[12] The question about whether these judgments on the Chinese state enterprises hold true for the Chinese state hinges on addressing two related questions. First, which are the Chinese state enterprises and in what ways are they similar to the generic state enterprises in

Western public economics? Second, how has the state enterprise sector performed in fulfilling its mandated functions since the economic transition in 1978? This section will focus on the discussion of the first question. The subsequent sections will deal with the second question. As already demonstrated in the last chapter, there is no shortage of literature on China's state enterprises, but characterizing today's enterprises is challenging because to distinguish between public and private enterprises using a set of generic attributes—the most evident of which are ownership, control, and performance—becomes problematic in the case of China. Ownership is the first defining attribute that differentiates state enterprises from private enterprises. Control is the second attribute related to institutional capability and governance. The third attribute, performance, arises from several theories about state enterprises that distinguish them from private enterprises. We review these attributes in the China context.

3.4.1 Ownership

This attribute that defines state enterprises presents major problems. First, in common with other countries, though China defines state enterprise by ownership (full and majority), decentralization and interlocking holdings often make it difficult to tell which part of the state—the central, provincial, or local—is the owner. Further, due to numerous reform experiments, state ownership of enterprises ranges from 100% (for strategic enterprises) to minority shareholding, is differentiated according to administrations (central, provincial, and local governments) and also includes quasi-state entities whose ownership is ambiguous (Hu, 2005; Scissors, 2011).[13] There are overlaps too in central enterprises (Yangqi), which currently number 98 enterprise conglomerates and are controlled by the central government, including both strategic enterprises and those in which the government holds more than 50% of the stocks. At the same time, non-state enterprises are not entirely private sector enterprises because township and village enterprises that are collectives are also included.

An example of the difficulty of classification is provided by Milhaupt and Zheng (2015: 673–674) who reported on the mixed ownership of Ping An Insurance, reported to be the world's most valuable insurance brand in 2016 (Olano, 2017) in Table 3.3. In its 2015 Annual Report, the company proudly proclaimed its 96th place listing on the "Fortune Global 500" and was top-ranked among *non-state-owned Chinese enterprises* (ital-

Table 3.3 Top ten shareholders of Ping An Insurance (Group) of China Ltd.

Type of Enterprise	*Shareholder*	*% Shareholding*
State	Shenzhen Investment Holdings Company Ltd.	6.08
	Shum Yip Group Ltd.	2.27
Domestic non-state	Yuan Trust Investment Co. Ltd.	4.8
	Linzi New Horse Investment Development Co. Ltd.	4.03
	Linzi Jingao Industrial Development	3.46
	Shenzhen Wuxi Yufu Industrial Development Ltd.	2.27
	Gongbujiangda Jiangnan Ind. Development Company Ltd.	1.76
Foreign	HSBC Ltd.	7.76
	HSBC Insurance Holdings Ltd.	4.58
	All Gain trading Ltd.	1.04

Source: Milhaupt & Zheng (2015), Table 1

ics ours). It also ranked at No. 32 on "Forbes Global 2000" (Ping An Insurance, 2015: 3). However, Milhaupt and Zheng (2015: 674) noted that "Ping An did not appear on an influential ranking of China's top 500 private companies, suggesting that it was not considered a POE by the domestic organization that conducted the ranking." Given that the company is part of the financial sector and its size, and despite its self-designation, the likelihood that state control is exercised, though indirectly, is real indeed. This example shows not only the difficulty of classification but also that of clarifying who exercises control.

3.4.2 Governance

Ownership ambiguities have prompted attempts to distinguish enterprises by their exercise of control (Chen, Firth, & Rui, 2006). In this regard, the appointment of CEOs of state enterprises by the government reflects the latter's control of these enterprises (Fan, Wong, & Zhang, 2007). This, as has been argued, is inimical to performance of state enterprises. However, much has changed in the state enterprise sector. Since the formation of the SASAC in 2003, CEO appointments for the central enterprises were conducted by SASAC mainly from within the ranks of these enterprises (The State-owned Assets Supervision and Administration Commission, 2009). For state enterprises in general, a growing body of literature also points to such appointments being made on commercial rather than political grounds (Knowledge@SMU, 2012; Li, 2005).

Nevertheless, appointment of the top management level matters much less than governance. To the extent that exceptions to the state enterprise stereotype abound among China's enterprises, the nature of governance cannot be easily categorized. Guthrie & Wang (2007), in reviewing various enterprise structures, concluded that many state enterprises are managed and run like private firms. In terms of reward for performance, state enterprises that are listed on international stock exchanges compete for talent and link executive compensation to corporate performance like any other private enterprise. Some state enterprises have attracted foreign investors and hence have multinational representation on their boards. The level of compensation is now sufficiently high to attract top managers and executives from the private sector.[14] Listing on the international stock exchanges like Hong Kong and New York, which bring in private and foreign investors, clearly also subjects these enterprises to market discipline, as well as improved corporate governance and some degree of shareholder influence. China has also embarked on an international talent hunt for high-caliber executives, including foreigners and Chinese émigrés, for its leading state enterprises to ensure they achieve international competitiveness. Thus, state enterprises pit themselves against the domestic private sector and even multinational enterprises in their talent hunt. By offering attractive employment terms, state enterprises have an edge in recruiting talent. Evidence has also shown that the global managerial labor market is a strong determinant of compensation of state enterprise CEOs (Li, Moshirian, Nguyen, & Tan, 2007).

Further, Kato & Long (2004), who studied executive compensation in firms listed in China's stock markets, concluded that Chinese enterprises tend to associate executive compensation (in cash) and firm performance much more strongly than enterprises in the US and Japan, although state enterprises manifest a much weaker link. Corroborating these findings, Conyon & He (2011) conclude that the factors determining executive compensation in China were no different from those in the US, and that China's corporate governance reforms were reasonably effective in aligning managerial with shareholder interests.[15] Thus, it should not be surprising if state enterprises such as Baoshan Iron and Steel, Legend Computers (now Lenovo), China International Marine Containers Corporation, the Pearl River Piano Group, and Guangzhou Metro Corporation were said to be among the best managed firms in China since as early as 2001

(Knowledge@Wharton, 2001; Tse, 2006). In reconciling the weak link between cash compensation and corporate performance despite strong management performance of state enterprises, Cao, Lemmon, Pan, & Tian (2010) argued that political incentives can offset any shortfall in economic incentives which disadvantage managers of state enterprise.

3.4.3 Performance

The third attribute is enterprise performance, which state enterprises are expected to fare below par.[16] Public enterprise theory measures performance by taking into account enterprises' economic inefficiency and/or poor profitability. State enterprise inefficiency arises from the monopoly power of state enterprises in their respective markets and the obligation to satisfy multiple and conflicting objectives. The latter factor, together with bureaucratic management, has been argued to account for their poor profitability. The inability to innovate, a critical attribute in the discourse on economic convergence and technology catch-up, is also said to be a contributory factor to poor performance.

Studies undertaken for the period up to the 1990s have confirmed the theoretical hypothesis about loss-making state enterprises, citing factors such as employment costs, market competition, social welfare costs, power relations with different levels of government, government policies during economic transition as well as historical factors (Holz, 2002; Hu, 2005). Principal-agent problems, exacerbated by the reforms in the 1990s, also emerged as a result of asset stripping especially at the subnational level (Smyth, 2000). However, with reforms undertaken since the early 1990s, the situation reversed in the mid-1990s (Tian & Estrin, 2008). A research project completed recently by the Unirule Institute of Economics on China's state enterprises reported that the net profit of state-owned and state-holding enterprises in 2008 was more than three times higher than that in 2001 as a result of subsidies, lower tax burdens, and financing cost, compared to non-state enterprises (Jiang, 2011).

Are state enterprises technological laggards? The China Chemical National Corporation (ChemChina), created from a merger between China Blue Star Chemical Cleaning and other state enterprises affiliated with the Ministry of Chemical Industry, has upgraded its technology through international acquisitions (Koch & Ramsbottom, 2008). In the clean energy sector, state enterprises such as State Grid Corporation, which dominates China's electricity supply, are said to be a leader not only in

China but also the rest of the world in clean energy research and development (R&D) and the technology's eventual commercialization.[17] Local jurisdictions like Shanghai have also supported the national strategy through creating environments for innovation. These initiatives reflect the fact that large enterprises, many of which are state-owned, take up a dominant share in R&D funding and expenditure, and that China's R&D expenditure as a share of GDP is now comparable to those in developed countries. There is also evidence that enterprises rather than the government are increasingly driving innovation, a positive outcome of the Chinese government's strategy launched in 2006 to promote indigenous enterprise-based innovation (Ren, Zeng, & Krabbendam, 2010; Zhang, Zeng, Mako, & Seward, 2009). Further, Zheng, Liu, and Bigsten (2000) find that large state enterprises are more likely than non-state enterprises to generate technical progress while Yang also reports that state enterprises did respond to technological catch-up (Gong, 2004; Zheng, Liu, & Bigsten, 2000). Thus, some Chinese state enterprises are currently at the forefront of innovation in an environment that still faces many challenges.

Despite their good performance, state enterprises are still subject to criticism that their success is attributable to their reliance on state power, or the preferential treatment being granted as a monopoly or near-monopoly and for being in heavily regulated sectors with little competition from the private sector. In fact, state enterprises found in intensively competitive industries are also facing competition from both the domestic and foreign private sectors as well as other state enterprises.[18] The stiff competition was attributed to the large number of state enterprises (except the central enterprises which number slightly over a hundred) owned by different levels of government operating in China's fragmented market. These enterprises face tough competition as they move beyond their local market (Knowledge@Wharton, 2006), resulting in some highly competitive state enterprises. The automobile and steel industries are such examples. Under competition, Chinese automobile makers are beginning to achieve original capabilities and R&D (Li, 2009). The government has also promoted competition by introducing a bidding process for enterprises attempting to make acquisitions abroad. Dyer & McGregor (2008) cited the case of Chinalco's share acquisition of Rio Tinto being approved by the government after it won the bid against other state enterprises. They also noted that China Airlines' success in beating Singapore Airlines over the intended purchase of China Eastern Airlines is not simply an exercise of raw state power. As a matter of fact, China Airlines had to pay a higher price than Singapore Airlines to take over China Eastern Airlines. Given these developments, Woetzel (2008) notes that while the playing field remains in favor of the state enterprises, especially in terms of access to finance, the competitive conditions facing state and private enterprises were converging. Internationally, state enterprises face the even greater handicap of being viewed with suspicion by foreign governments.[19]

The role of reform and privatization is central to the existence of Chinese state enterprises. Privatization has taken different routes during implementation and resulted in different corporate entities. For instance, the state enterprise reform introduced a decade ago had promoted greater autonomy in not only enterprises but also various levels of government. The various routes to privatization include privatization of control with no ownership change, leasing, mergers, sale to employees to form joint-stock companies, as well as ownership participation from individuals, and groups of individuals, including foreign investors. Profitable enterprises have been listed on international stock exchanges while enterprise groups were formed with a view to develop national champions. The myriad experiments—many were unsuccessful but others helped enterprises rise to become behemoths that are looked upon with suspicion by the West today—simply illustrate the dynamism of a sector that has been labeled as "dying" and "a dinosaur".[20]

The existence of these specific cases still leaves open the criticism that besides state favoritism,[21] cases of successful state enterprises represent exceptions to a subsector wallowing in failing and failed enterprises. However, as noted earlier, while successful enterprises may account for a tiny fraction of the total enterprises, they are, nevertheless, often among the largest in the country, if not in the world, and they still account for a sizeable share of industrial output.[22]

More importantly, the crux of the above discussion is not about the argument that the state enterprise sector as a whole is efficient, competitive, and innovative, though this is to a certain extent true for some enterprises but that the general characterization of the sector as moribund, loss-making, or inefficient is no longer appropriate. Nor is it easy or meaningful to draw a contrast between private and the state sectors, given how some state enterprises are professionally managed. Indeed, as Scissors (2011) notes, the contrast perpetuates a mistaken notion that what China officially refers to as "non-state" is synonymous with private (Scissors, 2011).

Even more importantly, the above discussion illustrates the limited applicability of the state-private dichotomy that has served as the implicit assumption in many studies. Further, what the world is seeing is a form of enterprise, neither fully public nor private, that defies stereotyping, which however fits well with the historical and socio-cultural development of China. Given the special environment in which they exist, these enterprises bear little resemblance to the Japanese keiretsu and Korean chaebol, which are private entities albeit with extensive government intervention.[23] The Chinese enterprises, many beginning to rival their Japanese and Korean counterparts in size, are public-private hybrids. While their closeness to government and political leadership has given them the advantage to tap state resources, they do enjoy sufficient autonomy to be managed like private enterprises at the same time.

3.5 The State Enterprise Sector and Economic Growth

Given the size of the state enterprise sector, commentary on its sectoral and/or macroeconomic role has also been framed in terms of its contribution to economic growth. Empirical studies on economic growth of the state enterprise sector until around 2000 have largely been unfavorable. A host of empirical studies have found that total factor productivity—a source of economic growth—of these enterprises was reported to be zero or negative, and many reasons were attributed to their poor performance (Sachs & Woo, 2003). By comparing state enterprises' productivity with that of non-state and/or private enterprises, Sachs & Woo (2003) report higher and more rapidly rising profitability among non-state enterprises but declining profitability for enterprises with increasing share of state ownership.

At the macroeconomic level, there were commentaries critical of state enterprises for inhibiting China's economic growth as the country's economic growth moderated considerably and state enterprise losses mounted at the onset of the Asian Financial Crisis (AFC) in 1997 (Dorn, 2000; Rawski, 2000). While these commentaries were mostly not supported by research, a few studies have attempted to make that link empirically. Chen and Feng (2000) analyzed cross-provincial data for the 1978–1989 period and found evidence of a growth-enhancing effect of "private and semi-private enterprises" and growth-diminishing impact of public enterprises. Similarly, Phillips and Shen (2005) discovered that the size of the state enterprise sector (measured in terms of its share in total industrial output) was negatively related to provincial growth rates.

In empirical studies conducted since the turn of the twenty-first century, an increasing number of positive analyses has replaced and eclipsed the mostly negative findings as state enterprise reform—which was initially aimed at stemming losses but gradually reoriented to nurture globally competitive enterprises—has produced an economic turnaround for the state sector. Recent literature surveys have indicated that there are signs of productivity growth in the state enterprise sector in the period leading up to 1993 and after, and that the existing gap between the state enterprise sector and the non-state and foreign enterprise sectors is narrowing (Jefferson, Rawski, & Zhang, 2008). These results were corroborated by the estimates made by Park (2010), who also documented the impressive rise in total factor productivity (Table 3.2).

An important reform that will likely have a major impact on growth is the consolidation of state enterprises into conglomerates under the supervision of the central government (SASAC). The objective of forming central enterprises or "Yangqi" is to help them achieve global competitiveness in both scale and technology. Adopting Korea's "picking winners" system, China chooses industries with cutting-edge and green technology, selected forms of manufacturing, and production of industrial materials of strategic importance like steel, cement, aluminum, and rare earth elements as "pillar industries". Restructuring and mergers were supported by incentives such as tax credits and financing from state banks and asset management companies (The Central People's Government of the People's Republic of China, 2010). These enterprises number fewer than 100 and efforts are being made to consolidate further.[24] These enterprises, together with selected state enterprise giants, will be key players in the government's strategy of "state-led" growth.

None of the studies discussed earlier dealt with data of an appropriate level of generality to offer a reasonable macroeconomic view. It does not seem possible to explicitly associate macroeconomic growth and productivity data with the role of the state enterprise sector. For instance, as Table 3.4 has shown, China's economic growth rate for various years bears little relation to changes in the state enterprise sector. It is therefore hard to refute Li and Putterman's (2008) argument that "it is implausible that China's economic growth could have progressed so rapidly if the country has been dragging along its state sector like an albatross round its neck for all of these years."

Table 3.4 Selected macroeconomic indicators of China's economic growth and income distribution (1980–2009)

Year	*GDP growth rate (%)*	*Period*	*TFP growth rate (%)*	*Year*	*Gini coefficient*	*Income share held by poorest 10%*
1980	7.8			1981	0.291	
1984	15.2	1980–1990	2.93	1984	0.277	
1988	11.3			1987	0.299	3.3
1990	3.8			1990	0.324	3.5
1992	14.2	1990–1900	3.72	1993	0.355	3.2
1994	13.1			1996	0.357	3.1
1996	10.0			1999	0.392	2.1
1998	7.8					
2000	8.4			2002	0.426	2.3
2002	9.1	2000–2007	6.04	2005	0.425	1.8
2004	10.1					
2006	12.7					
2008	9.6					
2010	10.4					

Sources: World Bank database at http://data.worldbank.org/indicator/, and Park Jungsoo, "Projection of Long-term Total Factor Productivity for 12 Asian Countries", ADB Working Paper No. 227, October 2010, Table 3.

Finally, it should be noted that mainstream Western economics, which recognizes the productive and redistributive role of state enterprises, cannot be criticized for the research focus and emphasis on efficiency. Responsibility lies in the dominance of neoliberal ideology toward the end of the twentieth century, with the Washington Consensus holding sway with multilateral lending institutions. Consequently, the larger important role of state enterprises in general and China's in particular has been neglected (Chai, 2003). This missing role is examined in the next section.

3.6 State Enterprises and Social Protection: Missing in (Research) Action?

In the quote at the beginning of this chapter, Confucius' prescription for good government was for the population to have adequate food, the country to have a strong army and the confidence of the people. Although not explicitly stated, food adequacy speaks to a welfare goal of government, a goal Chinese state enterprises were entrusted with from the beginning.

There is a plethora of research directed at measuring state enterprise performance in terms of efficiency, but there is little research linking state enterprises to their social security role. To be sure, there are however a few exceptions. Bai, Li, and Wang (2003) stressed the importance of state enterprises playing both productive and distributive roles during the transition period as independent institutions get ready to become fully operational in the provision of a social safety net. Huang, Li, and Lotspeich (2010) recognize that by preventing large-scale unemployment, state enterprises facilitated the growth and development of non-state enterprises through a positive externality—social stability—but at the cost of reduced productive efficiency. Their estimates have shown that incorporating this externality would have aligned state enterprises' contribution to economic growth with that of non-state enterprises. While relieving enterprises of their distributive role has strengthened their profitability, it has left a void in the social safety net that has not been filled even today.

How did state enterprise reforms change the enterprises' original mandate? Before the start of China's economic transition in 1978, state enterprises accounted for three-quarters of China's industrial output, employed two-thirds of all industrial employees, and were responsible for employee welfare, including pension and housing. They also contributed to 90% of the state's fiscal revenues (Dong & Putterman, 2003). Hence, the distributional role of state enterprises as provider of social protection and as income source to fund social provisions needs no further emphasis. Together with enterprise employees' security of tenure, all employees were said to be protected by the iron rice bowl (Fig. 3.4). During the first 15 years of transition, state enterprise reforms had improved financial discipline through restructuring incentives and increasing competition, but that had not given enterprise managers the autonomy to dismiss workers. By the mid-1990s, as the state enterprises' share in total output plunged, the share in total employment has decreased much more gradually. This implied that despite the serious losses suffered by state enterprises due to asset stripping by managers, inefficiencies arising from a long history of soft budget constraints, and large labor redundancies (Hashiguchi, 2008; Mako & Zhang, 2003),[25] the social safety net had remained largely intact. However, the severe losses had attracted attention from the international community, which suggested privatization as a solution. Little attention was given to alleviating the social burden of state enterprises though privatization, as a remedy, was in place.[26] The "iron rice bowl" was thus under threat (Fig. 3.4).

Fig. 3.4 The civil servants' scramble for the "iron rice bowl". Note: Xiao (2010), in his description of those bidding for government employment, noted "with almost guaranteed stability and generous welfare package, a civil servant has long been regarded as (having an) 'iron rice bowl'." Source: Xiao, Q. (2010) "Top 10 'tribes' in 2009", China Daily, January 11, 2010. Retrieved from http://www.chinadaily.com.cn/china/09tentopnews/2010-01/11/content_9289602.htm

The Chinese government reacted to the growing losses of state enterprises by making a shift in the reform strategy, retaining only the largest state enterprises while "releasing" the small ones (Zhuada, fangxiao抓大放小) through sale, privatization, or closure (Zhou, 2000).[27] However, so long as the retained enterprises are not relieved of their social burdens, they would be forced and continue to rely increasingly on bank loans, which have become harder for state enterprises to obtain since then as a result of the reform. Hence, state enterprises' debt burden soared, while struggling even to fund their operations.

Despite the reluctance to shed labor, an estimated 3.6 million workers were laid off between 1995 and 1997, although some were rehired (Zhou, 2000). That it did not prove to be socially destabilizing could be due to the fourfold increase in employment in the non-state sector during the period.

Corporatization and shareholding reform, including the admittance of foreign ownership and listing on international stock exchanges, did eventually erode the provision of social safety net, however (Moore & Wen, 2006).[28] This is the result of successful listing and foreign investor participation that required a clean set of accounts without any data on social costs and that solely displays the information about income of the listed enterprise (Walter, 2010).[29]

A by-product of the reforms was the creation of social security experiments to take over the role formerly played by state enterprises. These experiments ranged from the rehiring of laid-off workers and provision of compensation packages for laid-off workers to the establishment of the National Social Security Fund in 2001. They helped relieve some of the hardships caused by the layoffs and restructuring under state enterprise reforms, but did not seem sufficiently comprehensive to form a national social security system. Discussions of forming the national social security system continued in the lead-up to China's 12th Five-Year Program (FYP) (Lim & Spence, 2010).[30] State enterprise reforms that are based partially on Western-style corporate restructuring had therefore obliterated the traditional distributive role of Chinese state enterprises, leaving a vacuum in the wake that had to be filled by piecemeal experimentations of social security.

Interestingly, in today's extensive discussion on social security, there are very few references made to the state enterprises' distributive role, which until slightly over a decade ago was a prominent function (Barnett & Chalk, 2010; Li & Piachaud, 2004; Organisation for Economic Co-operation Development, 2010). While it is the case that the social security protection afforded by state enterprises at that time is no longer adequate today given the large number of rural-urban migrant workers to be covered, there is little from existing Western research that recognizes state enterprises' distributive role.

Even after being relieved of their social responsibilities, state enterprises did make an impact on income distribution. In housing reform, the state has made a retreat in the provision of public housing, while promoting the development of the private housing market and construction industry. State enterprise employees were encouraged to and did purchase their housing units at subsidized prices. Financing for house purchase was made available through the Housing Provident Fund to which employees have to contribute, as well as through commercial mortgage financing. The latter had driven up the demand for housing, with housing prices rising sharply.[31] Regardless of their core business, state enterprises, whose original mission included building and providing housing for employees, began to undertake construction of residential (and commercial) units for profit on land that they owned or acquired from profit retention. The state enterprises' foray into real property had driven up land, and hence housing, prices, thus putting housing out of the reach of lower-income and rural-urban migrant households (Barboza, 2010; Li, 2011; Lim & Spence, 2010). Efforts by the central government to rein in these enterprises have had limited success. Thus, not only do state enterprises no longer provide social safety nets, they have contributed to increased inequality in access to housing.

Despite their focus on the market, state enterprises should be given due credit in recognizing their social responsibility for continuing to support the government in such activities as disaster relief and diplomatic confidence-building. For instance, in the post-disaster reconstruction in Yushu, Sichuan province, four central enterprises—Sinohydro Group Ltd., China Railway Construction Corporation, China State Construction Engineering Corporation, and China Railway Group Ltd.—played a significant role (China State Enterprise News, 2011). Central enterprises are also involved in China's engagement with Africa, for example, a unit of the China State Construction Company was responsible for the construction of the African Union Conference Centre (The Ministry of Commerce of the People's Republic of China, 2012). Also, as China's largest state enterprises move toward international standards of governance, there is an increased focus on corporate social responsibility. This represents the state enterprises' formal return to the pursuit of social objectives that were once a part of their mission (Knowledge@Wharton, 2010).[32]

As substantial resources are required to fund a comprehensive social safety net, state enterprise profits, estimated to be as much as 20% of the national budget in 2010, are naturally regarded as the source of funding (Mattlin, 2009). Although the state as a shareholder is entitled to dividends, the largest state enterprise holding companies, empowered by the 1994 tax reform law, have been retaining the bulk of the profits they earn.[33] At the same time, the successes of national champions and enterprises in strategic sectors have built powerful corporate interests that are able to resist pressures to distribute part of their earnings as dividends to the government, monies that could have been used to fund social security. The challenges faced by SASAC (established in 2003 to exercise the government's ownership rights) in fulfilling its mandate serve as a cautionary tale (Lam, 2011; Mattlin, 2009; Naughton, 2008).

On a final note, the absence of micro-level research, coupled with the lack of macro-level data, implies that assessing the distributional impact of state enterprise reform at the macroeconomic level is an impossible undertaking. Indeed, official data on income distribution at the national level were no longer published after 2005 (Table 3.2). Existing data show rising income inequality, whether measured by the Gini coefficient or by the share of income accruing to the bottom decile of income earners. The extent to which state enterprise reform contributed to this deterioration cannot be determined; factors like growing urbanization and unequal regional growth have been also important factors.

3.7 Conclusion

The Chinese state today is the product of its political and cultural history, both past and recent, and is deeply embedded in Chinese society. To the extent that external influences impact this state-society nexus, they are assimilated and/or adapted to China's situation, never copied wholesale. There is no better illustration of this than how state enterprise reforms have been conceived and implemented. That strengthening rather than diminishing the state enterprise sector is the prime directive of the Chinese leadership shows that the Chinese concept of the role of this sector is intact. The emergence of state-private hybrid enterprises is also distinctively Chinese. Nevertheless, efforts to increase efficiency and competitiveness through layoffs, public listings, M&A represent the incorporation of Western governance practices. And state enterprises shedding of social obligations smack of a degree of neoliberalism. The result of this blending of indigenous and external influences is the emergence of state enterprises that do not fit a simple dichotomy of state and private.

Yet the dichotomy between state and private enterprises forms an essential part of the Western theories about public enterprises. In these theories, state enterprises are stereotyped as performing poorly in comparison with private enterprises. The standard solution being proposed is to privatize the state enterprises, which would also shrink the state sector. Save for the notable exceptions discussed in this chapter, existing research on China's state enterprises has relied heavily on these Western theories and paradigms.

Given the particularities of the Chinese state, benchmarking its enterprises using Western theories, as has been extensively done, has several adverse consequences. First, the misinterpretation of Chinese state enterprises has resulted in the failure to recognize the emergence of a new type of enterprise—the state-private hybrid—that with full state support will play a growing global role. Second, underestimating their historical and future roles has rendered assessments of their performance partial and unreliable. This historical role has been detailed in this chapter. Chapter 6 will provide a detailed account of their future role, a role no other state enterprise in the world has been called upon to shoulder. Third, while the pursuit of efficiency in enterprise operations is advocated in neoliberalism rather than the Western theories per se, this is effected at the expense of the state enterprises' initial role in the provision of a social safety net. In its drive to create globally competitive corporations, China's own reforms have led to the demise of this preexisting social safety net. With widening disparities, the implementation of a plethora of social security reform initiatives to date is strong evidence that the destruction of a system is far easier than rebuilding one.

This chapter, like other existing research, has not been able to establish the link between the performance of the state enterprise sector and macroeconomics. In addition, there is scant evidence of how losses incurred by state enterprises and the relief from social burdens could impact economic growth; neither is it simple to dissociate state enterprises' distributional impact from the impact of urbanization and regional differences in growth. This will definitely warrant future research should more data become available.

Last but not least, whether the Chinese experience has relevance for other countries in transition, like Vietnam, or countries whose governments play a major role through government-linked corporations, like Malaysia, is unclear, but it should make for interesting comparative study. Clearly, China's historical trajectory is unique and cannot be emulated; however, if the evolution of the Chinese state enterprise sector is but a phase of the country's experiment with market socialism, China's many experiments have much to offer by way of lessons of successes and failures.

Notes

1. Other attacks on the Chinese system may be even less grounded. Two examples from credible sources suffice to prove the claim. John Micklethwait opined that "the country's rulers are acutely aware that their government does not serve ordinary Chinese well". This judgment was based on a single person's view, and the article was not even entirely about China (The Economist, 2011). Arthur Kroebar (2012), in explaining China's continued resilience to the global finance crisis, ended his article with the account of China's "second-rate society" being built upon inequality, and this is ironic considering the revelations about what unfettered capitalism had produced in twenty-first-century US (Kroeber, 2012).
2. This term is used also by Hsiung (2012). Zhang Weiwei (2012) calls China a civilizational state with "its own intrinsic logic of evolution and development".
3. Since the Institute was launched in 2004, there are currently (as of 2017) nearly 500 such institutes globally (Confucius Institute Headquarters, 2017).
4. "Yu zhi qi guo zhe, xian qi qi jia" (欲治其国者,先齐其家) (To rightly govern the state, it is necessary first to regulate one's own family) (Dawson, 2005).
5. James C. Hsiung (2012) noted that "the state, as the certifying agent of social mobility, in what became a 'one-career society', invariably became larger than society itself."
6. "Legal person" is a concept relative to a natural person, which refers to legal organizations including state, corporations, institutions, and so on to execute rights and obligations in law.
7. A Party Committee is an organization (similar to Board of Directors and Board of Supervisors) established in China's state enterprises. It functions to ensure that the Communist Party of China's policies and strategies are executed. It participates in decision-making, supervision, day-to-day operations, employment of key persons, coordination of internal relations, and other corporate governance details. It is compulsory for state enterprises to set them up but not for private enterprises.
8. Corporate system reform refers to the type of enterprise transforms from enterprise owned by the whole people to wholly state-owned companies with only one single-large stockholder that is the state. For example, in December 2017, China Mobile Communications Group Corporation reformed into China Mobile Communications Group Co. Ltd. (Stcn.com, 2017).
9. Joint-stock system reform refers to ownership structure is diversified to not just one single-large stockholder. For example, in October 2017, a case of

cross holdings among "Yangqi" was that Ansteel Group transferred 650 million A-shares to China National Petroleum Corporation (Xinhuanet, 2017)

10. Mixed ownership reform refers to welcoming non-state stockholders' participation. For example, in August 2017, China Unicom launched the mixed ownership reform to let Alibaba, Tencent, Baidu, and other companies invest in China Unicom to become stockholders (Stcn.com, 2017).
11. The census enumerated 154,000 state enterprises that are wholly or majority-owned by the government, representing only 3.1% of the total number of enterprises in the industrial and service sector (Gao, 2010). The appearance of China's state enterprises in the Fortune 500 list of companies is another indicator of the enterprise size. In 2011, China had 61 companies in this list, compared to 19 in 2005. The Sinopec Group is ranked fifth (23rd in 2005), China National Petroleum sixth (39th), and State Grid seventh (32nd) (Fortune Online, 2011).
12. This state-private dichotomy is encapsulated in catchwords such as "China state enterprises advance, private sector retreats" (Chovanec, 2010).
13. Marshall Meyer argued this was the case with Haier (Knowledge@Wharton, 2001).
14. A recent research report by Jiang (2011) found that employee salaries paid by state enterprises are 13% higher than that in the non-state sector, while the management level in central state enterprises earns over 60% higher than the private sector on average (Jiang, 2011).
15. Their findings echo those of Fung, Firth, and Rui (2003) that show corporate governance has a significant impact on CEO compensation among partially privatized state enterprises in China (Fung, Firth, & Rui, 2003).
16. "Enterprise performance" in this context refers to performance at the (microeconomic) enterprise level.
17. The developments and growing technological capabilities described here are reported in a number of studies (Ren, Zeng, & Krabbendam, 2010; Tong & Zhu, 2009; Wu, 2007).
18. However, Geng, Yang, and Janus (2009) argue that asset accumulation was the highest among what the state considered strategic industries (Geng, Yang, & Janus, 2009).
19. Even the sale of telecommunications equipment by Huawei, an employee-owned enterprise, to America's AT&T in 2009 was scuttled by the American fear of the Chinese use of such equipment to spy on the US (Pomfret, 2010).
20. By the mid-1990s, Mai and Perkins (1997) made this conclusion that "most SOEs are now able to operate, to a greater or lesser extent, in a market environment. Economic reform has enabled them to make their own production plans, set prices, purchase inputs and sell outputs within a market structure (Mai & Perkins, 1997)".

21. As the boundary between public sector and private sector becomes indistinct for many enterprises, the key to government support appears to hinge upon whether the leadership of the enterprise has close ties with the government, regardless of whether it is classified as public, private, or in-between.
22. In as early as 1997, Li and Putterman (2008) estimated that small state enterprises accounted for no more than 16% of total state enterprise output (Li & Putterman, 2008). This share in output would have fallen further with the government strategy of "retaining the large and releasing the small", since the bulk of state enterprise closures are likely to be small enterprises owned by local and provincial jurisdictions.
23. The large Chinese state conglomerates have been compared with their Japanese and Korean counterparts (The Economist, 1997).
24. The number of central enterprises had to be reduced to fewer than 100 by 2010, but progress was slower than expected (Yang, 2011).
25. From May 1998, those who were retrenched were able to receive assistance through a re-employment service. The International Labour Organization (ILO) reported that by the end of 1998, about 85% of those made redundant had registered (International Labour Organization, 2002). Dong and Putterman (2003) estimated that the ratio of state enterprise loss to before-tax profits rose from 5% in 1980 to 22% in 1995, reflecting a widening gap (Dong & Putterman, 2003).
26. The World Bank did undertake a program that aimed to reduce the social consequences of its enterprise reform program. However, the fund allocated was modest, and the activities, which were later assessed to be partially successful, were limited to management and retraining of laid-off workers (Carlier, 2001).
27. The strategy involved privatization, liquidation, and/or closure of numerous state enterprises at county and local levels, laying off about four million state enterprise employees, and restructuring of large enterprises through corporatization, mergers and listing on international stock exchanges.
28. Moore and Wen (2006) were of the view that the direction taken of state enterprise reform was driven chiefly by the state's concept of privatization and economic benefits derived rather than the need for a more balanced economic and social strategy (Moore & Wen, 2006).
29. Walter (2010) called these reforms "a social disaster" (Walter, 2010).
30. In the collection of papers that served as inputs to the FYP, 2 out of 9 chapters and 5 out of 20 background papers were devoted to social security issues and an additional paper co-authored by Edwin Lim and Michael Spence on housing.
31. As reflected from the data in the China Statistical Yearbook, the average residential housing prices increased two and a half times from RMB 1790 per square meter in 1997 to RMB 4459 per square meter in 2009.

32. Corporate social responsibility was first introduced into China by multinationals to meet the demand of Western consumers, but its adoption was accelerated by labor protests within China.
33. Listed subsidiaries of these holding companies are required to and do pay dividends to the holding companies, but these profits are retained at the holding company level.

References

Bai, C.E., Li, D., & Wang, Y.J. (2003). Thriving on a tilted playing field: China's non-state enterprises in the reform era. In N.C. Hope, D.T. Yang, & M.Y. Li (Eds.), *How far across the river? Chinese policy reform at the millennium* (pp. 97–121). Palo Alto, US: Stanford University Press.

Barnett, S., & Chalk, N. (2010). Building a social safety net China embarks on an effort to improve both pensions and health care in the world's most populous nation. *Finance & Development, 47*(3), 34–35.

Barboza, D. (2010). State-owned bidders fuel China's land boom. *The New York Times.* Retrieved from http://www.nytimes.com/2010/08/02/business/global/02chinareal.html?pagewanted=all&_r=0

Broadman, H.G. (1999). The Chinese state as corporate shareholder. *Finance and Development, 36*(3), 52–55.

Carlier, A. (2001). *Social dimensions of corporate restructuring (social safety net component)—TF-021191: Implementation completion report* World Bank. Washington, DC.

Cao, J., Lemmon, M., Pan, X.F., & Tian, G. (2010). *Political promotion, CEO compensation, and their effect on firm performance.* Paper presented at the FMA Asian Conference, Singapore.

Chai, J.C. (2003). Privatization in China. In D. Parker & D.S. Saal (Eds.), *International handbook on privatization* (pp. 235–261). Cheltenham: Edward Elgar.

Chang, G.G. (2010). China's economy to reach $ 123 trillion? *Forbes.* Retrieved from http://www.forbes.com/2010/01/07/china-economy-robert-fogel-opinions-columnists-gordon-g-chang.html

Chen, B.Z., & Feng, Y. (2000). Determinants of economic growth in China: Private enterprise, education, and openness. *China Economic Review, 11*(1), 1–15.

Chen, G.M., Firth, M., & Rui, O. (2006). Have China's enterprise reforms led to improved efficiency and profitability? *Emerging Markets Review, 7*(1), 82–109.

China State Enterprise News (2011). SASAC leading the central media team to visit Yushu. Retrieved from http://www.chinasoe.com.cn/news/soe/2011-08-29/11811.html

Chovanec, P. (2010). China state enterprises advance, private sector retreats. *Forbes*. Retrieved from http://www.forbes.com/sites/china/2010/08/31/guo-jin-min-tui/

Confucius Institute Headquarters (2017). About Confucius Institutes. Retrieved from http://english.hanban.org/node_10971.htm

Connell, D. (2013). *The role of national governments in river management*. Paper presented at the Global Water Forum, UNESCO and Australian National University.

Cooper, M.C. (2008). New thinking in financial market regulation: Dismantling the "split-share structure" of Chinese listed companies. *Journal of Chinese Political Science, 13*(1), 53–78.

Dawson, M.M. (Ed.). (2005). *The ethics of Confucius*. New York: Cosimo.

Dorn, J. (2000). State-owned enterprises continue to hinder Chinese growth. *Japan Times*. Retrieved from http://object.cato.org/publications/commentary/stateowned-enterprises-continue-hinder-chinese-growth

Dong, X.Y., & Putterman, L. (2003). Soft budget constraints, social burdens, and labor redundancy in China's state industry. *Journal of Comparative Economics, 31*(1), 110–133.

Dong, W., & Zhang, X. (2008). China: 30 years of reform and opening-up (1978–2008). Blue Book of Development and Reform. Beijing: Social Sciences Academic Press (China).

Dyer, G., & McGregor, R. (2008). China's champions: Why state ownership is no longer proving a dead hand. *Financial Times*. Retrieved from http://www.ft.com/cms/s/0/979f69c8-f35b-11dc-b6bc-0000779fd2ac.html#axzz1ZY4qTsAm

Fan, J.P.H., Wong, T. J., & Zhang, T.Y. (2007). Politically connected CEOs, corporate governance, and post-IPO performance of China's newly partially privatized firms. *Journal of Financial Economics, 84*(2), 330–357.

Fung, P.M.Y., Firth, M., & Rui, O. (2003). *Corporate governance and CEO compensation in China*. Chinese University of Hong Kong.

Fu, Z.Y. (1996). *China's legalists: The earliest totalitarians and their art of ruling*. London: ME Sharpe.

Fortune Online (2011). Global 500 listing for 2011. Retrieved from http://money.cnn.com/magazines/fortune/global500/2011/countries/China.html

Gabriele, A., & Schettino, F. (2012). Market socialism as a distinct socioeconomic formation internal to the modern mode of production. *New Proposals: Journal of Marxism and Interdisciplinary Inquiry, 5*(2), 20–50.

Gao, X. (2010). State-owned enterprises in China: How big are they? *East Asia & Pacific, World Bank*. Retrieved from http://blogs.worldbank.org/eastasiapacific/state-owned-enterprises-in-china-how-big-are-they

Geng, X., Yang, X.K., & Janus, A. (2009). State-owned enterprises in China: Reform dynamics and impacts. In R. Gaunaut, L.G. Song & W.W. Thye (Eds.), *China's new place in a world in crisis: Economic, geopolitical and environmental dimensions*: Canberra: The Australian National University E Press.

Goldman, M. (2000). Restarting Chinese history. *American Historical Review, 105*(1), 153–164.

Gong, Q. (2004). *Has China's economic reform improved enterprise performance? A DEA evaluation of China's large and medium enterprises.* Working Paper No. 287. ESRC Centre for Business Research, University of Cambridge.

Guthrie, D., & Wang, J.M. (2007). Business organizations in China. In H.W.C. Yeung (Eds.), *Handbook of research on Asian business* (pp. 99–124). Cheltenham, UK: Edward Elgar Publishing.

Hashiguchi, Y. (2008). China's reform of state-owned enterprises and their speed of employment adjustment. *International Cooperation Essays, 16*(1), 185–198.

He, P. (2011). The difference of Chinese legalism and western legalism. *Frontiers of Law in China, 6*(4), 645–669.

Holz, C.A. (2002). Long live China's state-owned enterprises: Deflating the myth of poor financial performance. *Journal of Asian Economics, 13*(4), 493–529.

Hu, F.Z.Y. (2005). Deconstructing state-owned enterprises in socialist China under reform: a scalar examination. *Environment and Planning A, 37*(4), 703–722.

Huang, P.C.C. (2008). Introduction to "The nature of the Chinese state: Dialogues among Western and Chinese scholars, I". *Modern China, 34*(1), 3–8.

Huang, X., Li, P., & Lotspeich, R. (2010). Economic growth and multi-tasking by state-owned enterprises: An analytic framework and empirical study based on Chinese provincial data. *Economic Systems, 34*(2), 160–177.

Hsiung, J.C. (2012). *China into its second rise: Myths, puzzles, paradoxes, and challenge to theory.* World Scientific.

International Labour Organization (2002). Reemployment in reform of state-owned enterprises: The case of China. Retrieved from http://www.ilo.org/public/english/dialogue/ifpdial/la/gp/china2.htm

Jacques, M. (2009). *When China rules the world: The end of the Western world and the birth of a new global order.* London: Penguin Press.

Jacques, M. (2011). How China will change the way we think: The case of the state. Retrieved from http://www.transatlanticacademy.org/publications/how-china-will-change-way-we-thinkthe-case-state

Jefferson, G.H., Rawski, T.G., & Zhang, Y. (2008). Productivity growth and convergence across China's industrial economy. *Journal of Chinese Economic and Business Studies, 6*(2), 121–140.

Jiang, H. (2011). *Revised report of the research on SOE reform.* Unirule Institute of Economics. Beijing. Retrieved from http://english.unirule.org.cn/Html/Events/20110704161121587.html

Kato, T., & Long, C. (2004). *Executive compensation, firm performance, and state ownership in China: Evidence from new panel data*. William Davidson Institute, University of Michigan. Working Paper No. 690.

Knowledge@SMU (2012). Why China's state-owned firms can still succeed. Retrieved from http://www.cfoinnovation.com/story/4938/why-chinas-state-owned-firms-can-still-succeed.

Knowledge@Wharton (2001). Think state-owned companies are inefficient? Look at China, from https://knowledge.wharton.upenn.edu/article/think-state-owned-companies-are-inefficient-look-at-china/

Knowledge@Wharton (2006). A crucible of competition: The emerging Chinese company. Retrieved from http://knowledge.wharton.upenn.edu/article/a-crucible-of-competition-the-emerging-chinese-company/

Knowledge@Wharton (2010). Corporate social responsibility in China: One more great leap forward—many more still ahead. Retrieved from http://www.knowledgeatwharton.com.cn/index.cfm?fa=viewArticle&articleID=2218&-languageid=1

Koch, T., & Ramsbottom, O. (2008). A growth strategy for a Chinese state-owned enterprise: An interview with ChemChina's President. *McKinsey Quarterly, 3*, 51.

Kroeber, A. (2012). Bear in a China Shop. *Foreign Policy*.

Kuhn, P. A. (2002). *Origins of the modern Chinese state*. Stanford University Press.

Kwan, C. H. (2010). Growing criticism over advancing state-owned sector and retreating private sector—China should be aiming for the reverse, *Research Institute of Economy, Trade and Industry, Tokyo*. Retrieved from http://www.rieti.go.jp/en/china/10020301.html

Lal, D. (2006). A proposal to privatize Chinese enterprises and end financial repression. *The Cato Journal*, 26(2), 275–286.

Lam, W. (2011). China's state giants too big to play with. *Asia Times Online*. Retrieved from http://www.atimes.com/atimes/China_Business/MA22Cb01.html

Li, B., & Piachaud, D. (2004) Poverty and inequality and social policy in China. *Research Paper No.87*: Centre for the Analysis of Social Exclusion, London School of Economics.

Li, C. (2005). The rise of China's yuppie corps: Top CEOs to watch. *China Leadership Monitor, 14*.

Li, C. (1997). Confucian value and democratic value. *The Journal of Value Inquiry, 31*, 183–193.

Li, D., Moshirian, F., Nguyen, P., & Tan, L. (2007). Corporate governance or globalization: What determines CEO compensation in China? *Research in International Business and Finance, 21*(1), 32–49.

Lim, E., & Spence, M. (Eds.). (2010). Thoughts and suggestions for China's 12th Five Year Programme from an international perspective. Beijing: Cairncross Foundation.

Li, S. (2011). Issues and options for social security reform in China. *China: An International Journal, 9*(1), 72–109.

Li, W., & Putterman, L. (2008). Reforming China's SOEs: An overview. *Comparative Economic Studies, 50*(3), 353–380.

Li, Z. (2009). *The role of international technology transfer in the Chinese automotive industry.* Discussion Paper No. 269. Manufacturing Management Research Centre, University of Tokyo.

Mai, Y.H., & Perkins, F. (1997). *China's state enterprises: Nine case studies.* Briefing Paper Series No. 7. Department of Foreign Affairs and Trade.

Mako, W., & Zhang, C. L. (2003). Management of China's state-owned enterprises portfolio: Lessons from international experience. *World Bank Office, Beijing.*

Mattlin, M. (2009). Chinese strategic state-owned enterprises and ownership control. *Brussels Institute of Contemporary China Studies Asia paper, 4*(6), 1–28.

Moore, S., & Wen, J.J. (2006). Reform of state owned enterprises and challenges in China. *Journal of Technology Management in China, 1*(3), 279–291.

Milhaupt, C.J. and Zheng, W. (2015). Beyond ownership: State capitalism and the Chinese firm. *Georgetown Law Journal, 103*, 665–722.

Naughton, B. (2008). SASAC and rising corporate power in China. *China Leadership Monitor, 24*(2).

Olano, G. (2017). Ping An is now the world's most valuable insurance brand. *Insurance Business Asia*, April 26. Retrieved from http://www.insurancebusinessmag.com/asia/news/breaking-news/ping-an-is-now-the-worlds-most-valuable-insurance-brand-65887.aspx

Organisation for Economic Co-operation and Development (2010). *China in the 2010s: Rebalancing growth and strengthening social safety nets.* Paper presented at the China Development Forum, Beijing.

Park, J. (2010). *Projection of long-term total factor productivity growth for 12 Asian economies.* Asian Development Bank.

Parker, E.H. (1908). *Ancient China simplified.* Whitefish: MT: Kessinger Legacy Reprints.

Pei, M. (2006). China is stagnating in its 'trapped transition'. *Financial Times, February 24. Retrieved* from http://carnegieendowment.org/2006/02/24/china-is-stagnating-in-its-trapped-transition/2cvo

People.com.cn (2015). Xi Jinping hosted the 11th Meeting of the Leading Group for Financial and Economic Affairs. Retrieved from http://cpc.people.com.cn/n/2015/1110/c64094-27799893.html

Phillips, K.L., & Shen, K.R. (2005). What effect does the size of the state-owned sector have on regional growth in China? *Journal of Asian Economics, 15*(6), 1079–1102.

Ping An Insurance (2015). *Annual Report 2015*. Shenzhen.

Pomfret, J. (2010). History of telecom company illustrates lack of strategic trust between U.S., China. *The Washington Post*. Retrieved from http://www.washingtonpost.com/wp-dyn/content/article/2010/10/07/AR2010100707210.html

Rawski, T.G. (2000). *Is China's state enterprise problem still important?* Paper presented at the China's SOE Reform and Privatization, University of Tokyo.

Ren, L., Zeng, D., & Krabbendam, K. (2010). Technological innovation progress in central China: A survey to 42 firms. *Journal of Knowledge-based Innovation in China, 2*(2), 152–170.

Sachs, J.D., & Woo, W.T. (2003). China's economic growth after WTO membership. *Journal of Chinese Economic and Business Studies, 1*(1), 1–31.

Scissors, D. (2011). *Chinese State-Owned Enterprises and U.S.-China Economic Relations*. Testimony before the U.S.-China Economic and Security Review Commission. Retrieved from http://www.heritage.org/research/testimony/2011/04/chinese-state-owned-enterprises-and-us-china-economic-relations

Shambaugh, D. (2000). *The modern Chinese state*. Cambridge University Press.

Smyth, R. (2000). Asset stripping in Chinese state-owned enterprises. *Journal of Contemporary Asia, 30*(1), 3–16.

Stcn.com (2017). Cross holdings among "Yangqi" can reduce the cost of state enterprise reform. Retrieved from http://www.stcn.com/2017/1017/13695096.shtml

The Ministry of Commerce of the People's Republic of China (2012). Focus on management and establishing a new milestone in the supervision of Africa Aid Program: Assistance to construct the African Union Conference Centre. Retrieved from http://jjhzj.mofcom.gov.cn/aarticle/z/201204/20120408073069.html

The Ministry of Finance of the People's Republic of China (2013). Statements regarding the central state-owned capital operation budget in 2013. Retrieved from http://yss.mof.gov.cn/2013zyczys/201303/t20130322_784806.html

The Ministry of Finance of the People's Republic of China (2015). Guidance on the function definition and classification of state enterprises. Retrieved from http://www.mof.gov.cn/zhengwuxinxi/zhengcefabu/201512/t20151230_1638704.htm

The National Bureau of Statistics of the People's Republic of China (2009). Letter regarding the opinions on the definition for state enterprises. Retrieved from http://www.stats.gov.cn/zjtj/tjfg/qtygwj/200905/t20090511_67312.html

The State-owned Assets Supervision and Administration Commission (2009). Notification on Disclosure of Information on the Supervision and Management of State-Owned Assets. Retrieved from http://www.gov.cn/zwgk/2009-02/12/content_1229068.htm

The State-owned Assets Supervision and Administration (2017) State enterprise reform began the "first shot" of mix-ownership reform. Retrieved from http://www.sasac.gov.cn/n2588025/n2588139/c2822453/content.html

The State-owned Assets Supervision and Administration Commission (2017). List of "Yangqi" (central enterprises). Retrieved from http://www.sasac.gov.cn/n2588035/n2641579/n2641645/index.html

Tian, L.H., & Estrin, S. (2008). Retained state shareholding in Chinese PLCs: Does government ownership always reduce corporate value? *Journal of Comparative Economics, 36*(1), 74–89.

The Central People's Government of the People's Republic of China (2010). The State Council's views on how to foster and restructure enterprises. Retrieved from http://www.gov.cn/zwgk/2010-09/06/content_1696450.htm

The Central People's Government of the People's Republic of China (2015a). The Roadmap of State Enterprise Reform. Retrieved from http://www.gov.cn/xinwen/2015-09/13/content_2930397.htm

The Central People's Government of the People's Republic of China (2015b). The Central Committee of the Communist Party of China and State Council's instructions on deepening the reform of the state enterprises. Retrieved from http://www.gov.cn/zhengce/2015-09/13/content_2930440.htm

The Economist (1997). China adopts the chaebol. Retrieved from http://www.economist.com/node/90635

The Economist (2011). Taming leviathan. Retrieved from http://www.economist.com/node/18359896

The State Council of the People's Republic of China (2004). Modifications for "interim regulations on social service organizations' registration and management". Retrieved from http://www.gov.cn/zwgk/2005-05/23/content_227.htm

Tong, S.Y., & Zhu, J. (2009). *China's rapidly growing enterprise-led innovation system*. EAI Background Brief; No. 461. Singapore: East Asian Institute, National University of Singapore.

Tse, E. (2006). *Transformation of a Chinese state-owned enterprise: Guangzhou Metro Corporation*. Booz Allen Hamilton.

Wakeman, F. (1993). The civil society and public sphere debate: Western reflections on Chinese political culture. *Modern China, 19*(2), 108–138.

Wallstreetcn.com (2015). About "supply-side reform". Retrieved from https://wallstreetcn.com/articles/226853

Walter, C.E. (2010). The struggle over ownership: How the reform of state-owned enterprises changed China. *The Copenhagen Journal of Asian Studies, 28*(1), 83–108.

Woetzel, J.R. (2008). Reassessing China's state-owned enterprises. *McKinsey Quarterly, 3*, 1–6.

Wong, R.B. (1997). *China transformed: Historical change and the limits of European experience*. New York: Cornell University Press.

Wu, W. (2007). State policies, enterprise dynamism, and innovation system in Shanghai, China. *Growth and Change, 38*(4), 544–566.

Xiao, Q. (2010). Top 10 'tribes' in 2009. *China Daily*. January 11. Retrieved from http://www.chinadaily.com.cn/china/09tentopnews/2010-01/11/content_9289602.htm

Xinhuanet (2016). Xi Jinping stressed during the State Enterprise Party Construction Work Conference: To unswervingly adhere to the Communist Party's leadership of state enterprises. Retrieved from http://news.xinhuanet.com/fortune/2016-10/11/c_1119697415.htm

Xinhuanet (2017). China Mobile Communications Group Corporation and China Telecommunications Corporation transformed into wholly state-owned companies with only one single-large stockholder that is the state. Retrieved from http://www.xinhuanet.com/fortune/2017-12/25/c_129775016.htm

Yang, X. (2011). China to rev up central SOE shuffle. *China.org.cn*. Retrieved from http://www.china.org.cn/business/2011-06/01/content_22693994.htm

Zhang, C., Zeng, D., Mako, W. P., & Seward, J. (2009). *Promoting enterprise-led innovation in China*. Washington, DC: World Bank.

Zhang, J., & Chen, J. (2017). Introduction to China's new normal economy. *Journal of Chinese Economic and Business Studies, 15*(1), 1–4.

Zhang, W. (2012). *The China wave: Rise of a civilizational state*. World Scientific.

Zheng, J., Liu, X., & Bigsten, A. (2000). *Efficiency, technical progress and best practice in Chinese state enterprises (1980–1994)*. Working Paper in Economics No. 30. Department of Economics, Goteborg University.

Zhou, H. (2000). *The challenges of China's economic reform: State enterprise reform and financial liberalization*. Master of Science thesis, University of North Texas.

Zhou, G. (2010). In search of a new China: State, society and the fate of modern China. Retrieved from http://ucsdmodernchinesehistory.wordpress.com/2010/03/27/841/.

Zhou, H. (2011). Confucianism and the Legalism: A model of the national strategy of governance in ancient China. *Frontiers of Economics in China, 6*(4), 616–637.

CHAPTER 4

The State's Role in a Strategic Industry—China's Banking Sector

Development of policy through seeking consensus, finding a middle road between extreme positions, and combining market economy with a strong ownership and guidance role for the government. These are key to understanding how the financial system has succeeded in supporting China's extraordinary growth.

(Stent, 2017: 253)

The available evidence persuades us that government influences, intentional or unintentional, will continue to constrain bank reform, with all the performance weaknesses that such influence implies.

(Dobson & Kashyap, 2006: 105)

4.1 Introduction

China's banking sector dominates its financial system. Efforts to improve the banks' efficiency have been made since liberalization. But the pace of these reforms has sometimes been halting, and this tardiness has been the subject of frequent criticism which is framed against the context of the Chinese state's domination of the banking sector. Criticisms became particularly shrill after the RMB 4 trillion stimulus to combat the GFC and also as China's growth slowed down (Mitchell & McGee, 2015). The danger cited was the possibility that China's banking sector may confront a financial crisis, jeopardizing its economic growth (Kollewe & Monahan, 2015). Because the banking sector is crucial, the Chinese state's role is crucial as well. This is because while Europe and North America have

R. Li, K. C. Cheong, *China's State Enterprises*,
https://doi.org/10.1007/978-981-13-0176-6_4

private-sector-driven financial systems, China's financial system is dominated by the government. In China, commercial banking and investment banking are highly controlled (Genevieve & Wei, 2005).

In line with its promotion of private sector involvement in China's banking system, Davis and Orlik (2013) have proposed the privatization of one of China's state commercial banks. Through this proposal, the entrance of foreign investment banks into China's market, and with less control of the state and greater consideration for shareholder interest, constitutes its initial objectives. The premise of this proposal was that greater private ownership and less state involvement would reduce the bad performance in terms of high non-performing loans (NPLs) and low efficiency in China's banking system. In other words, they considered state ownership and governance to be responsible for low profits and returns to shareholders.

Recognizing the sector's many weaknesses, China's leadership undertook reforms of the banking system as part of larger state enterprise reform since China began its marketization process in 1978. As already noted in the previous chapter, state enterprise reform had transformed China's state enterprises in terms of their governance mechanisms and ownership structures. However, financial sector state enterprises were treated differently from non-financial state enterprises with respect to both pace and substance. So the first question this chapter asks is whether the changes in China's banking sector that was affected by reform similar in magnitude and nature were comparable to those that result from non-financial state enterprise reform. Specifically, what does banks' ownership structure and governance mechanism look like today compared to before reform? How has the state-control mode evolved and what is the state-control mode today (how much of state control remains in both ownership and governance)?

To the extent that banking system reform differs from broader state enterprise reform, a second question that arises is why this is so. This chapter argues that the state's approach to banking reform is rooted in the system's history. The importance of history as lessons for the Chinese leadership's actions has already been discussed in Chap. 2. It is argued here that the government's policies with respect to the financial sector have as much to do with the history of Chinese banking as with economic ideology. Hence, the objective of this chapter is to provide the historical context as an explanation of the state's role in the banking sector. This role is manifested in the fact that the banking sector has been designated a strategic sector.

This objective is complemented by another objective. This is to chart the functioning of the banking sector in the context of the Chinese state's efforts to improve efficiency, manifested in indicators of financial robustness, the ability to remain profitable. But beyond this, the banking system is a major instrument of China's growth and internationalization strategies, and to support the state at critical times. How and how well do Chinese banks play these roles, and at what cost to the achievement of the system's commercial objectives?

The next section analyzes the historical role of China's banking sector since the Qing Dynasty. Section 4.3 then reviews the various steps of banking reform, especially after economic liberalization in 1978. Section 4.4 describes how this sector looks today, specifically linking state control to ownership structure and governance in major commercial banks. Section 4.5 examines the performance of the major commercial banks during two major events, China's entry into the WTO and the GFC, as well as China's strategic push into Africa. Section 4.6 offers some concluding remarks about this sector.

4.2 China's Banking Sector—A Historical Perspective

In the context of world history, the failure of the Paris Commune was partly attributed to its failure to take over the Banque de France, namely, to control the economic lifeline, that is, the central bank as the center of the financial system in France. Marx and Engels (1959) pointed out in the Communist Manifesto (1848) that if the proletariat wants to become the ruling class, then the state has to control all finance through a central bank with state capital. Lenin (1973) pointed out that the banking sector is in the central position of an economic system. After the establishment of the Soviet Union, the banking system under the state's control played a major role in its economic recovery. In 15 years, the Gross Industrial Production of the Soviet Union ranked second in the world (Wang, 2010). In reference to Chinese history, we also can see that the banking system is a crucial sector for the national economy.

4.2.1 The Qing Dynasty and British Economic Power

During the late Qing Dynasty, the Opium Wars[1] destroyed China's currency stability. At that time, multiple currencies were used by different jurisdictions. The absence of a central bank did not permit the issue of a single currency in China. There was also little credibility attached to the Qing Government's issued bank notes. In addition, several finance institutions were in existence. These were the "Qianzhuang" (钱庄) and "Piaohao" (票号) which focused on the currency exchange and bank draft businesses respectively. These institutions were the precursors of modern China's financial institutions. The Qing Government still had to repay loans from "Qianzhuang" and "Piaohao" which also financed foreign trade.

The modern banking sector in China did not emerge until quite late into the Qing Dynasty because the Qing Government underestimated the importance of creating a modern banking system. As a result, the history of modern banking in China started with the establishment of a foreign bank—the Hong Kong and Shanghai Banking Corporation (HSBC)—in 1865, founded by the British to control China's financial sector at that time. The capital foundation of HSBC stemmed from the opium trade and served to facilitate British Far East trade (Guo & Lu, 2013). HSBC proceeded to sweep away all financial institutions in Hong Kong and Shanghai to become the new leader of Far East foreign banks, and controlled China's international exchange business. Relying on British power, HSBC refused the Qing Government's request to reveal information about the bank's clients. Cheap deposits came to HSBC since it was considered the safest wealth vault. It also acquired banknote-issuing authority from the British Hong Kong Government. Finally, it controlled the capital sources of China's "Qianzhuang", "Piaohao", and the "Chaipiao" (拆票) businesses (Song, 2011). The "Chaipiao" business referred to short-term loans among those banks. Backed by British naval might, HSBC quickly established itself as the dominant institution in the Chinese banking system. HSBC's other businesses were political loans to the Chinese government, loans for railways, and advanced payments for the opium trade. It gradually took over the role of a central bank, which allowed it to exercise further control over the Qing Dynasty's financial system and to eventually dominate China's financial system's capital and credit flows (Song, 2011). HSBC's system of bank drafts and packing credit were major channels for China's trade finance and international exchange (Wu, 2006). HSBC controlled China's money supply and acted as a central bank due to the business limitations of the "Qianzhuang" and "Piaohao" institutions. Foreign banks also penetrated Chinese financial system and their agents monopolized financial markets.

4.2.2 The Establishment of the Bank of China (BOC)

In 1905, "Hubu"[2] (户部) Bank was established by the Qing Government. It was to play a dual role as both the central bank and a commercial bank. In the former role, it issued bank notes and acted as the national treasury, while in the latter it undertook basic commercial banking such as deposit-taking and granting of loans. In 1908, the Qing Government renamed the bank "Daqing" (大清) Bank and entrusted it with the sole functions of a central bank. "Daqing" Bank was a joint-stock bank in which the government owned half (5 million "Liang" (两)) (the silver currency) and private entities could purchase the rest (5 million "Liang"). The Qing Government officials assumed management responsibility.

The 1911 Revolution brought about the collapse of both the Qing Dynasty and its "Daqing" Bank. The revolutionary (Beiyang) government assumed that all the bank's shares belonged to the Qing Government and took steps to confiscate these shares. Private shareholders of the bank responded by holding a meeting to craft strategies to protect their shares (Caijing.com.cn, 2012).

In 1911, Chen Jintao, the Finance Chief for the Beiyang Government, sought to establish a central bank for the Beiyang Government by restructuring the "Daqing" Bank to become the Bank of China (BOC) (Fig. 4.1). It was to be a government private joint-stock bank and would perform a central banking role (China.com.cn, 2008). The new government's first step was to clean up businesses belonging to "Daqing" Bank and eliminated the shares (5 million "Liang") belonging to the Qing Government. Private shareholders' shares were converted from "Daqing" Bank to the BOC at par value. Next, the BOC attracted investments for 5 million shares (Caijing.com.cn, 2012). In 1923, Zhang Jiao, the Vice President of the BOC, raised private sector share capital to replace the government share capital to the amount of 5 million "Liang". In this way, the BOC was no longer controlled by the Beiyang Government as the private sector held 99% of the shares (Qu & Luo, 2011).

4.2.3 The Change of Government After the Qing Dynasty

After the 1911 Revolution, political turbulence saw several separatist warlord regimes establish several governments in different parts of China. In the north was the existing Beiyang Government, but in the center was the Wuhan Government, and in the south was the Guangzhou Government.

Fig. 4.1 The Bank of China, 1911. Source: Bank of China website, http://www.boc.cn/en/aboutboc/ab1/200808/t20080814_1601747.html

Chiang Kai-shek, who would eventually become the President of Nationalist China, was the head of the Guangzhou Government.

Between 1923 and 1926, the Soviet Union provided financial support in the amount of 30 million "Gold Rubles" to the Guangzhou Government to support the Northern Expedition by Chiang. In addition, the Soviet Union provided 10 million "Gold Rubles" for Chiang's government to establish a central bank. In 1927, the Northern Expeditionary Army finally reached Shanghai. There, the financial sector was controlled by Jiangsu and Zhejiang financial magnates, consisting of foreign banks, and the government's banks, the "Qianzhuang", and "Piaohao", and backed by British and American bankers. Agents for the foreign banks, through the Shanghai Chamber of Commerce, which included all important banks including "Qianzhuang", "Piaohao", and other commercial and industrial organizations, undertook to raise 60 million Yuan for Chiang with the condition that he "cleaned out" members of the Communist Party within the Wuhan Government (Song, 2011).[3]

In March 1927, the Wuhan Government sent Soong Tse-ven, its Minister of Finance, to Shanghai in an attempt to unify fiscal responsibility and secure financing for the Wuhan and Guangzhou Governments. This did not sit well with Guangzhou's Chiang, however, and he requested the Shanghai Chamber of Commerce, with which he maintained good relations, to ignore Soong. He also implemented an economic blockade on the Wuhan Government, and also reduced the financing channels for Jiangsu and Zhejiang Financial Magnates.

Feng Yuxiang, who was a powerful warlord independent of both the Kuomintang, which Chiang led—and the Communist party, was courted by Chiang as a way to neutralize the Wuhan Government. Chiang was in a stronger position than the Wuhan Government as he was able to offer Feng better financial benefits. In December 1928, the Nanjing Nationalist Government was established by Chiang to replace the Beiyang Government. The above maneuvers by Chiang meant that he needed financial resources in his struggle against other warlords and the Communist Party, as well as to consolidate his control of his "Nationalist" Government.

4.2.4 *The Establishment of the Central Bank of the Communist Party*

The growing Communist Party that called itself the Soviet Republic of China (SRC), which posed a threat to Chiang, was located in central China. In 1932, SRC established its own Central Bank. Chiang responded by implementing a tight economic blockade on this area. As a result, commodities were in short supply, the prices of commodities rose, and the SRC Government's issued bank notes depreciated. Additionally, Chiang produced counterfeit SRC currency that were injected into SRC-held areas and sought to exchange gold and silver from the reserves of the Central Bank of SRC on a large scale (Culture.china.com.cn, 2010). The objective was to deplete the bullion reserves of the SRC Central Bank.

For its part, the SRC Government had to have enough gold and silver reserves to back the bank notes it issued, knowing that it had to guarantee repayment in order to ensure its continued access to credit. It realized that as long as the currency-issuing authority had the trust of the people, it did not need to have the full backing of silver and gold reserves. Therefore, the ability of the SRC Government to resist the Kuomintang's siege and economic blockade largely depended on the credibility of this government's Central Bank rather than on its stock of bullion.

4.2.5 The Evolution of Chiang's Financial Autocracy

The establishment of the Nanjing Nationalist Government in 1928 to replace the Beiyang Government to enable Chiang's group to form the central government also came with the need to have an independent central bank. Soong, who had become the Minister of Finance under this government, wanted to restructure the BOC to become a central bank. However, at the time, the Nanjing Nationalist Government was not powerful enough to control the BOC, and this proposal was rejected by the Vice President of the BOC (Bank of China, 2014a). The largest shareholder of the BOC was the Xi Family, who was also the agent for the British-empire-backed HSBC. However, the Nanjing Nationalist Government was able to force the BOC and the Bank of Communications (BoCom)[4] to restructure and raise the proportion of government shares to become the majority shareholder.

Soong stated that there were three objectives in establishing a central bank: to unify the monetary system, consolidate the national treasury, and adjust the financial system (Qu & Luo, 2011). The Central Bank of Nanjing Nationalist Government was officially founded in Shanghai in 1928. The BOC was transformed into an international exchange bank, and from a government bank into a commercial bank. The BoCom was transformed into an industrial development bank. Nevertheless, the BOC and BoCom still shouldered the banknote issuance responsibility of a central bank. At that time, the BOC remained the number one financial institution in the sector, having the largest amounts of total assets, total loans, total deposits, and total money in circulation over both the Central Bank and the BoCom until the end of 1934 (Liu, 1999).

The Nanjing Nationalist Government implemented a financial monopoly policy and increased the number of government shares in the BOC in order to be able to exert control (China.com.cn, 2008). From March 1935, it issued government bonds to raise capital for the Central Bank, the BOC, and BoCom. It transferred out the Chairman of the Board and the Managing Director of BOC, and appointed Soong as Chairman of the Board. It tried to control the BOC totally through majority shareholding and restructuring at the management level. The capital of the BOC was 25 million Yuan with 20% (5 million) government shares. The Nanjing Nationalist Government raised government shares by 25 million Yuan to ultimately own 30 million Yuan out of 50 million Yuan or 60% of the total.

Shareholder objections were muted by the government's political pressure. Still these shareholders were able to force the government to accept several proposals to reduce the latter's power. One was to reduce the government's share to 50% from 60%, and the other was to reduce the number of government representatives to 9 (out of 21) among the Board of Directors, and to have the managing director appointed by the Chairman instead of by election by the Board of Directors. A "Chairman responsibility system" replaced the managing director responsibility system (Bank of China, 2014b).

At that time, the new Chinese financial system was known as "Four Banks & Two Bureaus"[5] and was fully under the control of government officials. In 1935, currency reform unified different currencies and made the "Fabi" (法币) legal tender. The four banks controlled the financial system. In 1942, the Nationalist Government assigned different functions to each of the four banks. The BOC's commercial banking functions were limited to mobilizing domestic savings and giving loans, supporting foreign trade and related investments and loans, and managing the government's foreign funds. Thus, the BOC became a specialized international trade bank. Most of its original businesses were finally gone (Bank of China, 2014c).

4.2.6 *The Collapse of Chiang's Financial Autocracy*

Not long after the currency reform, Japan launched its attack on China in 1937. As a result of the war and inflation, people sold "Fabi" for foreign currency. The "Fabi" devalued and the value of loans to the Chinese government in local currency correspondingly decreased. As a result, the Nationalist Government had to seek additional loans from Britain and America to support and stabilize the value of "Fabi". In 1939, the Sino-British Currency Stabilization Fund was established with a value of 10 million Pounds (the BOC—3.25 million; the BoCom—1.75 million; HSBC—3 million; and Standard Chartered Bank—2 million). In 1941, this fund was incorporated into the Sino-American-British Currency Stabilization Fund (SABCSF) in the value of USD 110 million (US—50 million, UK—40 million, and China—20 million). The Board of SABCSF managed this fund, the objective of which was to stabilize the "Fabi", intervene in the foreign exchange market, and manage exchange rates. At that time, the value of the "Fabi" was based on foreign currency reserves, the Board being the currency-issuing authority. In addition, it had the authority to set exchange rate policy. Thus, the Board of SABCSF played the virtual role of the central bank.

In 1942, America loaned China USD 500 million to support China's war with Japan. The Central Bank, BOC, established the Foreign Currency Management Committee to manage those loans. Because this amount was far larger than the USD 110 million commanded by the SABCSF, the BOC was then able to supplant the Board of SABCSF in foreign exchange management.

However, a series of policies by the Nationalist Government, such as Quantitative Easing in 1945, foreign currency liberalization in 1946, and currency reform in 1948[6] led to inflation, currency system collapse, and the loss of loan resources, all of which brought financial paralysis and contributed to the eventual collapse and defeat of the Kuomintang regime. When the Communist Party took over China, the People's Bank of China, established in 1948 to be the central bank, began to issue "Renminbi" (人民币), which was not based on foreign currencies until December 1948. The currency in mainland China was unified in 1950. Additionally, foreign banks pulled their businesses from mainland China.

As the above historical account shows, from the Qing Dynasty onward, successive governments' attempts to create a central bank have had limited success because they were unable to exercise effective control of monetary policy. To be fair, this lack of success was not entirely of their own making. For instance, the Chinese government's operation of a silver standard during the Great Depression was undermined by the US silver purchases to deplete the Chinese coffers (Friedman, 1992: 62). Nevertheless, blame must also be placed on the inability of the ruling Chinese government after the establishment of the Republic of China in 1911 to control its financial institutions as a result of either political weaknesses, infighting, and/or domestic strife. These weaknesses led to the need to bring in Western powers (especially the British but also increasingly the Americans) to ensure the functioning of China's fragile financial system. Both sets of factors have been detrimental to the creation of a strong Chinese financial structure regulated by a central bank.

Table 4.1 summarizes the evolution of the government and central banks in modern China. Controlling the banks bolstered the legitimacy of regimes. All regimes need money to run the state and to allocate resources for different uses. Therefore, the most effective way to control an economy is to control the currency and the banking system, which creates the currency.

Table 4.1 The evolution of government and central banks in the modern history of China

Period	*Government*	*Central Bank*
1865–1905	Qing Dynasty	HSBC acted as the central bank
1905–1912	Qing Dynasty	"Daqing" Bank
1912–1928	Beiyang Government	BOC and BoCom
1925.7–1926.12	Guangzhou Government	BOC and BoCom
1927.2–1927.8	Wuhan Government	BOC and BoCom
1927–1939	Nanjing Nationalist Government	The Central Bank
1939–1942	Nationalist Government	The Board of SABCSF
1942–1948	Nationalist Government	The Central Bank

Source: The authors

From this historical perspective, we can clearly see why state control is seen by the current leadership as vital for the banking sector and a strong banking system is needed to carry out government policies. For China's banking system, it is the single most important lesson of history Chinese leaders learnt. We also can see the paternal role of the state and socialist ideology after 1949. It is not surprising that control of the banking sector is a prime directive for the Chinese government. Its effort to strengthen this sector through reform that does not involve diluting state ownership must be seen in this light.

4.3 From Isolation to Banking Reform

Between 1949 and 1980, China remained closed, and there was no interference from outside. But inside China, the banking sector went through many changes. The PBC was established on December 1, 1948, by the consolidation of the former Huabei Bank, Beihai Bank, and Xibei Farmer Bank. Between 1950 and 1978, it was the only bank in China and was responsible for both central banking and commercial banking. All other banks, including BOC, which was taken over by PBC in 1949, and became one of its divisions in 1950 (Chinadaily.com.cn, 2006). The BOC website recorded "On October 27, 1953, Bank of China was authorized as a specialized foreign exchange bank under the *Articles of Association of Bank of China* issued by the Government Administration Council of the Central People's Government." Other banks were soon established. In 1951, the Agricultural Bank of China (ABC) was founded and merged into and separated from the PBC three times. It specialized in providing and managing agricultural funds for the state (Agricultural Bank of China, 2014). The initial establishment of the People's Construction Bank of China (PCBC) in 1954, which was affiliated to the Ministry of Finance, was to act as an "appropriation" institution that controlled and allocated budgeted infrastructure project funds (China Construction Bank, 2014). Before opening-up in 1978, the big three banks, the BOC, the ABC, and the PCBC, were not independent entities but subordinate to the state. They were specialized banks instead of commercial banks. When in 1978, the Chinese state began its state enterprise reform, the development of China's state banks was part and parcel of state enterprise reform but, as already stated, its reform pace differed from that of the non-financial sectors.

According to existing studies of China's state enterprise reform (Zhou & Xia, 2008) and China's banking sector reform (Liu, 2009), China's banking sector corporatization process could be described as occurring in two phases, the first until 1997, and the second from 1997.

4.3.1 *Dissociation of the Big-Four State Banks from the State, the Emerging Joint-Stock System and Corporate Governance Structure (1979–1997)*

The state-initiated financial reform began with the dissociation of the big-four banks from the state. In 1979, ABC was reabsorbed by the government for the fourth time and officially opened to the public to receive savings deposits. The BOC became a branch of the PBC to operate the foreign currency business and the PCBC was separated from the Ministry of Finance by the State Council. In 1984, the Industrial and Commercial Bank of China (ICBC) was established to undertake the PBC's industrial and commercial credit and savings businesses (Industrial and Commercial Bank of China, 2013a). Thus, in this stage, the specialized banks were transformed into commercial banks.

To an extent, the banking reforms tracked broader state enterprise reforms. From 1987 to 1988, a group of emerging joint-stock commercial banks was established to increase the competitiveness of China's banking system. The BoCom was the first joint-stock commercial bank in China. BoCom was also autonomous in its operations and a manager/contract responsibility system was adopted. As the pilot bank to implement joint-stock reforms, BoCom underwent ownership reform and governance reform by having its managerial autonomy increased. Since 1992, another group of banks such as the China Everbright Bank (CEB) emerged.

In 1994, three policy banks—the China Development Bank (CDB), the Agricultural Development Bank of China, and the Export-Import Bank of China—were established to provide policy-based lending for development, agriculture, and the export-import trade respectively. The policy-based functions of the big-four banks were formally removed and transferred to these policy banks. In 1995, the Commercial Banking Laws of the People's Republic of China were promulgated, emphasizing a modern corporate governance structure in which commercial banks were to act in accordance with the Company Laws of the People's Republic of China (The China Banking Regulatory Commission, 2008). These laws became the legal foundation of the banking system and commercialization and corporatization were formally stressed. In 1996, PCBC was renamed to the China Construction Bank (CCB). In 1997, CEB accomplished its joint-stock reform and became the first state commercial bank with foreign ownership, a part of its shares having been purchased by the Asian Development Bank (Berger, Hasan, & Zhou, 2009). CEB initiated foreign ownership participation in China's banking sector.

The year 1997 was also the year in which four Asian countries—Thailand, Malaysia, Indonesia, and South Korea in that order—succumbed to the AFC. By virtue of the non-convertibility of the RMB, China was protected from the scourge of currency speculators, who savaged the Thai and Malaysian currencies and even mounted an unsuccessful attack on the Hong Kong dollar. However, China's GDP growth slowed, especially in 1998 and 1999, reminding the Chinese leadership that the banking system's financial weaknesses, such as the substantial portfolio of NPLs had to be dealt with. The stage was thus set for the next phase of reform.

4.3.2 *Further Joint-Stock Reform by Listing (1998 to the Present)*

This stage was characterized by the state's preparations for public listing. Firstly, the big-four state commercial banks disposed of their NPLs and then were restructured into joint-stock enterprises with an aim to accelerate their corporatization and marketization processes (Kwan, 2009). In 1998, the Ministry of Finance issued RMB 270 trillion of special state treasury bonds to complement the big-four state commercial banks' capital base. With the capital adequacy ratio of 8%, they fulfilled the requirements of the Basel Accords. The following year, the state established four Assets Management Companies (AMCs) to take over RMB 1500 trillion of NPLs from the big-four. The state's strategies for the banking sector were to go international and import international competition because the Basel Accords rules represented international standards. In 2001, China's banking system qualified China to join the WTO as a member; and China's financial market was opened to foreign investors. Furthermore, the state encouraged foreign investors to become shareholders in joint-stock commercial banks as strategic investors.[7] Thus, both foreign ownership and foreign corporate governance mechanisms were introduced into China's banking sector (Matthews & Zhang, 2010).

Specific instructions from the state in 2002 were that the big-four state commercial banks were the only institutions able to deal in currencies. In 2003, the big-four state commercial banks and three policy banks started the process of preparing for public listing. The listing of this special sector had to overcome three thresholds, Company Laws and Commercial Banking Laws of the People's Republic of China, and the Basel Accords, with up to 8% capital adequacy ratio and no more than 10% NPL ratio required (Zhen, 2004). In 2003, the CBRC was established. China's banking sector has been supervised by the PBC, the CBRC, the CIRC, the CSRC, and the SAFE since 2003 (Zgjrjw.com, 2014).

In December 2003, to enrich the required capital base of the BOC and the CCB for joint-stock reform, the State Council made the decision to use state foreign currency reserves of USD 45 trillion. The Central Huijin Investment Limited (Central Huijin), a wholly state-owned enterprise, was established to supervising those funds. In June 2004, Central Huijin also injected RMB 3 trillion to BoCom. Thus, Central Huijin, which owned 6.68% of BoCom, became the sole shareholder of BOC and the largest holding shareholder[8] of the CCB. In April 2005, with permission from the state, joint-stock reforms of the ICBC started. The ICBC was injected with USD 15 trillion by Central Huijin and the Ministry of Finance and Central Huijin was given 50% of the equity of each.

In October 2005, the CCB listed through an Initial Public Offering (IPO) on the Hong Kong Stock Exchange (HKSE). Simultaneously, the ICBC issued A-shares through the Shanghai Stock Exchange (SSE) and H-shares through HKSE. In June and July 2006, BOC was listed on HKSE and SSE respectively. In September 2007, the CCB listed on SSE. In October 2008, ABC's joint-stock reform scheme was passed by the State Council. In July 2010, ABC went on a public listing at both the

SSE and HKSE. Thus, the banking sector opened up internationalization of bank ownership as part of these banks' efforts to globalize.

As with non-financial state enterprises, divestiture of ownership did not mean the erosion of state control. Following these reforms, most commercial banks were listed and began their split-share reforms (see Chap. 3) with the permission of the CBRC but with the proviso that the state had to maintain control. This meant that even when state shares became tradable on the stock markets, the state and state legal person shareholders could not sell their shares without the CBRC's approval. While other state enterprises were privatized and allowed to sell their tradable state shares, the banking sector remained under state ownership and followed state strategy.

Table 4.2 shows that the reform of the banking sector occurred in tandem with state enterprise reform except that the state's controlling position (through ownership and governance) was maintained. This meant that the reform process in terms of diminishing state control lagged behind that of non-financial state enterprises. Control has been given priority over ownership for state enterprises, but not for the banking sector which saw the state in the driving seat for both. After split-share reform, even though there is a potential trend to reduce majority shareholders' shares, the state made special policies to retain its controlling position in the banking sector in terms of ownership and governance. Thus, it is not hard to understand that the marketization and corporatization of China's banking sector has been at a slower pace than for other state sectors.

Additionally, during reform, the state continued to play an important role. In addition to efforts to boost their performance through preferences like low borrowing costs and shielding from competition, the Chinese state also paid attention to increasing efficiency within the confines of state policy. In addition, the state targeted the banking sector for public listing, joining WTO, and further opening to the international market to attract foreign equity and competition, that is, as part of its "Going Out" strategy (see Chap. 6). The state also offered substantial assistance such as helping their recapitalization and simultaneous transfer of NPLs and the injection of reserve funds to fulfill Basel Accord requirements. Listings on stock exchanges mandated these banks to conform to international corporate governance benchmarks. Moreover, and fortuitously, the GFC had decimated Western banks, some of which required government bailouts, with the result that Chinese banks had been propelled to the top in global rankings by asset size.[9]

Table 4.2 The link between state enterprise and banking sector reforms

Year	*State enterprise reform*	*Banking sector reform*
Governance Reform		
1978	More autonomy in operations and employees for own benefits	None
1984	The dissociation of state enterprises from the government and the separation of ownership rights and control rights were encouraged	1. BoCom was given autonomy in operations and manager/contract responsibility systems were adopted. 2. The policy-based functions of the big-four banks were formally stripped as the three policy banks was established. 3. No reaction for the separation of ownership rights and control rights policy. The state had the controlling power in terms of ownership and governance.
1993	The modern enterprise system	1. The Commercial Banking Laws of the People's Republic of China emphasized corporate governance structures for commercial banks. 2. Commercial banks had to act in accordance with the Company Laws of the People's Republic of China.
2005	Share incentive plans	Few
Ownership Reform		
1986	Joint-stock system	1. Two batches of joint-stock commercial banks emerged (For example, BoCom was the first joint-stock commercial bank; CEB accomplished its joint-stock reform in 1997, and became the first state commercial bank with foreign shares. 2. In December 2003, joint-stock reform of BOC and CCB started. 3. In April 2005, with the permission from the state, joint-stock reform of ICBC started. 4. In October 2008, ABC's joint-stock reform scheme was passed by the State Council.

(*continued*)

Table 4.2 (continued)

Year	*State enterprise reform*	*Banking sector reform*
1999	Listing	1. The Ministry of Finance issued special state treasury bonds to complement the big-four state commercial banks' capital base. 2. The state established four AMCs to strip NPLs from the big-four. 3. The State Council enriches the required capital base for BOC and CCB. 4. Central Huijin also injected RMB 3 trillion into BoCom. 5. ICBC was injected USD 15 trillion by Central Huijin.
2005	Split-share reform	Under the permission of CBRC, most state listed banks started the spilt-share reform.

Source: The authors

4.4 The Current Situation of China's Banking Sector

The above changes have produced a financial sector that continues to be dominated by government control through ownership and governance. Today, the financial institutions of the banking sector include policy banks, commercial banks, rural cooperative banks, urban credit cooperatives, rural credit cooperatives, finance companies affiliated to enterprise groups, trust and investment companies, financial leasing companies, auto financing companies, money brokers, and so on. Policy banks like the CDB, the Agricultural Development Bank of China, and the Export-Import Bank of China are joint-stock banks with 100% state ownership. Commercial banks consist of large commercial banks, joint-stock commercial banks, municipal commercial banks, rural commercial banks, and foreign investment banks. Major commercial banks (17 in total) include the big-four commercial banks and BoCom, which are now known as the big-5 commercial banks, and joint-stock commercial banks which consist of the China CITIC Bank, the CEB, the Huaxia Bank, the China Guangfa Bank, the Ping An Bank, the China Merchants Bank, the Shanghai Pudong Development Bank, the Industrial Bank, the China Minsheng Banking, the Evergrowing Bank, the China Zheshang Bank, and the China Bohai Bank, 12 banks in total (The China Banking Regulatory Commission, 2013).

Table 4.3 Fourth-quarter-end balances for major commercial banks (2003–2016)

Year	*The big-4/5 commercial banks*	*Total assets as % of all financial institutions*	*Total liabilities as % of all financial institutions*	*No. of joint-stock commercial banks*[a]	*Total assets as % of all financial institutions*	*Total liabilities as % of all financial institutions*
2003	The Big-4[b]	54.9	54.8	13	13.8	13.9
2004	The Big-4	53.6	53.5	13	14.9	15.0
2005	The Big-4	52.5	52.4	13	15.5	15.7
2006	The Big-4	51.3	51.0	13	16.2	16.5
2007	The Big-4	53.2	53.3	13	13.8	13.9
2008	The Big-5[c]	51.0	51.0	12	14.1	14.3
2009	The Big-5	50.9	51.0	12	15.0	15.1
2010	The Big-5	48.7	48.7	12	15.8	15.9
2011	The Big-5	47.3	47.4	12	16.2	16.3
2012	The Big-5	44.9	44.9	12	17.6	17.8
2013	The Big-5	43.3	43.3	12	17.8	18.0
2014	The Big-5	41.2	41.1	12	18.2	18.4
2015	The Big-5	39.2	39.1	12	18.6	18.8
2016	The Big-5	37.3	37.2	12	18.7	19.0

Source: Statistics of the China Banking Regulatory Commission 2003–2016. Retrieved from http://www.cbrc.gov.cn/chinese/home/docViewPage/110009.html

[a]13 joint-stock commercial banks included BoCom while 12 joint-stock commercial banks did not

[b]The big-4: ICBC, BOC, CCB, and ABC

[c]The big-5: ICBC, BOC, CCB, ABC, and BoCom

As will be seen later, despite the sector's diversification and expansion, the big-5 commercial banks remain the largest and account for the largest share of the sector's assets.

Table 4.3 shows the proportions of China's big 4/5 commercial banks' total assets in relation to those of all financial institutions in the banking sector, which saw progressive reductions in number although the number of those remaining was still considerable. Even though the joint-stock commercial banks outnumber by far the big-4/5 commercial banks, their total assets fall well short of those of the big-4/5 commercial banks.

Figure 4.2 shows the percentage share of assets of the big-5 commercial banks and joint-stock commercial banks (17 in total) of the banking sector. Together, they accounted for more than 50% of the assets of the banking sector. Thus, The Chinese state has tried to keep these institutions large and powerful. And despite their entry as mandated during China's

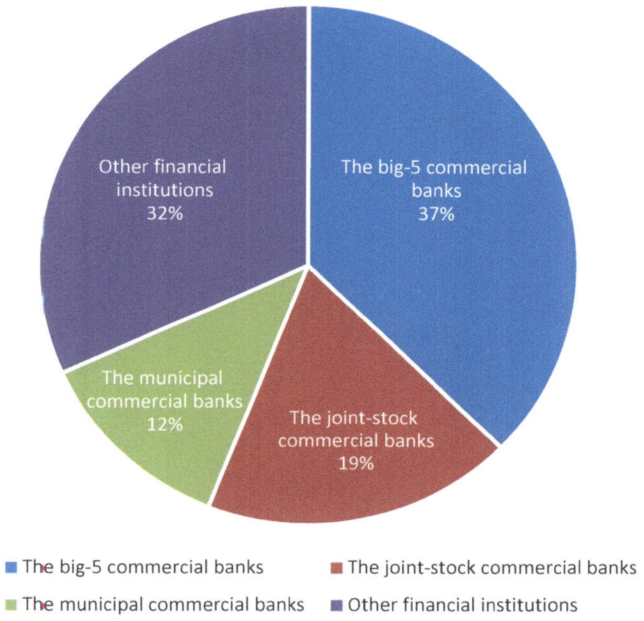

Fig. 4.2 Percentage share of assets of the banking sector in the fourth-quarter-end balances 2016. Note: Other financial institutions consist of policy banks, rural commercial banks, foreign investment banks, rural cooperative banks, urban credit cooperatives, rural credit cooperatives, finance companies affiliated to enterprise groups, trust and investment companies, financial leasing companies, auto financing companies, money brokers, and so on. Source: Statistics of the China Banking Regulatory Commission 2016. Retrieved from http://www.cbrc.gov.cn/chinese/home/docView/0539CAF58B2E4FE88540FCEAF0E1D8D6.html

accession to the WTO, foreign investment banks account for a very small share of total assets.

4.4.1 Ownership

Table 4.4 shows that among China's major commercial banks except Ping An Bank, China Minsheng Banking, and China Zheshang Bank, the state has a large proportion of ownership. By examining the top ten shareholders of those banks, the ownership concentration by the state and legal

Table 4.4 Ownership analysis of the major commercial banks

Bank Name	*Holding shareholder*[a]	*State share and state legal person share portion*[b] *(%)*	*Foreign investment share portion*[c] *(%)*	*Tradable shares*[d] *(%)*
BOC	Central Huijin (State shareholder)	67.57	28.08	100
ABC	Central Huijin	85.10	9.40	100
CCB	Central Huijin	59.99	37.16	100
ICBC	Central Huijin	71.34	24.27	100
BoCom	The Ministry of Finance of the People's Republic of China (State share holder)	30.95	38.82	100
China CITIC Bank	CITIC Group (State legal person shareholder)	76.06	25.89	100
CEB	China Everbright Group (State legal person shareholder)	63.91	11.9	100
Huaxia Bank	Shougang Group (State legal person shareholder)	67.58	0	100
China Guangfa Bank	China Life Insurance (State legal person shareholder)	93.01	0	N/A
Ping An Bank	Ping An Insurance (Group) Company of China, Ltd	5.16	0	85.21
China Merchants Bank	China Merchants Group (State legal person shareholder)	37.46	0	100
Shanghai Pudong Development Bank	Shanghai International Group (State legal person shareholder)	73.42	0	94.91
Industrial Bank	Fujian Provincial Department of Finance (State shareholder)	41.93	0	100
China Minsheng Banking	Hong Kong Securities Clearing Company Nominees Limited	0	18.91	100

(*continued*)

Table 4.4 (continued)

Bank Name	*Holding shareholder*[a]	*State share and state legal person share portion*[b] *(%)*	*Foreign investment share portion*[c] *(%)*	*Tradable shares*[d] *(%)*
Evergrowing Bank	Yantai Blue Sky Investment Holding Co. Ltd. (State legal person shareholder)	20.55	14.26	N/A
China Zheshang Bank	Hong Kong Securities Clearing Company Nominees Limited	25.04	15.56	N/A
China Bohai Bank	TEDA Investment Holding Co. Ltd. (State legal person shareholder)	62.01	19.99	N/A

Source: The authors' own calculation from latest annual reports of above listed banks, which are supervised by the CSRC through its Annual Report Standard

[a]The holding shareholder refers to the shareholder who owns largest share proportion

[b]The numbers are calculated among the top ten shareholders of each bank. Thus, the real number may be larger than shown here

[c]The numbers are calculated among the top ten shareholders of each bank. Thus, the real number may be larger than shown here

[d]"N/A" represents "Not Applicable"

person shareholders is relatively high. Moreover, as one of the shareholders in most of those banks, the state or a state legal person is the controlling shareholder. This means the state exercises control over those banks. Table 4.4 shows that foreign ownership is present among those banks, but compared to state ownership it is not significant.

Split-share reforms (see Chap. 3) had been undertaken for these banks. Most uncirculated shares could not be traded for a fixed period. After this period, state and state legal person shares became freely circulated on the stock market. Nevertheless, the state can also and does consolidate its controlling position by purchasing the tradable shares from the stock market. For example, the holding shareholder of the ABC, Central Huijin, bought A-shares through the Shanghai Stock Exchange to increase its ownership proportion in 2012. The listing and split-share reform was completed and well received by those banks as most are listed domestically or in Hong Kong, and the numbers of tradable shares for listed banks are very considerable.

4.4.2 Governance

Most of the Board of Directors and top management of China's big-4/5 commercial banks are hires of the financial and other fields from the government departments or other state enterprises. Key positions (Board of Directors, Board of Supervisors, and top management) in the big-4/5 commercial banks were filled by internal transfers among these banks as well as PBC, the three policy banks, CBRC, government departments (the Central Committee of the Communist Party of China, the National People's Congress, the State Council, the Chinese People's Political Consultative Conference, etc.), and state enterprises, which were all government institutions. They were considered experienced in China's reforms and opening-up as well as the transformation of financial institutions. In addition to strengthening internal collaborations and enacting strategies to boost performance, the control of management also ensures that government policies are followed by those banks.

The state's controlling power remains with the public officials. Among governments and government bodies, there are ten general administrative levels for public officials: National leader, Sub-national leader, Provincial-Ministerial level, Sub-Provincial (Ministerial) level, Bureau-Director level, Deputy-Bureau-Director level, Division-Head level, Deputy-Division-Head level, Section-Head level, Deputy-Section-Head level.[10] Administrative systems for non-financial state enterprises were eroded and eventually abandoned during state enterprise reform, but have been retained in big-4/5, joint-stock, and municipal commercial banks through a hidden administrative level system.

China's enterprise system had a Party Committee established within an enterprise. For a private enterprise it is an option, but for a state enterprise it is compulsory. The role of the Party Committee is determined by the proportion of state shares. It functions to ensure that the Communist Party of China's policies and strategies are executed. It participates in decision-making, supervision, day-to-day operations, employment of key persons, coordination of internal relations, and other corporate governance details. The state's controlling power in the banking sector is exercised also through the Party Committee.

The ultimate power to decide policy, but not day-to-day operations, is vested in the CBRC. The CBRC under the State Council regulates banks and ensures they follow the state's policies and strategies (diplomatic policy, national defense policy, monetary policy, etc.) (The China Banking Regulatory Commission, 2014).

For instance, directives given to the banks after the GFC included instructions to ensure real consumption contributed more to economic growth than gross fixed capital formation, and to ensure services are oriented toward the domestic middle classes than toward export-oriented manufacturing. Under the first directive, ICBC made more loans to individual consumption, small and medium-size enterprises, and middle-class consumers. ICBC bought government bonds, central bank bonds, and policy bank bonds, although it was not compulsory; ICBC's purchases of government or other bonds were based on their returns on investment.

Partial after-tax profits of selected state enterprises had to be submitted to the state. The after-tax profit retention was for the state enterprise's own development, which took the place of the financial allocation from the state since state enterprises reform began. Again, this policy was not adopted by the banking sector financial institutions (see below) (The Ministry of Finance of the People's Republic of China, 2013).

The state regulated pricing of commercial bank services, including charges for prices of basic service like bank bills of exchange, promissory notes, checks, credit transfers, and procuration services such as basic settlement prices. Pricing is the responsibility of the price administrative departments under the State Council, the banking regulatory authorities under the State Council, and the People's Bank of China (The Central People's Government of the People's Republic of China, 2012).

Big-4/5 commercial banks' remuneration of and benefits for key personnel were decided by the respective supervision institutions according to their administrative levels. However, their management is supposed to be in accordance with international standards, detailed in the Basel Accords III, and should include international audits and international financial statements.

At present, banks assume sole responsibility for their profits or losses. They do not submit their profits to the state. Four AMCs took over RMB 866340 million of the NPLs big-four commercial banks up to the end of March 2006 (The China Banking Regulatory Commission, 2006a). The state ultimately bought the rest of the NPLs. After that, the four AMCs transited from policy institutions to become commercialized companies. In addition, the proportion of NPLs in the big-four remained low. Therefore, the four AMCs did not have to play a role in taking over their NPLs.

Overall, the Chinese banks have major state ownership, follow state policies and regulations, and enjoy state favor over non-state commercial banks. The Chinese state through the CBRC still maintains absolute control over the banking sector with the control channels being mainly through ownership, governance, and the Party Committees (The China Banking Regulatory Commission, 2006b).

The need for state control, stemming from the unfortunate history of Chinese banking, has been stressed repeatedly by the leadership and top management of the banks. Zhou Xiaochuan, the president of the PBC, was reported to have said that the need to restructure the Central Huijin was to keep the absolute control of China's major banks (Hexun.com, 2007). Jiang Chaoliang, a director on the Board of BoCom, said that in order to ensure the absolute control position of the state in China's banking sector, China's banking sector should not relax the policy that foreign shares could not exceed a percentage[11] (Jiang, 2008). Cai Esheng, the Vice President of the CBRC, said the banking sector reform should be under the Chinese state's absolute control (Zhang, 2006).

4.4.3 *Performance*

Table 4.5 shows the main indicators of the big-5 commercial banks from 2007 to 2016 that embarked on a substantial reform effort. Because of banking sector reforms, the NPL ratio fell until 2012,[12] and indicators such as net profit were gradually increasing. The cost-income ratio decreased overall and indicated the costs from deposits were reduced. The bank capital to assets ratio (%) was substantially greater than the average level of total banks that saw good capital adequacy.[13] Loan-deposit ratios were increased overall and indicated that a leveraging strategy was adopted.

According to the fourth-quarter-end 2016 data, in terms of indicators such as cost-income ratio, capital adequacy ratio, loan-deposit ratio, and NPL ratio, the big-5 commercial banks performed better than the overall performance of all commercial banks (include the big-5, joint-stock, city, rural, and foreign commercial banks). For the year 2016, the net profit of big-5 commercial banks accounted for 57.42% of all commercial banks. And the big-5 commercial banks' overall performance was better than joint-stock commercial banks.[14]

4.5 Answering the Government's Call

The major commercial banks also have to assist other state enterprises. As initially specialized banks, China's banks were little more than fund disbursement institutions to fund state enterprises' economic activities. In

Table 4.5 Main performance indicators of the big-5 commercial banks (2007–2016)

	2007	*2008*	*2009*	*2010*	*2011*	*2012*	*2013*	*2014*	*2015*	*2016*
Profitability Indicator: Net Profit (RMB in billion)										
ICBC	82.25	111.23	129.40	166.03	208.45	238.69	262.97	276.29	277.72	279.11
BOC	62.02	65.57	85.35	109.69	130.32	145.75	163.74	177.20	179.42	184.05
BoCom	20.32	28.52	30.12	39.04	50.74	58.37	62.30	65.85	66.53	67.21
CCB	69.14	92.64	106.84	135.03	169.44	193.60	215.12	228.25	228.89	232.39
ABC	43.79	51.45	65.00	94.91	121.96	145.13	166.21	179.51	180.77	184.06
Profitability Indicator: Cost-Income Ratio (%)										
ICBC	35.02	29.84	33.18	30.99	29.91	29.24	28.80	27.93	26.69	27.40
BOC	33.70	31.52	34.92	34.16	33.07	31.73	30.61	28.57	28.30	28.08
BoCom	34.38	31.74	32.63	32.11	30.19	29.86	29.68	30.52	30.54	31.77
CCB	41.83	36.77	39.04	37.25	36.19	29.60	29.65	28.92	27.02	27.51
ABC	34.60	45.30	43.37	38.53	35.84	36.76	36.30	34.56	33.28	34.59
Capital Adequacy Indicator: Capital Adequacy Ratio (%)										
ICBC	13.09	13.06	12.36	12.27	13.17	13.66	13.66	14.53	15.22	14.61
BOC	13.34	13.43	11.14	12.58	12.97	13.63	12.46	13.87	14.06	14.28
BoCom	14.44	13.47	12.00	12.36	12.44	14.07	12.08	14.04	13.49	14.02
CCB	12.58	12.16	11.70	12.68	13.68	14.32	13.34	14.86	15.39	14.94
ABC	N/A	9.41	10.07	11.59	11.94	12.61	11.86	12.82	13.40	13.04
Liquidity Indicators: Loan-Deposit Ratio (%)										
ICBC	56.30	56.40	59.50	62.00	63.50	64.10	68.32	70.88	73.29	73.25
BOC	64.78	63.71	70.30	70.20	68.77	91.19	75.34	77.93	77.89	77.08
BoCom	64.87	64.91	71.97	72.10	71.94	72.71	73.40	74.07	74.08	73.98

(*continued*)

Table 4.5 (continued)

	2007	*2008*	*2009*	*2010*	*2011*	*2012*	*2013*	*2014*	*2015*	*2016*
CCB	61.27	59.50	60.24	62.47	65.05	66.23	70.28	67.53	69.80	68.17
ABC	65.71	50.84	55.19	55.77	58.50	44.97	47.34	49.91	49.31	49.50
Credit Risk Indicators: NPL Ratio (%)										
ICBC	2.74	2.29	1.54	1.08	0.94	0.85	0.94	1.13	1.50	1.62
BOC	3.12	2.65	1.52	1.10	1.00	0.95	0.96	1.18	1.43	1.46
BoCom	2.05	1.92	1.36	1.12	0.86	0.92	1.05	1.25	1.51	1.52
CCB	2.60	2.21	1.50	1.14	1.09	0.99	0.99	1.19	1.58	1.52
ABC	23.57	4.32	2.91	2.03	1.55	1.33	1.22	1.54	2.39	2.37

Source: Annual reports of big-5 commercial bank 2007–2016

the 1980s, the state started to transfer funds to newly founded state enterprises in the form of loans instead of appropriations ("loan replacing appropriation"). Thus, in playing the role of funding non-financial state enterprises, the state banks were transformed from financiers to lenders.

There were 6599 large and medium state enterprises with losses in 1997, which prompted the 15th National Congress of the Communist Party of China to put forward its "getting out of the difficulties within three years" to bring them out of the red (Huo, Wang, & Wang, 2001). The lending policy was framed such that bank lending would favor loss-making state enterprises. Moreover, technology innovation was rewarded with more loans, and appropriations of special funds for selected state enterprises were encouraged. Preferential channels such as access to borrowed funds at favorable interest rates, debt forgiveness, or loans to boost creditworthiness were provided by the state. The Chinese state directed lending to favored state sectors through policy implemented by commercial banks (The World Trade Organization, 2010).

The major commercial banks have to also answer the state's call under extraordinary circumstances as well as support state strategies overseas in addition to providing banking services to the Chinese people and financial support for the economy. Two such circumstances, China's entry into the WTO and the GFC, as well as an instance of supporting the state's "Going Out" strategy will be discussed next.

4.5.1 China's Entry into the WTO

As China globalizes, banks have an important role to play in facilitating trade with China's trading partners. To remove trade barriers, China wanted to be able to be fully competitive internationally. That was why it joined WTO in 2001. China's banks would engage with banks in WTO member countries under the WTO Financial Services Agreement, which is within the framework of the General Agreement on Trade in Services (GATS). GATS covered four modes of international service trade when applied to China's dealings with other members. Cross-border supply referred to services delivered within the territory of China from the territory of another member; consumption abroad referred to services delivered outside the territory of China in the territory of another member to a service consumer of China; commercial presence referred to service delivered within the territory of China through the commercial presence of the foreign supplier; and the movement of natural persons referred to service delivered within the territory of China, with the foreign supplier represented by a natural person. China's banking sector also opened itself to foreign stock ownership. This forced banks to face fierce competition as foreign investment banks' secured access to the Chinese banking market. China Unionpay was one product of China's entry into the WTO. China Unionpay is a Chinese bankcard association that provides an inter-bank, cross-region, and cross-border transaction settlement system among connected banks.

In compliance with the agreement under which China joined the WTO, the Chinese banking sector was opened to an international market in December 2006. Chinese banks also attracted foreign investment through international listings. Moreover, foreign financial institutions entered domestic markets as a stand-alone foreign bank or through acquiring shares of Chinese banks.

Foreign banks, however, did not operate on a level playing field when admitted and faced greater supervision from China's state supervision departments. In the early stages of foreign banking entering Chinese financial markets, the Chinese state worried that domestic financial institutions would be disadvantaged if opened too quickly to foreign competition. So supervision departments issued accreditation to foreign bank businesses with a cautious attitude. In fact, however, foreign banks were not a threat to domestic banks at all. They were not allocated any of the RMB 4 trillion stimulation during the GFC and their local customer bases and networks were small. However, the foreign banks' profitability came mainly from their investment in domestic banks. For instance, as at the end of 2012, HSBC Holdings owned 10.87% shares of the Industrial Bank[15] through Hang Seng Bank, which is the second largest shareholder. HSBC Holdings was also the third largest shareholder of BoCom, with 18.7% of ownership. It was the second largest shareholder of Shanghai Bank.

4.5.2 *Penetrating Global Financial Markets*

At the same time, the big-4/5 banks were important instruments of state policy to make acquisitions on global financial markets. Since the end of 2007, CCB acquired Bank of America (Asia) and BOC purchased Singapore Aircraft Leasing Enterprise. ICBC cooperated with the Kuwait Investment Authority to search for investment opportunities around the world. Since 1993, when the Singapore branch of ICBC was established, the globalization strategy was activated through purchased international banks to establish local branches. Since 2007, ICBC acquired Halim Bank in Indonesia and Seng Heng Bank (the biggest local bank of Macau), and purchased some stock equity from the largest local bank of South Africa (the Standard Bank of South Africa). In February 2013, China announced expansion of RMB exchange protocols with Singapore and the PBC appointed ICBC's Singapore branches to execute RMB clearing operations and to play an agency role between Singapore banks and the PBC (Industrial and Commercial Bank of China, 2013b). This protocol would build a bridge between Singapore and China and benefit the RMB's international progress. Of course, ICBC stands to profit from each transaction. In Malaysia, BOC was appointed by the Chinese government to play this role. Till July 2017, the PBC had designated 23 Renminbi clearing banks all around the world, and those banks were the branches of the big-5 commercial banks (SWIFT, 2017).

Beyond these acquisitions, China's big-4/5 banks are part of China's push to invest in other developing countries, especially Africa, as it operationalizes its "Going Out" strategy. And since 2013, the much more ambitious BRI will secure for these banks, together with the CDB and the newly established Asia Infrastructure Investment Bank (AIIB), a much larger international presence. Chapter 6 is devoted to elaborating this new role.

4.5.3 Global Financial Crisis

In 2008, the GFC rocked the whole world. As a consequence of this crisis, foreign demand for China's goods plummeted; and to maintain economic growth, China was seeking to stimulate domestic demand. In November 2008, Premier Wen Jiabao required the banking sector to provide support for China's economic growth by participating in the RMB 4 trillion stimulus plan. Enlarging credit access was a major part of this plan. According to the Statistics and Analysis Department of PBC, credit was expanded by RMB 9.59 trillion and the big-5 commercial banks accounted for approximately half of this expansion. Table 4.6 shows that loans by the big-5 commercial banks doubled from 2008 to 2012. This was mainly attributed to the state's policies to maintain economic growth.

The financial sector, strengthened through reforms and not having purchased much of America's toxic assets, remained resilient to the GFC shocks. China was also not overly dependent on foreign capital for its

Table 4.6 Total value of loans extended by big-5 commercial banks (2008–2012)

Bank Name (RMB in trillion)/Year	*2008*	*2009*	*2010*	*2011*	*2012*
ICBC	4436	5583	6623	7594	8583
BOC	3190	4797	5538	6203	6710
BoCom	1299	1801	2190	2505	2880
CCB	3683	4692	5526	6325	7310
ABC	3100	4138	4788	5399	6153
Sum Up	15,708	21,011	24,665	28,026	31,636
Total all financial institutions	30,339	39,968	47,920	54,795	62,991
Growth rate	16%	32%	20%	14%	15%
% of Big-5 in Total	52%	53%	51%	51%	50%

Sources: Annual reports from the big-5 commercial banks 2008–2012 and summary of sources and uses of credit funds of financial institutions 2008–2012, from the Statistics and Analysis Department, the People's Bank of China

development. Indeed, the troubles facing Western banks have catapulted Chinese banks to the forefront in global rankings.[16] Another impact has been that Chinese banks, which have traditionally focused on large enterprises, began to turn their attention to small and medium enterprises, especially after the government tightened credit in the aftermath of the stimulus package (Zhang & Cheong, 2011). In its assessment report, the IMF concluded that China's financial sector "entered the GFC from a position of relative strength" (The International Monetary Fund, 2011). However, it also outlined several risks, including the growth of "off-balance sheet exposures and of lending outside of the formal banking sector" that can reduce banks' loan portfolio quality.

The adverse impact of the GFC on export-oriented enterprises and construction firms was a major source of vulnerability for China. Another source was the large credit expansion that accompanied China's RMB 4 trillion stimulus package, which threatened to reverse the hard-won successes in containing a potential real estate bubble and cooling an overheated economy just prior to the onset of the GFC. In the housing sector, already low borrowing costs encouraged over-investment in housing,[17] while local municipal governments have directed state enterprises to invest in housing or channel funds to real estate developers (Xu, Yeh, & Wu, 2009). Even those worried about the banks' heightened vulnerability, however, were undoubtedly mindful of the considerable resources the Chinese government could deploy to support these institutions.

One consequence of the GFC is that it may well have a greater lasting impact that is likely to slow down financial reforms of the kind advocated by the IMF. Whether this consequence is positive or otherwise remains to be seen. While the IMF and others lament this development (Lipsky, 2011), it should hardly be surprising if the GFC led the Chinese leadership to exercise greater caution moving this reform forward.[18] "Backwardness" in financial innovation and cross-border financial intermediation as well as underdeveloped capital markets was what allowed Asia to limit contagions from the GFC were views that Asian leaders shared (Khor & Tan, 2011). An important difference between the AFC of 1997–1999 and the GFC is that while during the AFC, sizable NPLs signaled immediate danger to Chinese banks and, thus, spurred financial reforms, the weaknesses of banks during the GFC are nowhere as immediate. China's leadership clearly sees countering a continuing impact of the GFC having a higher priority than banking reforms. And, as the AFC clearly demonstrated, countering crisis impact is most effective under centralized decision-making followed by "unified action" (Yao & Wu, 2011).

Will financial reform continue, albeit with some delay or with greater caution? The answer will likely be yes. First, the lesson of the GFC is not so much that financial liberalization should be halted but that effective prudential regulation should have been enforced. The casualty is not financial liberalization but the neoliberal approach to liberalization. Second, the long-term costs to the Chinese economy of the weaknesses discussed above, in the form of distorting investment choices at the microeconomic level and of hampering the effective implementation of monetary policy at the macroeconomic level are persuasive arguments for continued liberalization (McCormick, 2008). These costs, not the accusation of Chinese culpability in the GFC in the form of adopting mercantilist policies (Wolf, 2008), will provide the impetus for continued reform.[19] Indeed, China's 12th Five Year Plan speaks of reform to move toward market interest rates.[20] As history shows and given its abundant stock of foreign reserves, China will not be pressured by external voices but will manage this process at a pace it deems appropriate.

4.6 Conclusion

The reform of China's banking sector took place in conjunction with state enterprise reform but followed a somewhat different path. Instead of privatization, China's banking sector underwent corporatization and governance reform but the state did not reduce its ownership much less relinquish control. To implement the governance reform, the big-4/5 banks acquired increasing autonomy and established a sound modern corporate governance structure. Through introducing the joint-stock system, the ownership structure was somewhat diversified with equity from private capital. They became joint-stock enterprises through public listing, joint venture, and cross holdings. However, the state still occupies a dominate position in much of the banking sector and regards banking as a strategic industry. Thanks to reform, however, this ownership is combined with an independent modern corporate governance structure. This structure means that while the state retained controlling power, it does not intervene in the banks' day-to-day operations. Thus, the reform of China's banking sector was in line with the state enterprises reform of corporatization but without losing state control (both ownership and governance).

Why has the state maintained its dominance through ownership of the major banks? First, as has been shown in detail in this chapter, this dominance has historical origins, stemming from lessons learned from the Qing Dynasty and the post-revolutionary period before the outbreak of the Second World War, when successive governments tried but failed to control the financial sector and currency system to manage the economy. The result has been frequent changes and policy reversals in the quest to form a central bank, control of currency, and financially manage the economy, with policies held hostage to political rivalry and leadership struggles. The role of foreign interests, be they states or private financial enterprises, in furthering their own interests (as demonstrated by HSBC) in or at the expense of (as shown by Roosevelt's silver purchases) China's financial system, and Chinese reliance on them to bolster the latter must have been another lesson not lost on later generations of the Chinese leadership.

Second, the central role of the state as a political philosophy, which is also rooted in China's culture and history as discussed in Chap. 2, calls for banks to be major instruments of Chinese policy under its state-led model. This means banks are called upon in extraordinary situations when the stability of the economy is threatened and when the state seeks to advance its interests beyond its borders. This role can clearly be seen when the GFC hit China in 2008–2009 and when the Chinese government sought membership in the WTO to increase its international footprint.

At the same time, the government is aware of the inefficiencies associated with not privatizing these banking institutions. It has attempted modernizing their governance, strengthening efficiency, and distancing them from the central government in their day-to-day operations, which has resulted in their operating like and fulfilling the role of commercial banks in the country's financial system. It has however also accorded them preferential treatment.

With state protection, they are performing well, perhaps to the detriment of truly private banks. China is pursuing and its leadership is clearly aware of the transitional costs of the state role in banking for the development of a private banking sector, which is consonant with the state-led growth model. However, they must feel this cost is outweighed by what they believe to be the benefit from being able to use banks to support and implement state functions in ways that Western commercial banks have not or could not. China's enormous pool of external reserves undoubtedly gives the government comfort in managing whatever costs such a system may engender. Therefore, it is likely that the Chinese state will live with the costs for as long as the state-led growth is pursued and as long as these banks continue to be perceived as effective instruments of policy.

Finally, the jury is still out as to whether banks, through their profligate lending, pose a major threat to economic stability. In the years before liberalization, and even after, state banks were just instruments of state policy, disbursing funds/loans to state enterprises at the state's command. Thus, the NPLs that had accumulated in the 1990s were the products more of state policy—the need to fund state enterprises without the ability to lay off staff—than of mismanagement. The solution to the NPL problem, in the form of their takeover by newly created asset management companies, also has a precedent in the US Resolution Trust Company, established to do exactly the same in that country's Subprime Crisis. This does not exonerate banks from abetting such practices as shadow banking.[21] But it is not fair to blame the banks for implementing what their owners, the state, wanted implemented.

Notes

1. The First Opium War took place between 1839 and 1842 and saw the defeat of the Qing forces by the British. The Treaty of Nanking in 1842 that concluded the war saw the cessation of the island of Hong Kong to the United Kingdom in perpetuity, and it established five treaty ports at Shanghai, Canton, Ningpo, Fuchow, and Amoy. A Second Opium War was fought in 1856–1869 that resulted in the opening of more "treaty ports" to Western powers.

2. “Hubu” was the Ministry of Finance of the Qing Government.
3. Since the Communist Party cooperated with Kuomintang (国民党) to resist the warlord, in Wuhan Government, there were a group of members of the Communist Party joining as the officials.
4. BoCom was established with the capital of 2.5 million “Liang” by Qing Government in 1908 with 2/5 “Youchuanbu” (邮传部) (Ministry of Postal Service and Transmission of Qing Government) shares and 3/5 private shares.
5. Four banks: the Central Bank, BOC, BoCom, and Peasants Bank of China.
6. The currency reform in 1948 refers to using “Jinyuanquan” (金圆券) to replace “Fabi” as the fiat currency. “Jinyuanquan” was circulated from August 1948 to July 1949.
7. Strategic Investor refers to the legal person shareholder who subscribes newly issued shares from the issuer and has the long-term cooperation and investment relationships with the issuer. This legal person can be the domestic or foreign enterprises as long as it has capital, technology, management, market and talent advantage which can upgrade the industrial structure, expand the market share for the issuer, strengthen the core competition and innovative capacity for the issuer to acquire profit reward.
8. The holding shareholder refers to its having greater than 50% ownership, and if less than 50% but more than other shareholders’ ownership proportion in the same enterprise or if there are fewer shares than other shareholders had, but exercising control through other shareholders indirectly.
9. Relbanks data shows that for 2016, Chin’s ICBC, CCB, ABC and BOC occupy the first 4 positions in terms of asset holdings 2016 (Relbanks.com, 2017).
10. The administrative levels for public officials were regulated by the Civil Servant Law of the People’s Republic of China which had been approved by the 15th Meeting of the Standing Committee of the 10th National People’s Congress of the People’s Republic of China (The Central People’s Government of the People’s Republic of China, 2005).
11. It shall not exceed 20% of the shares of Chinese financial institution when a single foreign financial institution invests in a Chinese financial institution, and it cannot exceed 25% for the joint shares of multiple foreign financial institutions (China Banking Regulatory Commission, 2003).
12. Since 2012, the NPL ratio had increased gradually again. As the state enterprise reform in 2015 mentioned in Chap. 3, except for serious excess capacity, other indicators for China’s state enterprises’ low profitability were considerable numbers of “zombie enterprises” (mostly state enterprises) and the reported rise in NPLs in China’s big state banks which was caused by those “zombie enterprises” (Rfa.org, 2016). Even the reforms such as supply-side structural reform were conducted for state enterprises

during recent years, the positive effect would not be seen so soon in Table 4.5.

13. The average level numbers of capital adequacy ratio (%) of total banks from 2007 to 2016 (from the statistics of China Banking Regulatory Commission, various years) were not showed in Table 4.5.
14. The data was from the statistics of China Banking Regulatory Commission: http://www.cbrc.gov.cn/chinese/home/docView/A676043248BD4BEC896B4DDDFFCDF6D7.html and http://www.cbrc.gov.cn/chinese/home/docView/0C8F35BE17D74D01831FFC991F34D938.html
15. Industrial Bank is one of joint-stock commercial banks.
16. According to the global world's largest public companies list by Forbes 2017, ICBC, CCB, ABC, BOC and BoCom rank the 1st, 2nd, 6th, 8th and 34th respectively. The ranking is based on a comprehensive score by revenue, profits, assets and market value (Forbes, 2017).
17. However, Huang (in Carnegie 2011) provided an interesting justification for this financial repression. He argued that to the extent that the wealthy lose more from this repression through an inflation tax, the government used this as a progressive form of taxation at a time when few Chinese citizens fell within the tax net.
18. The need for caution in financial liberalization is shared by other Asian countries.
19. Huang, Wang, Wang, and Li (2010) found evidence that financial liberalization was helpful to China's economic growth while financial repression inhibited it (Huang, Wang, Wang, & Lin, 2010).
20. Okazaki, Hattori, and Takahashi (2011) drew lessons from the Japanese experience in financial liberalization to urge financial reform to facilitate internationalization of China's banks, in line with that for the RMB (Okazaki, Hattori, & Takahashi, 2011).
21. Shadow banking refers to alternative funding that does not show up as loans in banks' accounts. The most popular, according to PBC, are "entrusted loan agreements and trust loans. Under the former, a company lends money to another firm with the bank as the middleman, while for the latter, banks use money raised from wealth-management products to invest in a trust plan, with the proceeds eventually going to a corporate borrower" (Bloomberg, 2017).

References

Agricultural Bank of China (2014). The development history of Agricultural Bank of China. Retrieved from http://www.abchina.com/cn/AboutABC/nhfm/nhlch/

Bank of China (2014a). The important turning point for Bank of China—restructuring to the international exchange bank (1928). Retrieved from http://www.boc.cn/aboutboc/ab7/200809/t20080926_6925.html

Bank of China (2014b). National government's financial monopoly forcing Bank of China to restructure again (1935). Retrieved from http://www.boc.cn/aboutboc/ab7/200809/t20080926_6916.html

Bank of China (2014c). Nanjing government establishing four-joint headquarters, adjusting the division of four banks (1939). Retrieved from http://www.boc.cn/aboutboc/ab7/200809/t20080926_6915.html

Berger, A.N., Hasan, I., & Zhou, M. (2009). Bank ownership and efficiency in China: What will happen in the world's largest nation? *Journal of Banking & Finance, 33*(1), 113–130.

Bloomberg (2017). China's $8.5 trillion shadow banking industry is back in full swing, April 19. Retrieved from https://www.bloomberg.com/news/articles/2017-04-18/china-s-8-5-trillion-shadow-bank-industry-is-back-in-full-swing

Caijing.com.cn (2012). The republic of China was established, Bank of China came into being (1912)). Retrieved from http://www.caijing.com.cn/2012-01-17/111626505.html

China.com.cn (2008). From Daqing Bank to Bank of China: The epitome of modern Chinese banks. Retrieved from http://www.china.com.cn/international/txt/2008-01/11/content_9517627.htm

Chinadaily.com.cn (2006). People's Bank of China. Retrieved from http://www.chinadaily.com.cn/bizchina/2006-11/16/content_734959.htm

China Construction Bank (2014). The brief history of China Construction Bank. Retrieved from http://www.ccb.com/cn/investor/history.html

Culture.china.com.cn (2010). Chiang Kai-shek attempts to spare none through economic blockade, Soviet area communists and civilians wisely fight. Retrieved from http://www.china.com.cn/culture/lishi/2010-05/20/content_20082076_2.htm

Davis, B., & Orlik, T. (2013). World Bank design comprehensive reform blueprint for Chinese economy. Retrieved from http://cn.wsj.com/gb/20130802/bch072538.asp?source=whatnews

Dobson, W. and Kashyap, A.K. (2006). The contradiction in China's gradualist banking reforms. *Brookings Papers on Economic Activity, 2*, 103–162.

Forbes (2017). The world's biggest public companies. Retrieved from https://www.forbes.com/global2000/list/

Friedman, M. (1992). Franklin D. Roosevelt, silver and China. *Journal of Political Economy, 100*(1), 62–83.

Genevieve, B. D., & Wei, S. J. (2005). Pitfalls of a state-dominated financial system: The case of China. National Bureau of Economic Research.

Guo, X., & Lu, G. (2013). *The capital thief staring on China: HSBC in China 150 years*. China Youyi Press.

Huang, Y., Wang, X., Wang, B., & Lin, N. (2010). *Financial reform in China: Progress and challenges*. Paper presented at the Conference on Financial Liberalization in China, Japan and Korea, Seoul, Korea.

Industrial and Commercial Bank of China (2013b). ICBC officially started RMB payment and clearing services in Singapore. Retrieved from http://www.icbc.com.cn/icbc/gxk_1/12452.htm

Industrial and Commercial Bank of China (2013a). Looking back to Industrial and Commercial Bank of China's history (1984–2006). Retrieved from http://www.icbc-ltd.com/ICBCLtd/关于我行/历史回眸/

Jiang, C. (2008). The President of BoCom: The authority of foreign equity participation in domestic financial system should not be enlarged. Retrieved from http://money.163.com/08/0918/07/4M3TMKHV00251LIE.html

Khor, H.E., & Tan, K.S. (2011). An Asian response to international financial reforms. *East Asia Forum*. Retrieved from http://www.eastasiaforum.org/2010/11/10/an-asian-response-to-international-financial-reforms/

Kollewe, J. and Monahan, A. (2015). Analysts fear China financial crisis as deflation looms. *The Guardian*. January 9. Retrieved from https://www.theguardian.com/business/2015/jan/09/china-economic-crash-bank-of-america-analysts

Kwan, C.H. (2009). Reform of China's state-owned banks a success. *Nomura Journal of Capital Markets, 1*(4). Retrieved from http://papers.ssrn.com/sol3/papers.cfm?abstract_id=1566662

Lenin, V.I. (1973). V.I. Lenin collected works, Volume 32, December 1920—August 1921. Moscow: Progress Publishers.

Lipsky, J. (2011). China: Economic transformation and financial reform. *The International Forum of Sovereign Wealth Funds*. Beijing, China.

Liu, H. (1999). The Set up and role of the Central Bank of Nanjing Nationalist Government. *Republican Archives, 3*, 76–87.

Liu, M. (2009). *30 years of reform and opening up of China's banking sector*. Beijing: China Finance Press.

The Central People's Government of the People's Republic of China (2005). The Civil Servant Law of the People's Republic of China. Retrieved from http://www.gov.cn/flfg/2005-06/21/content_8249.htm

The Central People's Government of the People's Republic of China (2012). Seeking for opinions on commercial bank service price management measures. Retrieved from http://www.gov.cn/gzdt/2012-02/10/content_2063605.htm

The China Banking Regulatory Commission (2003). Management measures on foreign financial institutions investing to joint shares in Chinese financial institutions. Retrieved from http://www.cbrc.gov.cn/chinese/home/docDOC_ReadView/295.html

The China Banking Regulatory Commission (2006a). Disposal of non-performing assets by the four AMCs in 2006. Retrieved from http://www.cbrc.gov.cn/EngdocView.do?docID=2464

The China Banking Regulatory Commission (2006b). Q&A on WTO and opening up of China's banking sector. Retrieved from http://www.cbrc.gov.cn/chinese/home/docView/2864.html

The China Banking Regulatory Commission (2008). The Commercial Banking Law of People's Republic of China. Retrieved from http://www.cbrc.gov.cn/chinese/home/docView/2421.html

The China Banking Regulatory Commission (2013). Main performance index sheet of commercial banks (legal person). Retrieved from http://www.cbrc.gov.cn/chinese/home/docView/123C72BD103540C2B679F0A4BA19E903.html

The China Banking Regulatory Commission (2014). The main functions of China Banking Regulatory Commission. Retrieved from http://www.cbrc.gov.cn/chinese/yjhjj/index.html

The Ministry of Finance of the People's Republic of China (2013). Statements regarding the central state-owned capital operation budget in 2013. Retrieved from http://yss.mof.gov.cn/2013zyczys/201303/t20130322_784806.html

The International Monetary Fund (2011). People's Republic of China—Financial system stability assessment. Washington D.C.

The World Trade Organization (2010). *Trade policy review: China (Revised)*. Geneva: WTO, 2010.

McCormick, D. (2008). No time for retrenchment—Why China should push ahead with financial liberalization. *International Economy, 22*(3), 66–69.

Matthews, K., & Zhang, N. (2010). Bank productivity in China 1997–2007: Measurement and convergence. *China Economic Review, 21*(4), 617–628.

Marx, K., & Engels, F. (1959). *The communist manifesto*. London: Penguin Books.

Mitchell, T. and McGee, P. (2015). World Bank warns China to reform its 'distorted' financial system. *Financial Times*. July 1. Retrieved from http://www.ft.com/cms/s/0/bf01a54c-1fa1-11e5-aa5a-398b2169cf79.html#axzz4GvCAB1Iw

Okazaki, K., Hattori, M., & Takahashi, W. (2011). The challenges confronting the banking system reform in China: An analysis in light of Japan's experience of financial liberalization. Institute for Monetary and Economic Studies, Bank of Japan.

Qu, M., & Luo, W. (2011). The history of Chinese banking industry: From the late Qing Dynasty to the moment. City University of HK Press.

Relbanks.com (2017). Top 100 banks in the world. Retrieved from https://www.relbanks.com/worlds-top-banks/assets

Rfa.org (2016). China's four big state-owned Banks reported rising non-performing loans. Retrieved from https://www.rfa.org/mandarin/yataibaodao/jingmao/nu-08302016112129.html

Song, H. (2011). Currency wars 3: Financial high frontier. Beijing: Chinese Chamber of Commerce and Industry Publishing House.

Stent, J. (2017). *China's banking transformation: The untold story*. Oxford: Oxford University Press.

SWIFT (2017). Whether the Belt and Road can revive the internationalization of the Renminbi? Retrieved from https://www.swift.com/zh-hans/resource/rmb-tracker-july-2017

Wang, Z. (2010). The rise of Soviet Union. *Operation Barbarossa*. Beijing: Foreign Languages Press.

Wolf, M. (2008). *Fixing global finance*. Baltimore: Johns Hopkins University Press.

Wu, Y. (2006). On Hong Kong and Shanghai banking corporation and modern China's trade financing and international exchanging. *Journal of Beijing Union University (Humanities and Social Sciences)*, (2).

Xu, J., Yeh, A., & Wu, F. (2009). Land commodification: New land development and politics in China since the late 1990s. *International Journal of Urban and Regional Research, 33*(4), 890–913.

Yao, X., & Wu, X. (2011). Transition of China's financial system after the Global Financial Crisis. *The World Economy, 34*(5), 792–804.

Zgjrjw.com (2014). The banking sector memorabilia of economic reform and opening up 30 years. Retrieved from http://www.zgjrjw.com/zt/jr30/index.html

Zhang, W. (2006). China's SOE reform: A corporate governance perspective. *Corporate Ownership and Control, 3*, 132–150.

Hexun.com (2007). Zhou Xiaochuan: Central Huijing's transformation to Temasek. Retrieved from http://futures.money.hexun.com/1992245.shtml

Huo, S., Wang, X., & Wang, W. (2001). Cadres' reader on some current significant social and economic problems. Beijing: Party School of the Central Committee of China Communist Party Publishing House.

Zhang, Z., & Cheong, K.C. (2011). *China's SMEs and the Global Crisis: Challenges and opportunities*. Paper presented at the 8th SMEs in a Global Economy Conference, Nong Khai, Thailand.

Zhen, S. (2004). How to use RMB 450 trillion of fund injection when the big-4 banks are conducting the ownership reform? Retrieved from http://www.china.com.cn/chinese/2004/Feb/490751.htm

Zhou, T., & Xia, X. (2008). The progress of China's state enterprises reform. In Zou, D. (Eds.), China: 30 years of reform and opening-up (1978–2008). Beijing: Social Science Academic Press.

CHAPTER 5

China's "Commercial" State Enterprises—A Case Study of ZTE Corporation

China's state enterprises are not retreating but advancing. This is bad for China and for the world.
(Article heading, the Economist, July 20, 2017)

5.1 Introduction

The state has played a dominant role since the establishment of the People's Republic of China in 1949, with this role fulfilled by state enterprises. This role began to change with economic liberalization in 1978. Reform of state enterprises was a central area of reform in the country's transformation toward a socialist market economy. As already indicated, one product of this reform which saw enterprises transformed to different degrees at varying paces is that it is very hard to identify and characterize what can be referred to a typical state enterprise in China today. Some enterprises are 100% owned by the state, while others are partially owned with varying degrees of state control. Some are held by a state enterprise which is a subsidiary of another state enterprise. In addition, there are enterprises over which the state has control despite having less than a controlling ownership share. Because of the complicated ownership of those enterprises, as well as an unclear link between ownership and control, characterizing state enterprises is not a simple matter.

This situation raises questions that have implications for both the applicability of theory as well as the meaning of state enterprise as currently

R. Li, K. C. Cheong, *China's State Enterprises*,
https://doi.org/10.1007/978-981-13-0176-6_5

understood. The Western concept of public enterprise is defined by ownership, whether in whole or in part, by the state. Through ownership, control is exercised. To the extent it is the latter which really matters for the state, two related questions are, first, how is control exercised, and second, how does this control affect enterprise performance. Existing theories do not focus on the first question, simply assuming majority ownership means effective control. They answer the latter question by pointing to the inferior performance of state enterprises compared to their private counterparts.

Gaining insights into the above issues are the research objectives of this chapter. Specifically, these objectives are to (1) clarify the meaning of state and state enterprise in the Chinese context, (2) assess the applicability of extant Western theories of public enterprise in light of objective (1) above, (3) link the complexity of Chinese state enterprises ownership and governance and performance to the reforms that brought the situation about, and (4) view all the above through analyzing the case of ZTE Corporation, a large enterprise officially classified as a "state-holding enterprise". Since objectives (1), (2), and (3) have also been partially dealt with in previous chapters, this chapter focuses on objective (4).

Using a case study approach, we profile ZTE Corporation in Sects. 5.2 and 5.3, relating its development to the reforms mentioned earlier. The discussion is centered on the evolution of the magnitude and nature of state ownership and governance. How these link with the state impact enterprise performance is the subject of Sects. 5.4, 5.5, and 5.6. The concluding section draws together the main findings and highlights several qualified implications, including for the application of existing theories.

5.2 Rationales for Choosing ZTE Corporation

The case study method cannot allow conclusions to be generalized. However, one way to ensure the significance of case-study-based research is to select a case that is important to a major industry or the economy, this importance deriving from its scale of operations, or its contribution to national strategy. These criteria led us to select ZTE Corporation, a major manufacturer of electronic communications equipment (ZTE Corporation, 2016a). Understanding ZTE Corporation requires an appreciation of its holding company, ZTE Holdings. Since ZTE Holdings is not listed, a fair amount of information in this chapter is gleaned from interviews and/or conversations with its management.

This study is also embedded and longitudinal. Embedded in this case are key players in the enterprise—top managers and officials with knowledge of state enterprises—with whom interviews were conducted. The period covered is from the enterprise's inception to the present. Secondary data were from existing online databases and also annual reports of ZTE Corporation. Selected other state enterprises were used to provide supporting data including the shareholder structure, assets, profits, and so on.

In terms of size, ZTE Corporation is one of the largest firms in the integrated communications manufacturing industry, with 2012 revenues of RMB 84,219,400,000. From the government's perspective, it, together with firms like Huawei Technology Co. Ltd., spearheads the country's drive to upgrade national technological capability under the Medium and Long-term Plan for Science and Technology Development 2006–2020.

ZTE Corporation provides global communications network solutions. Its businesses focus on design, development, distribution, installation of various advanced telecommunications systems and equipment including wireless, access and bearer, value-added services (VASs),[1] operators' networks, terminals, and so on. It was listed in the Shenzhen Stock Exchange domestically and the HKSE internationally. This corporation not only cooperates with China's leading telecommunications services operators like China Mobile to provide telecommunications products but also delivers its innovative products and business solutions across 140 countries through building operators' networks.

5.3 ZTE Corporation—A State Enterprise in Transition

ZTE Corporation is a multinational company producing telecommunication equipment and systems company headquartered in Shenzhen, Guangdong province. According to its website, its products include "wireless, switching, access, optical transmission, data, handsets and telecommunications software (and it) provides end-to-end solutions tailored to the specific needs of customers" (ZTE Corporation, 2016a).

ZTE Corporation is officially classified as a state-holding company by two of the criteria stated above—the state, though a minority shareholder, is the largest shareholder among all shareholders, and it also exercises control through its holding company—ZTE Holdings. Its corporate history, divisible into phases, is an eloquent documentary of the progress of state enterprise reform. The period from its formation in 1985 as the Shenzhen Zhongxing Semiconductor Co. Ltd. to about 1992 marked its first phase.

As the workshop director and the chief technology officer of the state military industry enterprise Aerospace System 691 Factory, Hou Weigui was selected as the enterprise's representative to go to the Shenzhen Special Economic Zone to look for cooperation partners to form a new technology enterprise. In May 1985, with the approval of the Shenzhen government, Shenzhen Zhongxing Semiconductor Co. Ltd. was founded with Hong Kong's Yunxing Electronics Trading Company as the foreign partner, and two state enterprises China Great Wall Industry Corporation Shenzhen Branch (now merged into Shenzhen Aerospace Guangyu Industry Group Corporation) and Aerospace System 691 Factory as equity owners. With registered capital of RMB 2800,000 and 66% of ownership from Aerospace System 691 Factory, the new company appointed Hou as president. The contract responsibility system was adopted when the board chose one of the three main shareholders to take the operating responsibility through a contract against which its share capital and dividends were pledged. In December 1992, a group of technicians and managers from Shenzhen Zhongxing Semiconductor Co. Ltd. incorporated a private enterprise Shenzhen Zhongxing WXT Equipment Co. Ltd. with registered capital of RMB 3,000,000. This company would have a significant role to play in ZTE Corporation's development. It should also be noted that while Shenzhen Zhongxing WXT Equipment Co. Ltd. was legally a private enterprise, its owners were employees of a state enterprise. As will be demonstrated later, this ownership pattern has major implications for ownership and control.

The second phase began with the enterprise's transformation into the ZTE Holdings and lasted just three years until 1996. In March 1993, Shenzhen Zhongxing WXT Equipment Co. Ltd. merged with two state enterprises—Shenzhen Aerospace Guangyu Industry Group Corporation and Aerospace System 691 Factory to form a joint venture company "ZTE Holdings" with the state owning 51% of shares. It was run by Shenzhen Zhongxing WXT Equipment Co. Ltd. and owned by both state and private parties. Thus ZTE Holdings is an example of the "state holding and private operating" system referred to earlier in which the state as holding shareholder delegated management to the operator (private) but the operator had to pledge its share rights. Under this system, the letter of authorized operating responsibility was signed between the Board of Directors (that the state is the holding shareholder) and the operator to ensure the state assets have increase in value. If there was a mismanagement, the operator had to pay out shares and share allocation earnings as compensation. If it performed better than planned, the operator would be rewarded (ZTE Corporation, 2013a). State ownership with private management occurred with state enterprise reform to loosen ownership but retain control. A degree of control also existed through management by former employees of state enterprises who were familiar with state enterprise objectives and modes of operation. In 1995, ZTE Holdings began its internationalization strategy.

Phase 3 (1997–2003) saw the enterprise listing on the Shenzhen Stock Exchange. In November 18, 1997, ZTE Holdings incorporated Shenzhen ZTE Co. Ltd. that issued 65,000,000 shares with the price of RMB 6.81 per share as its initial public offering at the Shenzhen Stock Exchange. It was the first listed Chinese enterprise manufacturing large-scale telecommunications equipment. Shenzhen ZTE is thus also an example of a state enterprise listing to tap outside capital and at the same time subjecting itself to the discipline of the market. Since then, the share structure of Shenzhen ZTE became a combination of three kinds: state legal person shares, other legal person shares, and public shares.

It was in this period that Shenzhen ZTE's technological potential was recognized by the government. In 1998, the State Economic and Trade Commission identified Shenzhen ZTE Co. Ltd. as one of the national technology centers, rendering it eligible to enjoy preferential treatment in the form of duty-free import of new technologies, instruments, and materials for research and development (R&D) (ZTE Corporation, 2003). Tax exemptions and relief were also accorded to expenditures for pilot projects and fixed assets investment for science and technology facilities. But the last two were terminated since 2000.[2] As evidence of its growing capability, Shenzhen ZTE cooperated with the Guangzhou Railway Corporation to construct the first home-engineered railway telecommunications system, thus breaking the monopoly held by foreign enterprises in this area.

The most recent stage focusing on shareholding reform was from June 2003, when Shenzhen ZTE Co. Ltd. was renamed ZTE Corporation to enter the international market, which is also a part of the government strategy of state enterprise reform to build internationally competitive firms. In November to December 2004, ZTE Corporation was the first A-share listed enterprise[3] which listed in the Hong Kong Stock Exchange and issued HK$ 3.1 billion H-shares (Fig. 5.1).[4]

Fig. 5.1 ZTE listing in the Hong Kong Stock Exchange. Scurce: Huang, G. (2005). Twenty years' history of ZTE Corporation. Retrieved from http://wwwen.zte.com.cn/endata/magazine/ztecommunications/2005year/no2/articles/200506/t20050622_162340.html

In accordance with the shareholding reform mentioned earlier, Instructions from the document "Directions for ZTE Corporation's split-share reform" announced by the board on November 23, 2005, was adopted by ZTE Corporation on December 25, 2005, as part of the country-wide split-share reform.[5] Because seven state-holding enterprises were state legal person shareholders of ZTE Corporation, SASAC's review and approval of this proposal was required (The Shenzhen Stock Exchange, 2005).

In accordance with this reform, the non-tradable shares could not be traded or transferred in the first 12 months of their issue, no more than 5% of the general share capital from ZTE Holdings could be circulated after 12 months, 10% after 24 months, and 37.41% after 36 months. Further ownership protection for the state and state-related parties was accorded holders of non-tradable shares through the setting of a higher price than tradable shares when the former became tradable.

In 2006, in order to support its expansion in the international market, ZTE Corporation transferred competent management staff overseas to support its international expansion (ZTE Corporation, 2016b). This subphase is detailed in the next chapter.

Finally, according to the annual report of ZTE Corporation, with the approval of the CSRC, the first phase of equity incentive plans for employees was implemented on March 13, 2007, and 85,050,238 shares were allotted to 4022 qualified employees. This step could be seen as using incentives to boost employees' performance in state-controlled enterprises, bringing ZTE in line with private enterprises in terms of employment incentives.

5.4 Ownership and Control, Governance and Control

Changes in ZTE's ownership structure have major implications for the degree of state ownership, while the institution of split shares has a major bearing on control. How this control is exercised has to do with governance of the enterprise. And all these factors affect ZTE Corporation's performance.

5.4.1 *Ownership Changes*

Table 5.1 tracks ZTE Corporation's state ownership changes based on milestones in its corporate history. At the end of 1998, state ownership in the form of legal person shares numbered 223,600,000, amounting to 68.80% of the general capital. There was no foreign owned shareholding. The state legal person shares were owned by seven state enterprises, and ZTE Holdings was the holding company with 62.80% of the general capital. Since ZTE Corporation listed in Hong Kong in 2004, Hong Kong Securities Clearing Company Nominees Limited (HKSCCNL), the foreign shareholder, was the second largest shareholder. Individual owners included top management and other qualified employees who were beneficiaries of the equity incentive scheme. ZTE Holdings held the most number of shares among state legal person shares, the remaining state legal person shares accounting for only a small proportion (6%) of the total.

With each corporate milestone, state ownership, reflected by the percentage of shares held by state legal persons, diminished. By 2004, state ownership had fallen to below 50%, making it no longer a majority

Table 5.1 Change in state ownership of ZTE Corporation (1998–2015)

Year	*% Shares held by state legal persons*	*Reason(s) for change in % of state ownership*	*% shares held by ZTE holdings*	*% shares held by HKSCCNL*
1998	68.80	Share structure at formation of Shenzhen ZTE Corporation.	62.80	N/A
1999	64.90	Share placing was adopted to all shareholders with total 19,500,000 shares. But state legal person shareholders gave up the placement. As a result, the general capital was increased without the state legal person shares' increases.	59.24	N/A
2001	57.90	Since March 13, 2001, 50,000,000 shares were issued to the public.	52.85	N/A
2004	48.18	ZTE Corporation issued 160,151,040 H-shares which were circulated in at Hong Kong Stock Exchange on December 9. It regulated that the state corporation shareholders had to reduce to hold some shares as the amount as 0.9% of those H-shares.	44.10	14.8
2005	40.86	Since ZTE Corporation adopted the split share structure reform, holders of non-tradable shares paid 2.5 shares for every 10 shares to holders of tradable shares as a sort of compensation.	37.41	16.62
2008	39.07	Through share placement, 58,294,800 H-shares were issued.	35.52	16.66
2009	37.25	A total of 85,050,238 shares were granted to 4022 qualified employees.	33.87	15.89
2010	35.73	A total of 58,294,800 H-shares were issued and a warrant call "ZTE ZXC1" exercised the option at the price RMB 42.39 per share and 21,523,441 A-shares was subscribed successfully.	32.45	18.27
2011	34.04	On June 13, ZTE Holdings reduced the holding shares 48,495,000 of ZTE Corporation through Shenzhen Stock Exchange.	30.76	18.27

(*continued*)

Table 5.1 (continued)

Year	*% Shares held by state legal persons*	*Reason(s) for change in % of state ownership*	*% shares held by ZTE holdings*	*% shares held by HKSCCNL*
2015	33.88	A-shares increased 25,741,682 shares because the employees of equity incentive plans exercised stock options. A-shares increased 687,508,255 shares because of the implementation of the 2014 annual profit allocation and capital accumulation fund turning into share plan in July 17, 2015.	30.59	18.17

Source: Annual reports of ZTE Corporation, 1999–2016

shareholder, and, by conventional definition, no longer a state enterprise. Under the Chinese classification, however, ZTE Corporation remains a state-holding enterprise. By 2015, state ownership has fallen to a third, of which 30% is held by ZTE Holdings. Much of the state ownership decline is attributable to the fall in the share ownership of ZTE Holdings.

Throughout this transformation, ZTE Holdings remains the key entity for ZTE Corporation. It is therefore important to understand the ownership structure of ZTE Holdings itself. As shown in Fig. 5.2, "Yangqi" (central enterprise), China Aerospace Science and Technology Corporation was the second largest shareholder that owned 34% of ZTE Holdings in 2015. Another "Yangqi" China Aerospace Science and Industry Corporation owned 17% of ZTE Holdings. In total, these two state-owned enterprises owned 51% of ZTE Holdings. Since state enterprises had over 50% ownership, the conventional definition of a state enterprise applies to ZTE Holdings. More importantly, that state enterprises have 51% ownership translates into effective control of ZTE Holdings by the state. The largest single shareholder (49% of shares), however, was Shenzhen Zhongxing WXT Equipment Co. Ltd. which was technically a pure private enterprise owned by individuals (albeit former state enterprise employees).

With ZTE Holdings owning just 30.59% of ZTE Corporation in 2015 (Table 5.1), the 51% state ownership of ZTE Holdings translates into just 15.60% of state ownership of ZTE Corporation. However, because ZTE Holdings is the holding company of ZTE Corporation, as stated in both

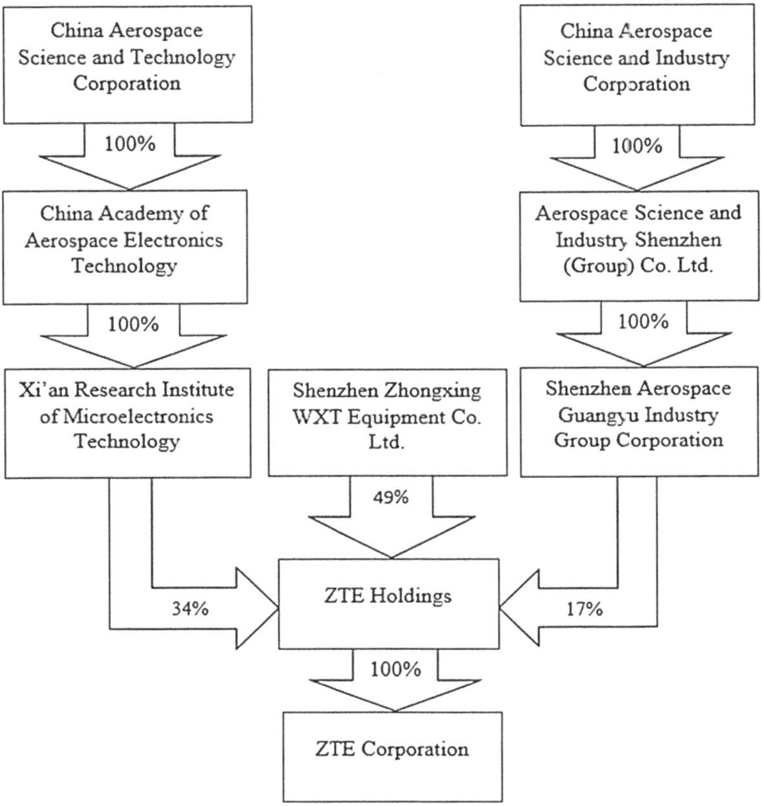

Fig. 5.2 Ownership structure of ZTE Holdings, as of 2016. Source: China Aerospace Science and Industry Corporation (2014). Corporate structure. Retrieved from http://www.casic.com.cn/n101/n127/index.html, and annual reports of ZTE Corporation (1999–2016)

companies' annual reports, and the largest of the shareholders (HKSCCNL owns 17% and all other shareholders less than 1% each), it retains full control of the latter. Thus, while state ownership had fallen to the point that it was only a minority shareholder, the state retained control through its majority ownership of the holding company.

There is more to this ownership than these numbers suggest. Although the state through ZTE Holdings has an equity stake of only 15.60% in

ZTE Corporation, the other shareholders of ZTE Holdings are former employees of the original state enterprise.[6] Together with the state, these shareholders can be considered "insiders" in the Corporation. There would also be other "insider" minority shareholders who are beneficiaries of the Corporation's incentive program. To the extent that these "insiders" grew up with the Corporation, their "ownership" counts for much more than ownership as legally defined. They, together with HKSCCNL the nominee company voting with ZTE Holdings which appointed them, would ensure that there would be de facto state ownership and little contest in board decisions.

The nature of private sector ownership in ZTE Corporation—the private sector participation coming from employees of state enterprises—is not uncommon in China. While new private enterprises have undoubtedly emerged as a result of the gradual liberalization of the economy, many of today's private enterprises began life as collectives[7] and township and village enterprises (TVEs) (Gregory, Tenev, & Wagle, 2000). Others were small state-owned enterprises that were privatized, especially under the "grasp the large and let go the small" state enterprise reform policy beginning in 1995. Thus, the public-private enterprise distinction, already less well defined given the embedded nature of the state in civil society described earlier, is made even more opaque by China's state enterprise reform experience.

5.4.2 *Corporate Governance*

How is this control exercised? It can be exercised through governance of the enterprise on the one hand and its relations with the state on the other. Apart from the letter of authorized operating responsibility signed between the Board of Directors (that the state is the holding shareholder) and the operator, the state's control over ZTE Holdings is reflected in the composition of its Board of Directors. The Board of Directors is made up of nine directors from the three shareholders: Shenzhen Zhongxing WXT Equipment Co. Ltd. (four), Xi'an Research Institute of Microelectronics Technology (three), and Shenzhen Aerospace Guangyu Industry Group Corporation (two). State-appointed directors outnumber non-state directors, five to four.[8]

ZTE Holdings is represented on ZTE Corporation's Board by five directors, a third of the total number of directors, while the remaining directors have been selected for their expertise rather than to represent any single shareholder or group of shareholders.

Board directors and senior managers had worked in management in various capacities within the related entities of ZTE Corporation and its parent companies.[9] There are no bureaucrats among them. As already indicated, this close connection to the holding company also bolsters ZTE Holdings' de facto control of ZTE Corporation. That all members of the Board are "insiders", those who grew up in or had been part of the component entities of ZTE Corporation and were knowledgeable about both the operations and the technology of the business, is likely to be more material to the success of the Corporation, given the technology intensity of the business, than the much touted autonomy from state control (Li, Xia, Long, & Tan, 2012).

The Board of Directors of ZTE Corporation held office for three-year terms. In the five terms since its incorporation, Board members made all the major strategic decisions about the Corporation. They also oversaw top management's appointments and dismissals. The top management took charge of day-to-day operations like recruiting management personnel, supervising enterprise operations, and setting market strategies.[10]

ZTE Corporation was independent of the holding shareholder ZTE Holdings in respect of management of its employees, assets, finance and accounting, as well as in its business and internal organization management. Thus, for major decisions, ZTE Corporation did not rely on the state but took decisions deemed to be in the best interest of the Corporation. For instance, the technology policies were set by the Chief Technology Officer and his team, who had the final say. And the state through ZTE Holdings did not exercise control over ZTE Corporation through finance. Employees of ZTE Corporation were paid by the Corporation and not by ZTE Holdings.[11]

Whether a de facto role is played by government officials in ZTE Corporation is unclear however. Although state enterprise reform had officially ended the role of government officials in these enterprises' administrative hierarchies, interviews with officials revealed that it was not uncommon for state enterprises to be supervised by central and local government officials under overt administrative systems.[12] ZTE Corporation is not under this category of major state enterprises, and there is the possibility that such an overt system did not exist or was of little importance.

However, in common with other state enterprises, ZTE Corporation has a (mandatory) Party Committee. Traditionally, this Committee functioned to ensure the policies of Communist Party were followed and implemented, participating in decision-making, supervision, employment of key persons, and even day-to-day operations. However, interviews with bureaucrats suggest that the Committee in ZTE Corporation functioned far less intrusively than those in major state enterprises. There could be some truth to ZTE Corporation President Hou's testimony in a Congressional hearing in Washington, DC, on September 14, 2012, that the Party Committee had no say in major decision-making and the day-to-day operations of the Corporation. He added that he was not a Communist Party member or a member of ZTE Corporation's Party Committee.[13]

Finally, two indicators point to ZTE Corporation's autonomy from state control. First, while it is customary for part of the after-tax profits of state enterprises to be surrendered to the state (The Ministry of Finance of the People's Republic of China, 2013), ZTE Corporation made no such repatriation. Second, prices of major state enterprises products that are closely associated with people's life had to comply with state pricing guidelines (The Central People's Government of the People's Republic of China, 2005a). But again for ZTE Corporation, it is free to set prices based on market determined.[14]

Since ZTE Corporation's listing in Hong Kong, financial reports were prepared according to Hong Kong accounting standards which conformed to international accounting standards (International Financial Reporting Standards) and Chinese accounting standards (Generally Accepted Accounting Principles) and were audited by professional accounting firms. Generally speaking, employees were hired and fired by the human resource department according their capacities and performance. Additionally, employees were paid and rewarded according to industry benchmarks, with bonuses set based on profitability.[15]

5.5 Relations with the State

ZTE Corporation's relationship with the state took several forms. First, the state ensured that its policies were followed when President Jiang Zemin visited ZTE Corporation in 2000 and issued important instructions in regard to major issues like technology trade policy and stock options issue.

Second, the government leadership also motivated ZTE Corporation to embrace innovation and go global. In 2010, President Hu Jintao visited the ZTE Corporation booth at the Expo on "Emerging Industries of

Strategic Importance" in Shenzhen, giving his endorsement to TD-LTE deployment.[16] In 2011, a member of the Standing Committee of the Political Bureau of the Communist Party of China Central Committee, Li Changchun, visited China Content Broadcasting Network and motivated ZTE Corporation to persist in innovation to revitalize China.

Third, in 2003, Chinese President Hu came to the ZTE Corporation headquarters to encourage ZTE Corporation to accelerate the "going global" pace. Also when ZTE Corporation signed strategic cooperation plans with other countries' companies such as India's Sistema and Hi3G Sweden, the signing ceremony was attended by the presidents of both countries.

Not unexpectedly ZTE Corporation has a good relationship with the central and local (Beijing and Shenzhen) governments.[17] This relationship is built on compliance with and advancing the country's technology strategy. This compliance and promotion saw ZTE Corporation investing heavily in R&D and hiring many R&D staff (Table 5.2), including for "TD-CDMA", "TD-LTE", and "Gota"—related technologies and products. Also, consistent with the policy of collaboration with research institutes and universities, "Kejiao xingguo" (科教兴国) (Development

Table 5.2 Financial performance of ZTE Corporation (2001–2015)

Year	*Total sales (RMB in million)*	*Expenditure on R&D as % of sales*	*Net profits (RMB in million)*	*Rate of return (%)*	*R&D staff/ total staff (%)*
2001	9440.9	11.10	414.0	4.39	45.5
2002	10,795.9	10.45	703.6	6.52	42.0
2003	17,036.1	9.01	1028.3	6.04	37.6
2004	21,220.1	10.67	1272.5	6.00	32.5
2005	21,740.7	9.01	1287.7	5.92	31.2
2006	23,214.6	12.20	767.0	3.30	34.6
2007	34,777.2	9.23	1252.2	3.60	35.1
2008	44,293.4	9.02	1660.2	3.75	33.8
2009	60,272.6	9.59	2458.1	4.08	33.5
2010	69,906.7	10.14	3250.2	4.65	32.8
2011	86,254.5	9.85	2060.2	2.39	33.6
2012	84,118.9	10.50	(2840.9)	(3.37)	38.0
2013	75,233.7	9.81	1357.6	1.80	37.5
2014	81,471.3	11.06	2633.6	3.23	35.9
2015	100,186.4	12.18	3207.9	3.20	37.5

Source: Annual reports of ZTE Corporation, 2002–2016

through Promoting Science Technology and Education), ZTE Corporation founded a corporate training center ZTE University to deliver corporate training in 2013. Also, in order to acquire technological support for its products, ZTE Corporation established Industry-University-Research Institute Collaboration Forum to pursue long-term development. This forum makes full use of the advantages in R&D of the other members (universities). Publications by ZTE Corporation, such as the journal "ZTE Communications", "ZTE Technologies", and "Mobile World", update to track its technological development.

ZTE Corporation's support of the state has been well rewarded. ZTE Corporation was able to bid successfully for businesses with major state enterprise clients such as China Unicom, China Telecom, China Mobile, and Guangzhou Railway. When the central government promoted Chinese telecommunication industries and products overseas, ZTE Corporation would have the opportunity to follow through with bids for projects. An example is during celebrations for the 60th anniversary of the establishment of Australia-China relations in 2012, when the door was open to ZTE Corporation as part of China's proposed cooperation with Australia. ZTE Corporation also plays a role when the Chinese government provides assistance to third-world countries. When the state offered telecommunication projects which enjoyed preferential treatments, ZTE Corporation was asked to submit the tender. And when China offered preferential loans to Papua New Guinea for infrastructure development including the installation of a telecommunication system, ZTE Corporation was one of the companies selected.

Another dimension of this recognition is the state's favored treatment of the enterprise in recognition of its achievements in technology. In the early years of ZTE Corporation's establishment, its products were recognized by the Ministries of Posts and Telecommunications and of Information Industry and the State Science and Technology Commission. And this Corporation itself also received both central and local governments' recognition. In 1996, ZTE Corporation was recognized by the State Science and Technology Commission as one of key high-tech enterprises under the National Torch Program and by the State Council as one of the 300 key state enterprises. This recognition arises from the state's drive for indigenous innovation under the Medium and Long-term Plan 2006–2020 referred to above. As early as 1998, the State Economic and Trade Commission identified ZTE Corporation as one of the national technology centers which rendered it eligible to enjoy preferential treatment in the form of duty-free imports of materials, income tax exemption on the sale of technology products, and incentives for investment. In 1999, ZTE Corporation was also involved in the State Council's National High Technology Research and Development Program. State recognition of ZTE Corporation's contribution also came in the form of the presence of state dignitaries in major ZTE Corporation events. For instance, ZTE Corporation's Pakistan branch was opened in 1999 with Premier Li Peng present, while in 2000, President Jiang Zemin and Vice Premier Wu Bangguo's visited ZTE Corporation.

It is relatively easy for ZTE Corporation to secure special state funds like science and technology innovation supporting funds and awards. For exports, the state provided export tax rebates for ZTE Corporation. Other export incentives were also offered to ZTE Corporation. For instance, the CDB contracted with ZTE Corporation to buy some of the latter's accounts receivable if it was able to meet its export quota. ZTE Corporation could also get loans at lower than market interest rates from CDB.[18] And for specific projects in developing countries, ZTE Corporation could secure preferential loans from CDB. In 2012, CDB announced it would increase its strategic cooperation with ZTE Corporation in the next five years in the amount of USD 20 billion (ZTE Corporation, 2012). According to its financial statement, ZTE Corporation had government subsidies and tax preference for many years till the present.

Beyond financial incentives, the state was prepared to allow a change in "Hukou"[19] to attract talented workers to ZTE Corporation and retain productive employees. Cheap land was offered by local governments to ZTE Corporation to construct research centers, factories, and affordable housing. For normal commercial loans, ZTE Corporation had better access to credit than private enterprises.

The above suggests that state control of the enterprise is exercised through ensuring compliance of and support for state strategies rather than through the placement of bureaucrats on the board or intervention in the management of the Corporation. Indeed, the last function is "outsourced" to professional managers familiar with and who make all the key decisions for the Corporation. Financial support comes not from direct payment of employee wages but from preferential financial arrangements available to the Corporation. These arrangements represent just one dimension, albeit the most important, of the state's support of the Corporation.

5.6 Corporate Performance

How has this enterprise model of minority state ownership, state control over policy but enterprise autonomy in day-to-day operations performed over the years? Table 5.2 shows performance indicators based on sales and profits for the period 2001–2015. These show growing sales yielding a healthy rate of return of 3.7% or more during the decade.

In 2012, however, ZTE recorded a loss of nearly RMB 3 billion, its first loss since its IPO in 2004, caused by the US Congress judgment that because of its connections to the Chinese government, ZTE and its larger rival Huawei posed a security risk to the US if allowed to install equipment in the US (Montlake, 2012). In 2015, total sales reached RMB 100,186.4 million, a 23% increase over the previous year, the highest within this industry. International sales made up 47% of total sales, having grown 15%, elevating it to become the world's fourth largest mobile phone manufacturer.

What might account for the Corporation's overall success? One explanation may lie in the model of light state control only in the form of ensuring national strategy compliance combined with autonomous management. However, the many areas of state support would also have given ZTE Corporation an edge over private sector competitors.

A better measure of ZTE Corporation's performance is its achievements in technology. As a technology company, ZTE Corporation's success must necessarily be built around technology. The innovation theme of ZTE Corporation was from "Made in China" to "Created in China". Pursuing this objective, the company had indeed progressed from basic material processing to the forefront of the Chinese technology sector. It made efforts in indigenous innovation while also introducing foreign advanced technologies to reach international standards. For these efforts it was rewarded and recognized by both Chinese government and other countries' governments. As early as 1986, an R&D team created the first generation of 68-lines stored program control exchange which it named ZX-60. Sequential improvements led to the licensing and adoption of ZTE Corporation's equipment for use in China. In August 1995, it became the first within the industry to receive ISO9001 Quality Certificate, and in 2000, it also received the 2000 edition 9001 standard authentication. With a total 3906 Patent Cooperation Treaty (PCT) applications in 2012, ZTE Corporation was ranked No. 1 globally by the WIPO (The World Intellectual Property Organization, 2012), surpassing Huawei, the

Table 5.3 The global top five PCT applicants and the number of international applications (2008–2014)

Year	*Rank 1*	*Rank 2*	*Rank 3*	*Rank 4*	*Rank 5*
2008	Huawei 1737	Panasonic 1729	Philips 1551	Toyota 1364	Robert Bosch 1273
2009	Panasonic 1891	Huawei 1847	Robert Bosch 1586	Philips 1295	Qualcomm 1280
2010	Panasonic 2154	ZTE 1863	Qualcomm 1677	Huawei 1528	Philips 1435
2011	ZTE 2826	Panasonic 2463	Huawei 1831	Sharp 1755	Robert Bosch 1508
2012	ZTE 3906	Panasonic 2951	Sharp 2001	Huawei 1801	Robert Bosch 1775
2013	Panasonic 2881	ZTE 2309	Huawei 2094	Qualcomm 2036	Intel 1852
2014	Huawei 3442	Qualcomm 2409	ZTE 2179	Panasonic 1682	Mitsubishi El 1593

Source: PCT Newsletter by the World Intellectual Property Organization (WIPO), 2009–2015 at http://www.wipo.int/pct/en/newslett/year.jsp

perennial No. 1 for China (Table 5.3). In terms of authorizations and applications of the domestic patent for invention, ZTE Corporation was No. 1 in China (ZTE Corporation, 2013b).

These technology indicators point to an enterprise that is competitive in its core area of competence. This competence is less a reflection of state support, although it helped to attract talent, than of management capability. In this sense, it provides a degree of vindication for the state enterprise model exemplified by ZTE Corporation, a model that is at variance with the stereotype implicit in existing conceptualizations of state enterprises and more akin to the so-called government-linked companies that exist in many countries.

Since ZTE Corporation launched its internationalization strategy, its share of revenue from outside China has soared. The year 2007 saw international revenues account for 60% of the total revenue—the first time it exceeded domestic revenues (ZTE Corporation, 2016b). It also cooperated with international high-technology companies like IBM. In all, its equipment is used by more than 500 telecommunications companies in more than 140 countries and regions. For some of these countries, like Malaysia, it had a significant market share.

5.7 Conclusion

Although the role of the Chinese state and its enterprises has been viewed through the lens of Western theories as generally negative, a systematic reading of China's history suggests that this view should be contested. Add to this history China's unique state enterprise reform experiments and an assessment of Chinese state enterprises that is far from clear-cut emerges. Thus, while numerous studies have espoused a negative view of Chinese state enterprises, research endorsing the opposite view, both theoretical and empirical, is also growing.

This chapter has not attempted this assessment but instead focused on one enterprise, ZTE Corporation, tracing its origins and linking its growth and transformation to China's stepwise state enterprise reform. Because of these changes, it has come to embody the state's strategy of reducing ownership but maintaining control. Yet the term "control" may be a misnomer—ZTE Corporation retains almost complete management autonomy although complying with national strategies of technology development. Even board members, who are instruments of state control, are chosen from within the Corporation and its affiliates.

At the same time, state support in the form of tax preferences has undoubtedly helped ZTE Corporation's performance. Such support weakens arguments that attribute state enterprise competitiveness principally to autonomy and/or the absence of state control. However, since, as shown by the many loss-making state enterprises with state support, preferential treatment by the state does not necessarily translate into better performance, arguments that autonomy begets better performance remain intact (Li, Xia, Long, & Tan, 2012). Still, ZTE Corporation does not easily fit the modes posited of state control, diversified control, and private control in that it embodies elements of both state and private control. What appears to be critical to ZTE Corporation's success, apart from managerial autonomy, is the presence of "insiders" both in the state and private entities owning ZTE Corporation who are well versed with the company's operations at the helm. Since these insiders were there from the beginning, it is also not very meaningful to refer to ZTE Corporation's management as being "outsourced".

As a "state-holding company", ZTE Corporation embodies much less "state" than what is normally understood in a state enterprise. Its management is also not in the hands of bureaucrats. Although no generalization is warranted, ZTE Corporation's performance attests to the relative success of the state strategy to stress control over ownership. And this control is limited to providing a strategic direction. In moving from state-owned to state-controlled, more appropriately state-led, China's state enterprises can be said to be at the forefront of the model of state capitalism. Yet, despite these changes, Western views of China's state enterprises have not been modified. This is clear from the quoted header from a recent issue of the Economist at the beginning of this chapter.

The ZTE Corporation experience speaks also to how not only agency costs have been reduced but also public choice issues have been resolved. It also shows that the importance of property rights can be exaggerated. What has emerged from the interviews is that ZTE Corporation's personnel, from the management down, take pride in what they have created, despite owning very little of the enterprise. This sense of collective pride, attributable to Confucian concepts of collective identity and increasingly recognized as an East Asian trait, this trait—of collective pride and shame—has most recently been discussed in the context of a South Korean jetliner crash in San Francisco (Klug & Lee, 2013), can contribute materially to enterprise performance.

Also little discussed is the intensity of competition between state enterprises themselves. The large number of state enterprises, at central, provincial, and local levels, has not only brought this about but made this inevitable among the commercial state enterprises. This phenomenon, likely unique to China, is again not taken into account in mainstream theories of state enterprises. An example of this is the competition between ZTE and the much larger employee-owned Huawei. Another example is the competition by different provincial and/or local agencies to establish export processing zones. This competition has the salutary effect of boosting efficiency, but also increases the chances of wasteful spending.

Finally, the relevance of neoliberal theories has been muted by the complexity of ownership in the specific case of state enterprises like ZTE Corporation and in general by the embeddedness of government in Chinese society. China's state enterprise reform experience has blurred further the lines between state and private enterprises which are central to Western public enterprise theories. Many of China's private enterprises today began life as state enterprises or as collectives. Some, like the private enterprise which is an equity partner of ZTE Corporation, have been formed by state enterprise employees.

With these enterprises, a calculus of ownership and control that is different from that predicated on existing theories has emerged. We believe it is this calculus, as much as the management autonomy to which much research is directed, that helps to explain good state enterprise performance.

Notes

1. VASs refer to non-core services that complement basic telecommunications services like phone calls. Examples are voice mail, short message service (SMS), and dial back, services which telecoms operators typically charge extra for.
2. The last two preferences were terminated in 2000.
3. A-shares in this case refer to RMB-denominated shares which can only be traded in the Shenzhen Stock Exchange.
4. H-shares are shares of a company incorporated in the Chinese mainland that is listed on the Hong Kong Stock Exchange or other foreign exchange. Although H-shares are regulated by Chinese law, they are denominated in Hong Kong dollars and trade the same as other equities on the Hong Kong exchange.
5. For details of the slit-share reform, see Chap. 3.
6. Hou, ZTE's founder, stated in an interview that ZTE was a private company answerable to its shareholders, and, being publicly listed, also has operations that are transparent and meet international standards (Mountlake, 2012).
7. Some collectives had been leased out to private entrepreneurs to run, with the option of taking the enterprise private eventually (Ralston, Terpstra-Tong, Terpstra, Wang, & Egri, 2006).
8. Questions answered by Top Management H of ZTE Holdings on August 15, 2012, but due to confidentiality, this information was not disclosed.
9. For example, Hou is the President of ZTE Corporation and Shenzhen Zhongxing WXT Equipment Co. Ltd.; Xie Weiliang is the vice-resident of ZTE Corporation, the president of ZTE Holdings, the general manager of Shenzhen Aerospace Guangyu Industry Group Corporation, and the president and general manager of Aerospace Science & Industry Shenzhen (Group) Co. Ltd.
10. Questions answered by Human Resource Manager S of ZTE Corporation on September 2, 2012, but due to confidentiality, this information was not disclosed.
11. Questions answered by Top Management S of ZTE Corporation on October 18, 2012, but due to confidentiality, this information was not disclosed.

12. Peoples Republic of China's Law on Public Officials had been approved by the 15th Session of the Standing Committee of the 10th National People's Congress (The Central People's Government of the People's Republic of China, 2005b). There are five general administrative levels for public officials—national, provincial, bureau, county, and rural.
13. The hearing was held because ZTE was suspected by members of the US Congress that it would do the bidding of the Chinese government and would pose a threat to American national security if allowed to do business (supply equipment to American companies) there (ICEO Online, 2013).
14. Question answered by Top Management S of ZTE Corporation on October 18, 2012, but due to confidentiality, this information was not disclosed.
15. Questions answered by Human Resource Manager S of ZTE Corporation on September 2, 2012, but due to confidentiality, this information was not disclosed.
16. TD-LTE stands for Time Division-Long Term Evolution, one of two 4G high-speed mobile communications standards, the other being FD (Frequency Division)-LTE. According to Capacity Media (2012), TD-LTE has its roots in China. ZTE is a leading developer of this technology.
17. Question answered by Top Management S of ZTE Corporation on October 18, 2012, but due to confidentiality, this information was not disclosed.
18. Questions answered by Managing Director Z of ZTE Corporation on November 22, 2012, but due to confidentiality, this information was not disclosed.
19. The "Hukou" system refers to the country's household registration system, which specifies for each household a particular residential location. Residents have full rights and enjoy education and social welfare benefits offered by the state as long as they remain in their specified location, but lose these rights and benefits if they move away without official permission.

References

Capacity Media (2012). What are FD-LTE and TD-LTE? January 11. Retrieved from http://www.capacitymedia.com/Article/2959693/What-are-FD-LTE-and-TD-LTE

China Aerospace Science and Industry Corporation (2014). Corporate structure. Retrieved from http://www.casic.com.cn/n101/n127/index.html

Gregory, N.F., Tenev, S., & Wagle, D.M. (2000). China's emerging private enterprises: Prospects for the new century. Retrieved from http://documents.worldbank.org/curated/en/923231468744007740/Chinas-emerging-private-enterprises-prospects-for-the-new-century

Huang, G. (2005). 20 years' history of ZTE Corporation. Retrieved from http://wwwen.zte.com.cn/endata/magazine/ztecommunications/2005year/no2/articles/200506/t20050622_162340.html

Klug, F., & Lee, Y.K. (2013). Asiana crash a point of shame for Koreans. Retrieved from http://finance.yahoo.com/news/asiana-crash-point-national-shame-124939265.html

Li, S., Xia, J., Long, C.X., & Tan, J. (2012). Control Modes and Outcomes of Transformed State-Owned Enterprises in China: An Empirical Test. *Management and Organization Review, 8*(2), 283–309.

The Ministry of Finance of the People's Republic of China (2013). Statements regarding the central state-owned capital operation budget in 2013. Retrieved from http://yss.mof.gov.cn/2013zyczys/201303/t20130322_784806.html

Mountlake, S. (2012). Crossed lines: ZTE gets tangled in US-China telecom-gear 'Cold War'. *Forbes*. November 29. Retrieved from https://www.forbes.com/sites/simonmontlake/2012/11/29/crossed-lines-zte-gets-tangled-in-u-s-china-telecom-gear-cold-war/#1232990b8c2d

Ralston, D.A., Terpstra-Tong, J., Terpstra, R.H., Wang, X.L., & Egri, C. (2006). Today's state-owned enterprises of China: Are they dying dinosaurs or dynamic dynamos? *Strategic Management Journal, 27*(9), 825–843.

The Shenzhen Stock Exchange (2005). Directions for ZTE Corporation's split share structure reform (Abstract) (Revision edition). Retrieved from http://disclosure.szse.cn/m/finalpage/2005-11-23/16217014.PDF

The Central People's Government of the People's Republic of China. (2005a). The Law of Price of the People's Republic of China. Retrieved from http://www.gov.cn/banshi/2005-09/12/content_69757.htm

The Central People's Government of the People's Republic of China. (2005b). People's Republic of China Civil Servants Law. Retrieved from http://www.gov.cn/flfg/2005-06/21/content_8249.htm

The World Intellectual Property Organization (2012). PCT Newsletter. Retrieved from http://www.wipo.int/edocs/pctndocs/en/2013/pct_news_2013_03.pdf

ZTE Corporation (2003). Introduction of ZTE Corporation's R&D system. Retrieved from http://www.zte.com.cn/cndata/magazine/zte_communications/2001/1/magazine/200311/t20031126_149782.htm

ZTE Corporation (2012). China Development Bank bolsters partnership with ZTE, financing facility expanded to $20 billion. Retrieved from http://www.zte.com.cn/global/about/press-center/news/201212/372570

ZTE Corporation (2013a). ZTE model: State holding, private operating. Retrieved from http://www.zte.com.cn/cndata/magazine/zte_communications/2001/4/magazine/200312/t20031209_149903.html

ZTE Corporation (2013b). ZTE ranked world No. 1 in patent applications for second straight year. Retrieved from http://www.zte.com.cn/global/about/press-center/news/201303/391025
ZTE Corporation (2016a). Inroduction of ZTE Corporation. Retrieved from http://wwwen.zte.com.cn/en/about/corporate_information/
ZTE Corporation (2016b). The history of ZTE Corporation. Retrieved from http://wwwen.zte.com.cn/en/about/corporate_information/history/

CHAPTER 6

"Going Out", Going Global, and the Belt and Road

Somewhere ages and ages hence:
Two roads diverged in a wood, and I—.
I took the one less traveled by,
And that has made all the difference.
The Road Not Taken, by Robert Frost.

6.1 Introduction—From Investment Destination to Investor

The role of the Chinese state in the country's engagement with the global economy is arguably unique not only in terms of the scale of its involvement in an activity which is in most countries the domain of the private sector but also in the nature of this engagement. Whereas in the majority of countries, the state's role consists mainly of promoting and regulating trade and investment through favorable rules and supporting infrastructure, China, in addition to all these, has given its state enterprises a major role not only in producing for export and competing in international markets but also in investing abroad. In examining this role, this chapter argues that this represents a new phase of these enterprises' role in China's growth and development that will have major consequences for the rest of the world.

China's economic transformation has been associated with its progressive opening to the global economy, the pace of its opening being on the

R. Li, K. C. Cheong, *China's State Enterprises*,
https://doi.org/10.1007/978-981-13-0176-6_6

Chinese state's own terms. Export orientation is an essential feature of this opening, attraction of inward FDI the key instrument in this export-driven growth strategy. This began almost immediately after China's announcement of liberalization in 1978: in 1980, the first four special economic zones (SEZs) were established in the southern provinces of Guangdong (Shenzhen, Shantou, Zhuhai) and Fujian (Xiamen). The location of these SEZs in the south was no accident. They were adjacent to the rapidly growing commercial hub of Hong Kong and the emerging manufacturing powerhouse of Taiwan. Common dialects unite the SEZs with these territories. The area was also far enough from Beijing, the seat of power, that should the SEZ experiment prove a failure, its repercussions could be contained (Fallows, 2007).

Far from being failures, these SEZs proved to be resounding successes. While early foreign investors were mainly from Hong Kong and Taiwan, and total inward FDI was modest all the way to the early 1990s (Table 6.1), transnational corporations (TNCs) soon saw the potential of these SEZs as export platforms. These TNCs, like their Hong Kong and Taiwan counterparts, were attracted by the abundance of low-wage skilled labor,

Table 6.1 China: Inward and outward foreign direct investment (1990–2016)

Year	*Inward FDI*		*Outward FDI*	
	Flow ($b)	*Stock ($b)*	*Flow ($b)*	*Stock ($b)*
1990	3.5	20.7	0.8	4.4
1992	11.0	36.1	4.0	9.4
1994	33.8	74.2	2.0	15.8
1996	41.7	128.1	2.1	19.9
1998	45.5	175.2	2.6	25.1
2000	40.7	193.3	0.9	27.8
2002	52.7	216.5	2.5	37.2
2004	60.6	245.5	5.5	44.8
2006	72.7	292.6	17.6	75.0
2008	108.3	378.1	55.9	184.0
2010	114.7	587.8	68.8	317.2
2012	121.1	832.9	87.8	531.9
2014	128.5	1085.3	123.1	882.6
2015	135.6	1220.9	127.6	1097.9
2016	133.7	1354.4	183.1	1281.0

Source: The United Nations Conference on Trade and Development (2017). The World Investment Report, various years

attractive FDI terms, and the improving infrastructure in the SEZs. The success of this strategy could be gleaned from Sauvant (2011: i), who wrote that "over half of China's exports originate today from foreign affiliates located in the country, and this share has, if anything, grown, while total exports rose from US$ 149 billion in 1995 to US$ 1.2 trillion in 2009." The reference to China being "factory to the world" stems from this spectacular performance.

Although the government initially wanted firms in these zones to be fully export-oriented, TNCs were keenly aware of the potential of an already large but rapidly expanding domestic market to which they believed the government would eventually grant access. Over time, the government opened its domestic market to sales by TNCs and foreign enterprises located in the country. The Chinese economy's gradual move toward what its leaders termed a "socialist market economy" produced a period of sustained spectacular growth that increased the purchasing power of Chinese consumers and firms manifold. To meet this growing demand, FDI inflows rose substantially; while maintaining a level just below $50 billion in the second half of the 1990s, it more than doubled in the next eight years, reaching $108 billion in 2008, the year the GFC struck, continuing to rise more modestly since then (Table 6.1). The fact that since 1994 China has been the most important host country among developing countries and economies in transition is testimony to the magnitude of FDI inflows in China.

But China's integration into the global economy was not limited to FDI inflows. Beginning with a trickle in the last decade of the twentieth century, Chinese enterprises began to invest overseas. Although Das (2014: 2) considered China "a bit of a laggard" in OFDI, the converse is actually true. Despite rapid economic growth, China was still a lower middle-income country that, judging by the behavior of its peers, should be recipient of FDI rather than its source.[1] As explained later, China's early OFDI was motivated by the state's "Going Out" strategy announced in 1990. Although it was the state's intention that Chinese enterprises should hone their competitive skills in global markets, a few non-state enterprises felt confident in their ability to compete overseas. As a result, almost all enterprises that heeded the government's call in the early days were state enterprises. This picture progressively changed as Chinese enterprises, both state and non-state, grew in size, financial strength, and as a consequence, confidence. As Table 6.1 shows, OFDI nearly tripled from $5.5 billion to a still modest $15.7 billion between 2004 and 2006. But it more than tripled again over the next two years. By 2014, the volume of OFDI had nearly caught up with that of inward FDI. In 2016, at $183 billion, OFDI was far larger than inward FDI at $134 billion. Das (2014: Table 1) also noted that by 2012, the flow of Chinese OFDI had exceeded those of the UK, Germany, France, and Canada. China has thus emerged as a significant source of foreign investment in the global economy.

China's transition from a major recipient to a major investor has few parallels in the annals of development economics. With its much longer history, inward FDI in China has received considerable attention. Not so the phenomenon of OFDI. This chapter examines the phenomenon of China's OFDI with respect to (1) what motivates this already significant but still growing OFDI and (2) consonant with the theme of this book, what is the role of the state and state enterprises in China's rise as a leading investor.

6.2 "Going Out"—The Decision to Invest Internationally

Although outward FDI from China appears similar to OFDI from other countries, it is distinctive in several major ways. First, in terms of the volume of flows, it is much larger than OFDI from other countries at the same, or even at a higher level of economic development. Thus, as of 2016, China's OFDI of $183 billion compares with higher income members of the so-called BRICS—Brazil's $12 billion, India's $5 billion, Russia's $26.7 billion, and South Africa's $3.4 billion.[2] Most countries at China's stage of economic development would be accumulating scarce capital through, among other means, attracting inward FDI. Second, China's OFDI has been led by the state both through policy measures as well as by state enterprises. Both are discussed in this chapter. A third distinctive feature of China's OFDI is the manner of this investment. Where a considerable amount of FDI consists of setting up production facilities, as has been occurring with FDI in China, China's OFDI count many mergers and acquisitions (M&A). Xu (2011: 14) reported that "mergers and acquisitions increased from $60 million in 1999 to $30.2 billion in 2008, accounting for 54 percent of total Chinese FDI". Another distinctive feature that reflects the state's role in OFDI is its bundling with foreign aid in developing countries, especially in Africa.

Given the strong hand of the state, the first question to ask is whether Chinese enterprises that invest overseas subscribe at least to a degree to extant theories of FDI. These theories all assume that the decision-making calculus regarding making FDI abroad rests with the firms themselves.

6.2.1 *Internationalization and FDI Theories*

Impetus to undertake research on the internationalization of firms through making direct investment abroad had been provided by the emergence of Western multinational corporations (MNCs). Such research has produced several theories, each applicable to firms in particular situations.

For instance, Vernon (1966) saw international expansion as a way for firms producing mature products late in the product cycle to extend the competitiveness of these products. The assumption was that international destinations for FDI were less technologically advanced than in the firms' home markets.

A similar argument, but based on firms' resources, is the "resource-based view" (RBV) of FDI (Barney, 1991). This view sees firms as possessing resources, in the forms of physical, human, and organizational capital, which are heterogeneous across and not necessarily mobile between firms (Barney, 1991: 101). Its relevance for FDI arises from a firm's choice between exploiting its resources locally or externally. Internationalization then is not just about exploiting resources but also about strengthening them through acquisition of foreign knowledge. RBV has often been discussed in conjunction with the "industry-based view" (IBV) which posits that it is the conditions within an industry rather than a firm's resources that determine firm strategy, including whether to internationalize, and performance (Porter, 1980). Criticism of both views for ignoring formal and informal institutions that underpin competition at industry and firm levels led to a third view, the institution-based view that is applied especially to emerging economies (Peng, Wang, & Jiang, 2008).

Johansson and Vahlne (1977), in what is termed the "Uppsala Model", proposed a staged theory of internationalization, arguing that more gradual the internationalization, the higher the risks involved in doing so. These stages are sporadic export, export through an independent representative, establishment of a foreign sales subsidiary, and foreign production. FDI would occur from stage 3, intensifying in stage 4. Johanson and Mattson (1987) argued, however, that this staged process can be bypassed if a firm is able to identify and collaborate with foreign partners to form a network. Such a network would allow firms to take advantage of its partner's knowledge and market information, thereby accelerating the internationalization process.

Dismissing the assumption behind the foregoing theories, a group of researchers believe that some firms were "born global" (Mtigwe, 2006; Shrader, Oviatt, & McDougall, 2000). These "international entrepreneurial" firms were able to see international opportunities and are able to skip the more cautious approaches of the large firms (Oviatt & McDougall, 1994; Madsen & Servais, 1997). This theory likely applies to small firms that are able to see internationalization opportunities by leverage the Internet.

Arguably the theory that permits the widest generalization and is therefore most frequently used is that of Dunning (1980), whose "Eclectic Model" identifies both advantages as well as motives for undertaking FDI. Dubbed the "OLI Paradigm", the model sees ownership advantages in the form of firm-specific assets and skills in the home country, location advantages in the form of attractiveness of the destination country, such as low production costs and technological capability, and internalization advantages referring to the advantages of retaining assets and skills within the firm in situations of market failure or where there is risk of opportunistic behavior by corporate partners. He also suggested three motivations for FDI that have a bearing on its location—market-seeking, efficiency-seeking (cost reduction, higher technology), and resources-seeking (raw materials, including strategic resources) (Dunning, 1993).

While the above analysis is static, Dunning (1981) has extended his approach to a dynamic sequential macroeconomic model, the "Investment Development Path" (IDP) in which a country's FDI depends on its stage of development, proxied by GDP. The IDP hypothesizes the existence of five stages through which a country progresses from a net recipient of FDI to a net outward investor. The country begins with stage 1, during which its low income, small market, and poor infrastructure attract little FDI. As the country progresses to stage 2, it begins to attract inward FDI because of location advantages. By stage 3, not only does the country have location advantages but also its firms are developing ownership advantages that prepare them for making outward FDI. Stage 4 sees the country's outward FDI exceeding its inward FDI. By stage 5, the country would have become an advanced country attracting inward FDI but also making outward FDI through its firms leveraging all three—ownership, location, and internalization—advantages.

The applicability of this model lies in its identification of multiple advantages of and motives for FDI that permit broadening through extensions of the number and types of relevant factors. Thus, the Organisation for Economic Co-operation and Development (OECD) (2008) increased Dunning's motivations by including strategic assets-seeking and diversification. Si, Liefner and Wang (2013: 595) extended each dimension of the OLI model to include country and firm advantages (ownership), asset augmentation (location), and capabilities and institutions (internalization). The breadth of its scope has enabled it to incorporate other theories that postulate the same motives. For instance, the last motive, technology, was also Cantwell's (1998) focus, his argument being that firms internationalize to leverage their competitive edge in technology. More recently, Lee (2002) cites economies of scale and access to market niches as motives to accelerate internationalization.

While the IDP attempts to view FDI from a dynamic perspective, it is still built on static concepts. A model that overcomes this limitation is the "Linkage-Leverage-Learning" (LLL) model attributed to Mathews (2006). The model explains how latecomer firms develop to challenge established firms in the global economy through knowledge acquisition. Learning increases a firm's technological capability and unlocks new opportunities for LLL. Both inward and outward FDI play important roles. Thus, Si, Liefner and Wang (2013: 596) noted: "While inward FDI can be used to promote linkages within the domestic economy, outward FDI is a way of building linkages with the global economy." Also developed in phases, the LLL model describes how a firm strengthens its control over resources needed to compete globally.

6.2.2 *Does Chinese OFDI Fit These Theories?*

Research on Chinese OFDI has grown in tandem with the rapid growth of the latter. Considerable attention has been devoted to the uniqueness of Chinese OFDI, including the proactive role of government (e.g. Wei, 2010) and the preference for M&A (Globerman & Shapiro, 2009). These suggestions that China's unique OFDI situation implies the inapplicability of extant theories are accompanied by research that directly addresses this challenge to extant theories. In a review of research covering the period 1986–2012 in which major theories[3] were tested against the pattern of Chinese OFDI, Berning and Holtbrugge (2012: 174) found that only a small proportion concluded that existing internationalization/OFDI theories could be applied to Chinese OFDI without modification, about a third opined that these theories were inadequate to explain the pattern and behavior of Chinese OFDI while most concluded that traditional theories could not be directly applied to Chinese OFDI without modification or extension. For example, it was argued that the OLI model and even the IDP process could not explain latecomer catchup by some Chinese firms that undertook OFDI (Berning & Holtbrugge, 2012: 176). The presence of business groups and institutional support were also identified as factors being left out of the OLI model (Yiu, 2010).

That the bulk of the studies reject the idea that extant theories can be applied without modification is hardly surprising. Given the contextual significance of how any country and its firms progress from a focus on domestic production with or without inward FDI to becoming a source of OFDI, it would be a surprise if extant theories were fully applicable.

Compared to other countries, the China context is particularly salient for several reasons. First, as has been explained in earlier chapters, enterprise reform over the past decades has produced a large variety of enterprises ranging from 100% state-owned, through state-controlled and hybrid state-non-state enterprises, and to private enterprises as understood in Western economics. That enterprises exist at central, provincial, and local levels, and are located across geographic regions, each with its physical and institutional environment adds to this diversity. Thus, each type of enterprise has its resources, strengths, weaknesses, and other characteristics that together determine if, why, and how it invests abroad. Second, the evolution of the nature of China's OFDI has been as rapid as the amount of OFDI has grown. Just as with assessments of state enterprise reform described earlier, testing the Chinese OFDI experience against existing FDI models become rapidly outdated. For instance, by 2008, Africa had replaced Latin America as the second most important destination for Chinese OFDI, a process that took just five years (Ilheu, 2010: 54).

Looming large over all these factors is the dominating role of the state. This role is manifested in the "Going Out" strategy with state support for firms going out. Many "unique" features noted by researchers of Chinese OFDI are closely tied to this role. For instance, the role of state institutions especially state banks adds another dimension to Chinese firms' OFDI calculus. That Chinese OFDI is frequently linked to China's official development assistance is another area in supporting firms' undertaking OFDI.

Do these features merit creation of a new theoretical framework for China's OFDI? Or do they simply require modifications to or extensions of extant theory?[4] The uniqueness of China's experience does not necessarily translate into the need for new theory. Indeed, some unique features, such as the preference for M&A, do not even speak to the theories. Nor would exclusion from existing theory be sufficient reason to argue for the creation of a new theory. Since theories cannot possibly take into account all factors that are important in a specific context, the solution is to modify or extend existing theory rather than throw the baby out with the bath water. Thus, for instance, from the perspectives of Chinese firms, state support can be interpreted as representing an additional "ownership" advantage under Dunning's OLI framework (Wang, 2015a: 1).

Much has also been made of existing theories being built around MNCs from advanced countries and being not appropriate for China (e.g. Yin, 2015: 103). Also, Chinese OFDI represents a new approach of overcoming ownership disadvantages instead of Dunning's leveraging ownership advantages (Meyer, 2015). In reality, there is little new on offer—overcoming disadvantages and leveraging advantages both amount to strengthening ownership assets. An alternative interpretation that also fits into Dunning's OLI model is that the strategic assets in advanced countries that Chinese enterprises seek represent locational advantages in the host countries these enterprises want access to and are willing to invest to obtain it.

These and other examples claiming to require new theorizing can be shown to fit existing theories with modifications. Hence, Ilheu's (2010: 54) conclusion that "Chinese OFDI does not conflict with Dunning's general theory but cannot be explained only by it even after considering supplementary variables" appears to be a reasonable one.

New theorizing is required if existing theory is unable to explain a phenomenon or development. To the extent that existing theories are based on decision-making by private enterprises, the strong role of the state does present challenges to extant theory, although, as already explained, state ownership of an enterprise can be so explained. A point of departure, however, is the voice of the state in shaping decision-making by enterprises, especially those under state ownership or control. This is very different from OFDI in other countries and on which existing theories are built where private enterprises make the decisions to invest overseas. This complicates the question of whose motivation to undertake OFDI is being discussed—the state's or the enterprise's? As the next section shows, this is a source of considerable confusion in existing research on Chinese OFDI. In reality, both stakeholders' motivations are of importance.

A second fundamental difference between Chinese and other countries' OFDI relates to the type of firms undertaking OFDI. In China, state enterprises have led the foray into internationalization, including OFDI.[5] To the extent that these enterprises are obliged to follow state policies, the motivations of the state and these enterprises may merge. At the same time, even among state enterprises are those (state-controlled but market-oriented) enterprises the performance of which is measured by how they perform in the market. For these enterprises, state policies and strategies represent an extra layer of motivation for undertaking OFDI.

6.3 The State, State Enterprises, and "Going Out"

The first fundamental departure from existing theories is the role of the state in affecting enterprise decision-making regarding OFDI. This role consists of acting as "the supplier of information and assistance services, as well as promoter of incentives, simplification of administrative procedures and reductions in investment risks. There were also published guidelines, covering OFDI to some countries and sectors" (Timokhina, 2014: 5). This means that assessing the motivation for OFDI requires dealing with a sequence of questions. First, what are the state's motives for promoting OFDI? Second, how do state motives affect enterprise-level decision-making with respect to OFDI? Third, what motives independent of the state's strategies do enterprises themselves have in seeking OFDI? And finally, might there be conflict between state and enterprise motives and how do enterprises resolve such conflict?

Addressing these questions also helps clarify issues related to the second fundamental difference, that is a larger number of enterprises participating in OFDI and the earliest responders to the state's OFDI call are state enterprises. While there should be convergence between the state's and state enterprises' motives, many such enterprises, especially those listed on stock exchanges, also have performance benchmarks to achieve.

Failure to separate the motivation of the state from that of enterprises has unfortunate consequences. One is that of ascribing the wrong motives to stakeholders. For instance, even if excess capacity exists in an enterprise, OFDI is not necessarily the preferred option to solve its problem. Further, it leads to the erroneous belief by many Western governments that all OFDI from China is policy-driven. Specifically they believe that Chinese

OFDI in high-tech companies in the West signifies the Chinese state's attempt to steal technology when in fact Chinese companies in the high-tech area are those with the weakest ties to the state (Stratfor, 2015).

6.3.1 State-Level Motives for OFDI

A number of factors were stated as motivating China's call for its enterprises to internationalize. The first such factor is to leverage off the huge stockpile of reserves China accumulated (Xu, 2011: 16; Wang, 2016: 2). Two separate arguments have been adduced. The first is that China's huge stockpile, accumulated from the need to sterilize the inflow of export proceeds to prevent domestic inflation, is primarily invested in low-yielding US dollar denominated US Treasury instruments. This not only represented poor returns on investment but also put China's investment at the mercy of US policy. During the Global Financial Crisis in 2008, the fear was that the US would devalue the US dollar, at once reducing the value of China's holding of Treasury instruments. By using up a portion of these reserves for OFDI, dependence on US policy is reduced with Chinese investment more diversified. As to higher returns, however, there is no certainty that this will materialize. China's OFDI is closely bundled with the sizable overseas development assistance (ODA) especially to Africa.

A second motivation was said to be to deal with excess industrial capacity that has resulted from China's investment-driven growth model (China Hands, 2015; Poncet, 2010: 121). This overcapacity was exacerbated by the 4 trillion Yuan fiscal stimulus to counter the negative effects of the Global Financial Crisis in 2008, a significant proportion of which was expended on infrastructural construction (Badkar, 2013). OFDI, especially in infrastructure projects has been hypothesized to help absorb that excess capacity (Yang, 2015). Sluggish domestic demand was also cited as a push factor (Poncet, 2010: 121).

Logical as these factors are, they are not part of the government's policy statements, and cannot be viewed as such. China's official motive for promoting OFDI was to enhance the global competitiveness of its enterprises while also securing adequate primary resources to fuel the country's growth. On the former, Premier Wen Jiabao, in presenting the outline of the Twelfth Five Year Plan (2011–2015)[6] in October 2010, remarked:

> We must accelerate the implementation of the "Going Out" strategy, in accordance with market orientation and the principle of independent

> decision-making and guide enterprises with different kinds of ownership to invest overseas and co-operate in an orderly manner. (Davis, 2013: 35)

To fuel China's growth, raw materials, particularly in oil, iron ore, aluminum, and uranium, are needed, much of which needed to be imported from resource-abundant countries (Salidjanova, 2011: 1). The need to seek resources is therefore a stated policy of Chinese OFDI, this objective underpinning the country's investment first in Latin America and then Africa. In its 2004 guidelines to promote OFDI, the State Administration Reform Commission identified the following categories of preferred investment:

> (1) resources exploitation projects to mitigate the domestic shortage of natural resources, (2) projects that encourage the export of domestic technologies, products, equipment and labor, (3) overseas R&D centers to utilize internationally advanced technologies, managerial skills and professional contacts, and (4) mergers and acquisitions that could enhance the international competitiveness of Chinese enterprises. (Ilheu, 2010: 49)

The resource extraction motive is no better evidenced than in Africa, now the destination of substantial Chinese OFDI. Yet Chinese presence in Africa predates the arrival Chinese OFDI. Timokhina (2014: 2) noted that identifying itself with the Third World, "Its main objectives during the Cold War era were to compete with western and Soviet influences on the continent and to shore up votes for the eventual rejection of Taiwan's credentials at the United Nations". After the Cold War, China's focus turned to securing natural resources to power its growing economy, and resource-rich Africa was an obvious target for Chinese OFDI.

Yet, strategic motives remain important. In 2011, China's then-Premier Wen declared: "China had selflessly assisted Africa when itself was the poorest. We did not exploit one single drop of oil or extract one single ton of minerals out of Africa" (China.com, 2011). This, together with the China-Africa Summits,[7] was intended to assure African leaders that Beijing views Africa first through the lens of political ties rather than economic benefits. Even in developed countries where Chinese OFDI activities have been active, Davis (2013: 36) noted that China's OFDI is increasingly used as an instrument of "active investment diplomacy". Several failed high-profiled M&A deals[8] have caused China to re-examine lessons from these failures so that future M&A will have a better chance of success.

Finally, in the more recent phase of "Going Out", a new motivation for OFDI has emerged that prioritizes high-value manufacturing and technology. This is aptly expressed by Prime Minister Li Keqiang, in a press conference in 2014: "We cannot just export toys, apparel or shoes ... We also need to export Chinese equipment to ... raise its competitiveness as they are tested on the international market" (China Hands, 2015).

6.3.2 *Enterprises "Going Out" and Chinese State Priorities*

What impact might state pronouncements of strategic objectives have on enterprises' decision to "go out"? Since OFDI has been led by state enterprises, compliance with these objectives must have been a key consideration. And since the early phase of OFDI was to seek natural resources, the enterprises involved are typically fully state-owned "strategic" enterprises like PetroChina and Sinopec. To the extent that Chinese OFDI, especially in Africa, is closely tied with official development assistance, political affiliation and cooperation with host country governments likely rank as highly as economic objectives for these enterprises.

This raises the obvious question of risk management in unfamiliar environments. To the extent that the Chinese government issues and stands behind its strategic directives, enterprises responding to the government's call likely give less regard to risk assessment than would otherwise have been the case. The impact of layering strategic motivations over enterprise objectives is therefore to weaken risk assessment by the latter. Yet, incorporating government support in enterprises' decision-making regarding OFDI is also part of the latter's risk calculations. In addition, the guarantee of financial support at favorable terms from state-owned financial institutions like the China Development Bank would also help reduce enterprise risk. Another favorable factor would be favorable treatment by host governments anxious to capture Chinese OFDI as well as to cement bilateral political relations. Thus, Wang (2015a: 2) noted:

> Chinese MNEs are warmly welcomed by the host country government as a reflection of the friendship between China and these developing countries. As such investment is primarily targeted at helping the host country, to develop its own economy, the host country government would have every incentive to offer preferential treatments to have Chinese MNEs, including providing low-cost land, labor as well as supportive policies.

Wang (2015a: 2), citing Cui (2012) and Morck, Yeung, and Zhao (2008), also believed that the Chinese enterprises had "developed unique abilities when navigating complex bureaucracies and dealing with opaque political constraints in their home country. Such abilities enable them to mitigate the risk when operating in similar weak institutional settings and thus suit the fellow developing countries quite well". A third factor may be the absence of competition from established Western MNCs and the less favorable ODA terms offered by multilateral financial institutions that strengthened Chinese enterprises' bargaining position.

In the above circumstances, it has been alleged (Morck, Yeung, & Zhao, 2008; Wang, 2015a) that these enterprises were responsible for excessive OFDI with low efficiency. Although favored access to financing from state banks, opaque corporate governance and the lack of avenues for productive investment in China were explicitly cited as factors accounting for low efficiency OFDI (Wang, 2015a), the negative image of Chinese state enterprises still widespread in Western media likely also contributed to this perception, the paucity of supporting evidence notwithstanding. This may also explain why the possibility that low efficiency, if it indeed existed, could be the result of investing in environments of weak physical and institutional infrastructure and governance is hardly ever raised.

A third question of relevance to identifying OFDI motivation is of course the decision-making calculus of the enterprises making the OFDI themselves, aside from following state diktat. In summarizing studies exploring Chinese OFDI motivations, Yin (2015) distinguished between "conventional" (seeking to leverage Dunning's ownership advantages) and "unconventional" (seeking to overcome ownership disadvantages) motivations. It is worth remembering that this distinction notwithstanding, the issue of whether new theories are needed is not addressed. The motivations identified in each study cited are shown in Table 6.2.

Yin's study (2015: 103) also found a combination of conventional and unconventional motivators of OFDI. Despite the call for "a new, more systematic theory which can integrate these two directions of investment, that is, conventional and unconventional" (Yin, 2015: 103), these studies show the continued relevance of existing theories, with extensions, in accounting for Chinese enterprises' motivations for OFDI. And as Chinese enterprises' experience with OFDI deepens, this relevance is likely to increase.

Taken together, the distinctiveness of Chinese OFDI lies not so much in the factors existing theories omit but the structure of motivations that

Table 6.2 Chinese OFDI motivations identified by empirical studies

Study/Author(s)	*Motivations identified*
Cai (1999)	Export-market-seeking, resource-seeking, technology-and-management-skills-seeking, capital-raising
Wu and Chen (2001)	Resource-seeking, technology-and-management-skills-seeking, capital-raising, export-market-seeking, industry adjustment (market-seeking), foreign-exchange-securing
Deng (2004)	Resource-seeking, technology-seeking, market-seeking, diversification-seeking, strategic-asset-seeking
Hong and Sun (2006)	Resource-seeking, technology-seeking, market-and-diversification-seeking, strategic-asset-seeking
Buckley et al. (2007)	Market- seeking, resource-seeking, asset-seeking (technology, brands, local networks), political risk, cultural proximity, policy liberalization
Cheung and Qian (2009)	Market-seeking, resource-seeking, efficiency-seeking, institutions and political risk, cultural resemblance
Hurst (2011)	Market-seeking, resource-seeking, strategic-asset-seeking, efficiency-seeking
Cheng and Ma (2008)	Market-seeking, cultural proximity, tax havens and offshore financial center
Kolstad and Wiig (2012)	Resources, institutions
Quer et al. (2012)	Political risk, cultural distance
Amighini et al. (2013)	Market-seeking, resource-seeking, strategic-asset-seeking, human capital, political risk, infrastructure
Ramasamy et al. (2012)	Market-seeking, resource-seeking, strategic-asset-seeking, political risk

Source: Yin (2015), Table 1, p. 87
Note: For study sources in the table, see Yin (2015: 87)

enterprises undertaking OFDI are driven by. This structure has two layers, with state objectives providing overall guidance for all enterprises. While the enterprises themselves have their own motivations, these are subject to or constrained by state objectives. In quantitative terms, this amounts to constrained maximization. State motivations serve both to constrain enterprise and to limit their exposure to risks. For all the talk of distinctiveness, Chinese enterprises have motivations that broadly conform to those prescribed by existing theory and its extensions (see also Drogendijk & Blomkvist, 2013). As Chinese enterprises mature as OFDI providers, their decision-making should converge with that by established MNCs, subject, of course, to state imperatives.[9]

6.4 Phases of "Going Out"

To the extent that China's OFDI focus is constantly evolving, especially since "Going Out" was announced in 2000, the motivations, both of the state and enterprises, must also undergo significant change over time. The generalizability of conclusions by studies that cover a specific period of Chinese OFDI such as those cited above is therefore limited by the specific periods of coverage.

For a similar reason, attempts to divide China's OFDI experience into phases are dependent on the date of specific studies. For instance, Wong and Chan (2003) categorized China's OFDI as having developed in four phases. In the first stage (1979–1985), with foreign investment still under state guidance, only state-owned trading corporations and enterprises regulated by the State Economic and Trade Commission (SETC) allowed to invest overseas, the scale of OFDI was small. The second stage (1986–1991) saw the loosening of restrictive policies to allow more enterprises, including non-state firms, to apply for permission to establish subsidiaries led to a sharp rise in OFDI. The third stage (1992–1998) witnessed a big surge in provincial and local enterprises investing abroad with support from their respective jurisdictions. However, losses of state assets through mismanagement including stock market speculation put a brake on OFDI as more stringent monitoring of OFDI was put in place. The fourth phase, from 1999 to 2001, marked the announcement and early implementation of the "Going Out" strategy.

Writing seven years later, Poncet (2010) added to Wong & Chan's (2003) fourth stage—by adding the years 2002–2006. This stage coincided approximately with the announcement of the "Going Out" strategy and saw Chinese TNCs begin to make their presence felt on the world stage.

A similar set of steps was suggested in Ilhew (2010: 52), except that the brief period from 1999 to 2001 was named stage 4. This stage marked the early implementation of the "Going Out" strategy. The period since the launch of the policy and became official policy was then designated stage 5.

An even more recent effort to divide China's OFDI into stages is Fiala (2014: 14). He characterized the first phase, 1979–1991, as "testing the water", with 1979–1985 and 1985–1991 as sub-phases. The second phase, 1992–2001, characterized as "finding the stepping stones", also has two sub-phases—1992–1998, and 1999–2001—and ended with China's accession to the WTO. As with the earlier work, the latest phase began approximately with the announcement of the "Going Out" strategy.

From the point of view of this chapter, however, it is the latest stage that has the greatest significance not only from the point of view of the scale of OFDI reached but also because of the pace of change in the nature of OFDI. Ilheu (2010: 49–52) documented the diversification of OFDI motivations from resource-seeking, particularly in Africa, to market-seeking, evidenced by the increase in OFDI for business services, efficiency-seeking, as demonstrated by Chinese OFDI to relocate production in lower-wage countries in Southeast Asia, and strategic asset-seeking, these strategic assets being technology. M&A of firms in advanced countries have been the preferred route to technology Chinese enterprises need. Examples of such acquisitions are Beijing Automotive Industry Holdings' acquisition of Sweden's Saab for $200 million in 2009 and Zhejiang Geely's purchase of Ford's shares in its takeover of Volvo in 2010. Thus, the rapid rise of strategic asset-seeking OFDI can be seen by the escalating value of M&A made by Chinese enterprises from 2006 (Table 6.3).

The increasing role played by technology points to a future for Chinese OFDI that will be radically different from the past. China's drive to become a leader, not a follower, in the high-tech sector has seen its enterprises, both state and non-state catch up with Western conglomerates. The case of ZTE, already dealt with in an earlier chapter, is a good example of

Table 6.3 Major OFDI developments since the launch of "Going Out"

	OFDI				*Value of M&A*
	Total	*Africa*	*South America*	*Southeast Asia*	
2000	0.9				−0.4
2002	2.5				1.4
2003	2.8	0	0.0	0.1	1.6
2004	5.5	0.3	0.0	0.2	0.6
2006	17.6	0.5	0.0	0.3	12.2
2008	55.9	5.5	0.0	2.5	35.9
2010	68.8	2.1	0.9	4.4	29.8
2012	87.8	2.5	3.0	6.1	37.9
2014	123.1				39.2
2016	184.1				92.2

Source: The United Nations Conference on Trade and Development (2017). The World Investment Report, various years

catchup. Its international competitiveness can be seen in its being recently chosen, jointly with Nokia, by Indian public telecom operator BSNL to install Base Transceiver Stations (BTSs) to expand its mobile network (Hindustan Times, 2017). This major development, already unfolding with enterprises like Alibaba, Tencent, and Baidu vying for global leadership against much better known Western firms, and with China clearly leading in areas of green technology/alternative energy and nanotechnology among others, will see Chinese OFDI move in two directions. First, the adoption of a more collaborative approach to scientific research will see Chinese enterprises establish research facilities in advanced countries (Stratfor, 2015). Second, M&A by Chinese enterprises will intensify, Chinese enterprises no longer considered junior partners in technology.[10] Finally, with technology incubators like Shenzhen spawning many enterprises powered by Information and Communication Technology (ICT), internationalization can be a viable strategy almost as soon as they commence business—examples of "born global" enterprises referred to earlier (Lee, 2017). These enterprises are likely small when they launch, and privately owned. The internationalization of these enterprises in large enough numbers will mark a new phase of China's "Going Out", in which small- to moderate-sized private enterprises not only provide OFDI but also provide new models and methods to break the currently negative mold of "Made in China".

6.5 State Enterprise Internationalization—Two Case Studies

Motivation and the dynamics of internationalization differ from enterprise to enterprise. Review of these at the firm level can yield useful insights. In this section, the internationalization experience of two state enterprises is discussed. The first is a strategic state enterprise, fully government owned, in the financial sector. The second is a representative of a market-oriented state-controlled enterprise, a type that is gaining prominence as China seeks to compete internationally in the high-tech sector.

Because doing business in external markets also require knowledge of local conditions in the host countries and Chinese enterprises do not have the brand recognition of advanced country firms to sell standardized products, localization in the host country has to be undertaken. Thus, "Going Out" has to be accompanied by "coming in". The two case studies here deal with localization in Malaysia, China's largest trading partner since 2009.

6.5.1 *Case 1—Bank of China, a Strategic Enterprise*

Since China's state banks provide financial and network support for Chinese enterprises that venture into markets like the Africa, Middle East, and Latin America, they too must "go out". In addition to providing such support, Chinese banks promote the use of the RMB for international transactions, strengthening the hand of the Chinese government is strengthened in dealing with multilateral organizations like the WTO and IMF (Calkins, 2013).

BOC, the oldest of the state banks, had ventured overseas long before the Chinese government's promulgation of the "Going Out" strategy. BOC had established branches in Southeast Asia in the 1930s to capture the thriving remittance business. BOC Singapore opened its doors on June 15, 1936, while the first branch in Malaya began operation in 1939.[11] But that period was brief; within a matter of months, Malaya and Singapore fell to Japanese forces. BOC's return to Malaya after the Second World War was also brief, ended in 1959 by the fact that the People's Republic of China (PRC), which became BOC's new owner from 1949, had no diplomatic relations with Malaya, then Malaysia, until 1974.

The current phase of BOC internationalization is driven by a combination of pull and push factors. Pull factors include falling in line with the state's "Going Out" strategy, BOC's support strengthening the hands of enterprises "Going Out" while its greater familiarity with Chinese enterprises gives them an edge over other banks. The internationalization of the RMB is also seen by BOC as a major business opportunity. On the push side, China's slowing economy and the increasingly competitive business environment at home is also impelling overseas expansion.

BOC Malaysia reopened in 2001 to a much more cordial relationship between Malaysia and China than when it shut its doors. Over the last 15 years since its reopening, it has expanded to seven branches and set up two China Visa Centers across the country with more than 300 staff (Xinhuanet, 2016a).

BOC Malaysia today is focused on supporting Malaysia-China bilateral trade and other economic relations. Its Malaysian website (Bank of China, 2017) refers to its main business as follows:

> Bank of China (Malaysia) Berhad has been playing a pivotal role in business development and the facilitation of bilateral trade between Malaysia and China. Bank of China (Malaysia) Berhad has pioneered a wide range of Renminbi financial products and services such as pre-exchange Renminbi fund transfer, wholesale Renminbi notes and exchange, cross border Renminbi trade settlements, Renminbi deposit and loan, Renminbi prepaid card, Renminbi trade finance services, Renminbi money market and treasury services.

The motivation for BOC's reestablishment in Malaysia is manifest from the above. It is to support Malaysia-China trade relations and to promote Renminbi internationalization. This narrow focus on bilateral economic relations stands in contrast to the objective of commercial banks like Citibank and HSBC, which is simply to expand their business regardless of the nationality of their clients.

In its RMB internationalization role, BOC Malaysia was designated the RMB clearing bank in Malaysia by the central banks of both countries in 2015 (Malay Mail, 2015). With BOC as a clearinghouse in Malaysia, the ringgit can be directly converted to yuan, hence reducing transaction costs of conversion through intermediaries. Malaysia is only the second country after Singapore in ASEAN to establish an RMB clearing bank with China. With China's economic footprint growing through ramping up its outward FDI, including through the BRI, and with current adoption of the RMB rising in tandem (Lee & Ghosh, 2012), BOC Malaysia should see its business with the local Malaysian community and companies and investors from China grow.

The mode of operations described above both helps and hinders the state's objectives as stated earlier. On the one hand, support of Chinese enterprises internationalizing clearly strengthens the latter's competitiveness, and a ready portfolio of clients also benefits BOC's bottom line. This tilts the playing field in BOC's favor when it comes to competition with foreign banks. Yet, it does BOC no favor in terms of the Chinese state's objective of honing greater competitiveness for its financial institutions, their size notwithstanding. First, a good revenue stream may encourage BOC to avoid head-on competition with non-Chinese global banks. Together with the limited competition BOC and other state banks face at home, achieving global competitiveness in providing a full range of services to clients will be a tall order. Indeed, the view has been expressed that a truly global mentality has yet to emerge from Chinese state banks, and that "the sophistication of their banking operations, infrastructure and technology cannot yet be compared with those of banks in developed countries" (Camacho, 2011: 3–4).

What this means is that breaking into the already crowded Malaysian financial sector with local players well entrenched in delivering retail and personal services to local clients will be no easy task (Shane, 2015). It is therefore no surprise that customer deposits in the first half year ended June 30, 2016, grew a modest 2% to RM6.2 billion from the same period a year earlier, compared to 3% growth in loans and advances and 6% growth in total assets (Yong, 2016).

Potential competition for BOC can also come from other Chinese banks. In January 2010, the ICBC Malaysia was incorporated while the China Construction Bank (Malaysia) Bhd became the third Chinese state bank to be granted a banking license in Malaysia.[12] Both are fully owned subsidiaries of their parent banks in China. In practice such competition may not materialize—the Chinese state is likely to "manage competition" by allocating different projects to different banks.[13]

Full state ownership may also raise doubts as to the extent the Chinese state is involved in any consequential decisions by BOC. For example, the recent takeover by BOC Hong Kong of its parent's branch and sub-branch network in six ASEAN countries, Thailand, Singapore, Malaysia, Cambodia, Vietnam, and the Philippines so as to transform itself into a regional player has raised concerns, with explanations ranging from an attempt to offset business slowdown in Hong Kong to simply following state policy (Mak, 2016; Yong, 2016). Specific questions have been raised, for instance, as to why BOC Hong Kong, which has limited expertise in the ASEAN region (Shane, 2015), should be favored over an ASEAN country like Malaysia as a regional hub.

The take-away from this case study are several. First, despite its size, the role state banks like BOC plays in "Going Out" is decided limited. This is because the banks' objectives in supporting OFDI are subordinated to national strategies which are focused on enterprises actually internationalizing or undertaking OFDI. While close relationships between Chinese state banks and enterprises "Going Out" can give the latter an edge, it can also engender resentment among local financial institutions of host countries which cannot break into this relationship. Finally, this narrowly focused model exemplified by BOC in Malaysia does not leave much room for localization, which is essential if it is to compete successfully in host country Malaysia.

6.5.2 Case 2—ZTE Corporation, a Market-Oriented State Enterprise[14]

From its founding, ZTE's growth can partly be attributed to its ties to the Chinese state. These ties, reflected in the enterprise's alignment with the state's objective of developing a homegrown telecommunications sector, has brought the Corporation a range of benefits from finance to preferential access to business opportunities (Li & Cheong, 2016 254). In addition, state projects were directed ZTE's way—China's leading phone companies China Mobile, China Telecom, and China Unicom have all been clients of ZTE (Athreye & Chen 2009: 17). This is not to deny ZTE's technological prowess, which would have allowed it to hold its own, if not given the enterprise a competitive edge against its competitors. For instance, since 2000, when it launched the world's first CDMA handset with detachable SIM card, ZTE has been a leader in this area.

ZTE was an early starter in the internationalization process but a cautious globalizer. State support that produced lucrative contracts with other state enterprises and no shortage of funding from its dual market listing on the Shenzhen and Hong Kong stock exchanges meant that ZTE had little incentive to internationalize. Athreye and Chen (2009: 19) also argue that it was management conservatism that held internationalization back. Certainly, ZTE's CEO Hou Weigui, whose personal beliefs direct ZTE's corporate culture and business, is noted for his cautious approach to strategic leadership (Que, 2015: 67).

Yet ZTE has been a "model" state enterprise in terms of compliance with the state's directives. As shown in Chap. 5, it had been at the forefront of China's state enterprise reforms. It is therefore no surprise that ZTE's internationalization coincided with the Chinese government's launch of its "Going Out" strategy in 1999 and it was the first enterprise to respond to the call. Even before this, in 1998, ZTE had won a US$95 million turnkey project in Pakistan, the first large-scale overseas telecoms project contracted with any Chinese telecom company. However, only in 2007 did revenue from international sales exceed that from domestic sales (see Table 1). A likely push factor was the delay in the issue of 3G licenses by the Chinese government, a technology in which ZTE had invested heavily (see Que, 2015: 60).

ZTE's early internationalization efforts were focused mainly on emerging markets in Asian and North African countries. These countries have widely varying institutional and technological capabilities which made customization of its products essential. The enterprise's primary reliance on internally developed technology (Que, 2015: 65) made customization easier. In doing so, it adopted, taking advantage of its skilled but low-cost labor, and learned from existing technologies, before leapfrogging competitors by developing cutting-edge products, as shown by its launch of the world's first CDMA mobile phone with a removable SIM card in 2000.[15]

Acceptance of ZTE's products has been facilitated by the enterprise's endorsement of international standards, and also by the company's participation in international standard-setting bodies (ZTE Corporation, 2004). International standards are applied across the entire range of ZTE's processes and products, an area where it is ahead even of Huawei. This standardization has helped ZTE shorten R&D periods, reduce costs, manage processes from design to production, and improve the performance of new products.

ZTE's localization strategy has sought to leverage its low-cost advantage and willingness to adapt its products to local conditions, terms few established advanced country competitors would agree to (Que, 2015: 62). But by focusing on selling its products rather than its brand, ZTE not only saved on marketing costs but also kept its clients satisfied.

This strategy has served ZTE well in its entry into the Malaysian market through establishing a subsidiary company, ZTE Malaysia Sdn. Bhd., in 2004. Its sales pitch to Malaysia was its ability to provide the technology that the country needed to advance beyond middle-income to become a high-income country in 2020 (Sarkar, 2012) while also training and upgrading Malaysia's human capital, all at a cost competitors could not match. This cost advantage was achieved not only by the lowest cost of ZTE equipment but also the enterprise's ability and willingness to graft its new technology onto existing system, thus obviating the need to purchase completely new equipment. Adapting ZTE systems for use on existing Malaysian equipment also meant considerable workforce localization. Workforce localization not only facilitated on-time maintenance and repairs but also added to the cost savings.

At the same time, ZTE has collaborative research arrangements with TM R&D, the research subsidiary of Telekom Malaysia, that also involves the participation of Malaysian universities (Kumar, 2014). In addition, ZTE provided training to clients on how to use its equipment, and, in cooperation with Multimedia University Malaysia, ran a course for students that led to ZTE certification.

For a state-controlled enterprise like ZTE, the reception of the host country is crucial. ZTE is fortunate that unlike advanced countries like the US, Malaysia did not have technology security issues that could be used to stall ZTE's market entry. Indeed, ZTE technology is welcome not only on cost grounds but also because it can help upgrade Malaysia's technological capability. Also, contrary to Western country perceptions, state control is regarded positively as the Chinese government standing behind its enterprises. Malaysia itself is no stranger to government-linked companies (See Gomez, 2017).

To navigate Malaysia's political economy, ZTE's operating strategy is to work with major companies in the telecommunications industry favored or supported by the Malaysian government. The company brings its advanced technology, especially in 3G and LTE (Long-Term Evolution, a standard for high-speed mobile communication), and also a compatibility of new technology with existing setups. This approach was touted by ZTE's Vice President for Operator Solutions Sean Cai who argued that ZTE's LTE technology was unique as it offered continuity of 2G and 3G technologies as 4G was rolled out (Malaysian Insider, 2014).

ZTE's touted advantages, combined with the above strategy, have been successful. It did not take long for ZTE to gain contracts in Malaysia. In its first year of operation, ZTE had its first project—a US$4 million technical product for Telekom Malaysia. In December 2005, during Chinese Premier Wen's visit to Malaysia, ZTE signed a deal with Electcoms, Malaysia's leading trunking radio and radio paging operator. Since then, ZTE has formalized a strategic partnership with the telecom operator DiGi for which it has constructed 2G and 3G networks, followed by work on a 4G network. And in 2011, ZTE Malaysia signed an agreement with U Mobile to build a high-speed wireless network across the nation. ZTE is also a main supplier to Telekom Malaysia and Packet 1 Networks for their broadband and cellular networks respectively (China Daily October 4, 2013). And in 2015, ZTE signed an agreement to provide U Mobile with a Disaster Recovery system in the presence of visiting Chinese president Xi Jinping.

This case study speaks to the earlier discussion in several ways. First, ZTE is representative of state enterprises lightly controlled by the state that, while demonstrating compliance with state objectives, are able to pursue primarily commercial objectives. These objectives are not necessarily different from those described by existing theory. Second, in terms of strategic asset ownership, what it lacks in brand recognition it makes up for willingness to adapt equipment to suit local systems. Third, the enterprise's search for advanced technology from the West does not mean it is not cutting edge in some areas. Fourth, for market-seeking enterprises like ZTE, OFDI represents just one of several modes of market entry. In the case of ZTE, the establishment of a Malaysian subsidiary ensured protection of its proprietary technology.

6.6 The Belt and Road Initiative

The BRI, also referred to as One Belt One Road (still its Chinese name), was announced by President Xi in Astana, Kazakhstan, in 2013. To provide concrete support for this initiative, China created the Beijing-based Asian Infrastructure Development Bank, starting with 21 member states and a capital of $50 billion. To this was added a separate Silk Road Fund of $40 billion during the November 2014 annual Asia-Pacific Economic Cooperation (APEC) meeting (Deng, 2015: 127).

Ever since its launch, attention has been drawn overwhelmingly to this initiative, despite the fact that the precise form of this initiative has been evolving over time to also embrace projects before BRI's launch. The broad outline of this grand scheme is nevertheless clear. This initiative represents China's effort to rejuvenate the ancient silk roads through central Asia and at the same time establish a maritime route which is free from the choke-hold of the US, its Seventh Fleet, and its allies that might imperil critical energy supplies to China in times of tension.

Given the scale of the BRI, it should be no surprise that state enterprises will be at the forefront to drive the major projects. The precise role of state enterprises in the BRI depends on more than the latter's sheer size. It also depends on what strategies the Chinese state has set for the BRI. Hence, to the state's motivations for launching the BRI we need first to turn.

6.6.1 Motivation

The motivations behind the BRI have been much debated. They have been viewed as China's response to deal with existing issues like industrial overcapacity (Zhou, Hallding, & Han, 2015), keeping state enterprises alive by easing the slowdown in their activities (The Economist, 2017; Ivanovitch, 2016) and RMB internationalization (Zhang, Yu, Yu, & Jin, 2017). A more long-term view sees the BRI as another step China has taken to strengthen progressively its development strategies. Thus, if the "Going Out" strategy is seen as an exercise to enhance the competitiveness of enterprises to compete in global markets, then its sequel, the BRI can be viewed as the outcome of this competitiveness enhancing exercise, that is the unleashing of these newly competitive enterprises on the global economy. Indeed, Deng (2015: 119) postulated that the BRI was an outgrowth of the central government's efforts to develop China's western regions, as well as an effort to strengthen Chinese cooperation with Southeast Asia that was formalized under the China ASEAN Free Trade Area agreement that came into force in 2010.

While acknowledging that BRI can help deal with immediate challenges, other scholars see in its magnitude and complexity a much grander strategy. From a geostrategic perspective, the BRI is much more than an extension of existing policy. The progression from "Going Out" to BRI, it is argued (Deng, 2015), represents a major strategic shift from having its enterprises, both state and non-state, excel within the framework built by Western powers (the so-called international economic order) to China's attempt to remake that order. Deng (2015: 127) noted: "The Silk Road program is designed to infuse regional economic expansion with greater strategic purpose … The Silk Road clearly reflects China's ambitions to create a China-centric, albeit still open, Asian order." This transition, he argues, is from China moving from being a "responsible power" to a "post-responsible power".[16]

Other scholars echo Deng's sentiments even if they do not necessarily share his views. Wang Gungwu (2015b) in an opinion piece for the Singapore *Straits Times* argued:

> China's 'One Road, One Belt' strategy can be understood historically as a response to countering American naval influence by deepening its own links among Central Asian partners and East Asian economies. … We can expect to see a new kind of defensive interstate Great Wall that uses interconnected economic clout along the Indo-Pacific coasts, as well as overland, to ensure that the Eurasian continent remains inviolate.

McCoy (2015) elaborates on this strategy by citing McKinder's "World Island" theory that argues that control of the Eurasia landmass is more important than control of the oceans. Referring to the area between the Persian Gulf and the Yangtze River as the Heartland, he cited McKinder's prediction that "Whoever rules the Heartland commands the World-Island

(Eurasia). Whoever rules the World-Island commands the world." Although it might have been precipitated by Obama's "pivot to Asia", the BRI, these scholars contend, is the manifestation of a very long-term strategy that China has taken years to develop.

Consonant with this view, Callahan (2016: 226) commented:

> Beijing is combining new ideas (China Dream, Asia Dream), new policies (comprehensive diplomacy and security), new institutions (Asia Infrastructure Investment Bank (AIIB)) and new projects (BRI) to build what Xi calls the 'community of shared destiny.' The goal is to weave neighboring countries into a Sinocentric network of economic, political, cultural, and security relations. Beijing's grand strategy thus is to re-constitute the regional order—and eventually global order—with new governance ideas, norms, and rules.

This shift also coincides with the ideology enunciated in Xi's "China Dream" in which strength, prosperity, and happiness are the defining characteristics (Forde, 2013). At the 18th Party Congress in 2012, he set out two centennial goals—to build China into a moderately prosperous society by 2021, when the Communist Party Congress marks its centennial; and to achieve the great rejuvenation of the Chinese nation by 2049, when the PRC marks its centennial (Zhong, 2017). In a speech in late July 2017, Xi remarked: "The Chinese nation, which has experienced tribulations and hardships since modern times, has made a historic leap from standing up to becoming rich and then to getting stronger. Having stood up and become better off, getting stronger now becomes a new challenge to China. We must get prepared mentally, theoretically and systematically" (Zhong, 2017). Thus, for him, realizing this "dream" would take three phases: for the Chinese nation to stand up, to become wealthy, and then to become strong. Since Mao was credited with China standing up and Deng with making China prosperous, Xi saw his mission to make China strong. Promoted together with his policy concepts like "Asian security" and "Asia-Pacific Dream", the BRI is seen as the key instrument in realizing the "China Dream" (Deng, 2015: 127).

The focus on strength represents a departure of China's stance of "peaceful development". Callahan (2016: 238) noted that this focus on strength has caused China to bundle security with development, "organized according to Chinese interests and guided by Chinese values". Other departures from previous practice include the shift of attention away from the West to Asia—central to west Asia and Southeast Asia the recipients of much of BRI investment. Another distinctive feature of the BRI is it continued focus on international trade and investment as drivers. But, according to Callahan (2016: 238), the initiative is more than about "the hard power of building physical infrastructure" but also involves "the soft power connectivity of ideas, institutions and … diplomacy itself" to achieve Xi's vision of "a community of shared interests, destiny and responsibility".

6.6.2 *Substance and Scope*

Descriptions of the scope and size of BRI are numerous, although given the rapid changes the initiative is undergoing, any of this is likely to be outdated rapidly. In light of the discussion in the previous section, Godehardt's (2016: 19) characterization of the BRI appears most apt. Arguing that the BRI is not fully an alternative to the existing international order, she opined that the BRI is

> a proactive Chinese response to the growing complexity in the world that definitely has the potential to turn into an alternative concept of how international politics could be organized in the future. It represents a loose political concept in which new mechanisms of cooperation are created, or already existing institutions and ongoing projects are integrated. In this regard, OBOR is in fact very different from our rule-based Eurocentric model of international order.

According to her, it is characterized by (1) efforts to build up and strengthen cooperation among countries along the silk roads, (2) it being flexible, inclusive, and open, so that the geographical and institutional coverage and scope remains subject to change from time to time, and (3) the main task being to "build up a comprehensive economic and political network that promotes connectivity between countries" covered by the initiative (Godehardt, 2016: 20).

Given its many ambiguities, the BRI has been interpreted broadly to include Chinese projects in Africa and Latin America (Levine, 2015) and narrowly to refer to the successor of the ancient silk road (PwC, 2017). PricewaterhouseCoopers (PwC), in the most comprehensive and up-to-date report (PwC, 2017: 4), estimated that

> "more than 100 countries and international bodies committing to participate in the B&R initiative and 56 countries and regional organizations

> issuing joint statements and proposals, with China announcing a commitment to bilateral cooperation for implementing the B&R initiative. China is also working with more than 20 countries on capacity-building projects in the manufacturing sector." Still, just what exactly is the BRI has remained a question on many an interested observer's mind.

Announced by President Xi in Astana, Kazakhstan, in September 2013, the BRI represented a "reimagined" (Levine, 2015) Silk Road that is unprecedented in size and scope even narrowly defined. Although with several extensions, its geographic focus on the central Asian corridor (also referred to as "Eurasia") and Southeast Asia is clear. The Eurasia part involves the construction of roads, railways, and energy pipelines linking China, through the central Asian republics and West Asian countries Iran and Turkey to destinations in Europe. Already, a cargo rail route between the Chinese City of Yiwu and Madrid, a distance of over 12,000 km, had been opened, while a cargo shipment has also arrived in Yiwu from London on April 29, 2017. Although more symbolic than economic, these journeys are harbingers of things to come when the BRI reaches fruition. This east-west link will also open up trading and communications opportunities as well as strengthen financial links between Eastern Europe and China, the former's current trade with the latter being primarily through Western European ports.[17] This pan-Asian system will also include the development of a maritime gateway to the Arabian Sea through Gwadar port in Pakistan's Baluchistan Province, which will also be a terminal point of a railway from Kashgar in China's Xinjiang Province (Fig. 6.1).

For Southeast Asia, China envisages highways and a high-speed railway running from Kunming, Yunan Province, through Myanmar to Singapore. Another railway line will run south from Nanning, Guangxi Autonomous Region, which is connected to China's national grid, through Vietnam, Laos, Thailand, and Malaysia to Singapore.[18] Port construction is also taking place around Nanning, Guangxi in China, the coast of Peninsular Malaysia, Sri Lanka, and of course Gwadar. The Maritime Silk Road will then connect the South China Sea with the Indian Ocean and the South Pacific, with China developing the military capacity to protect these sea-lanes.

PwC (2017: 19–23) detailed no less than six economic corridors, four for the Eurasia land bridge and two for the Maritime Silk Road. As for types of projects, seven core infrastructure sectors were identified (PwC, 2017: 15). These were utilities, transport, telecommunications, social,

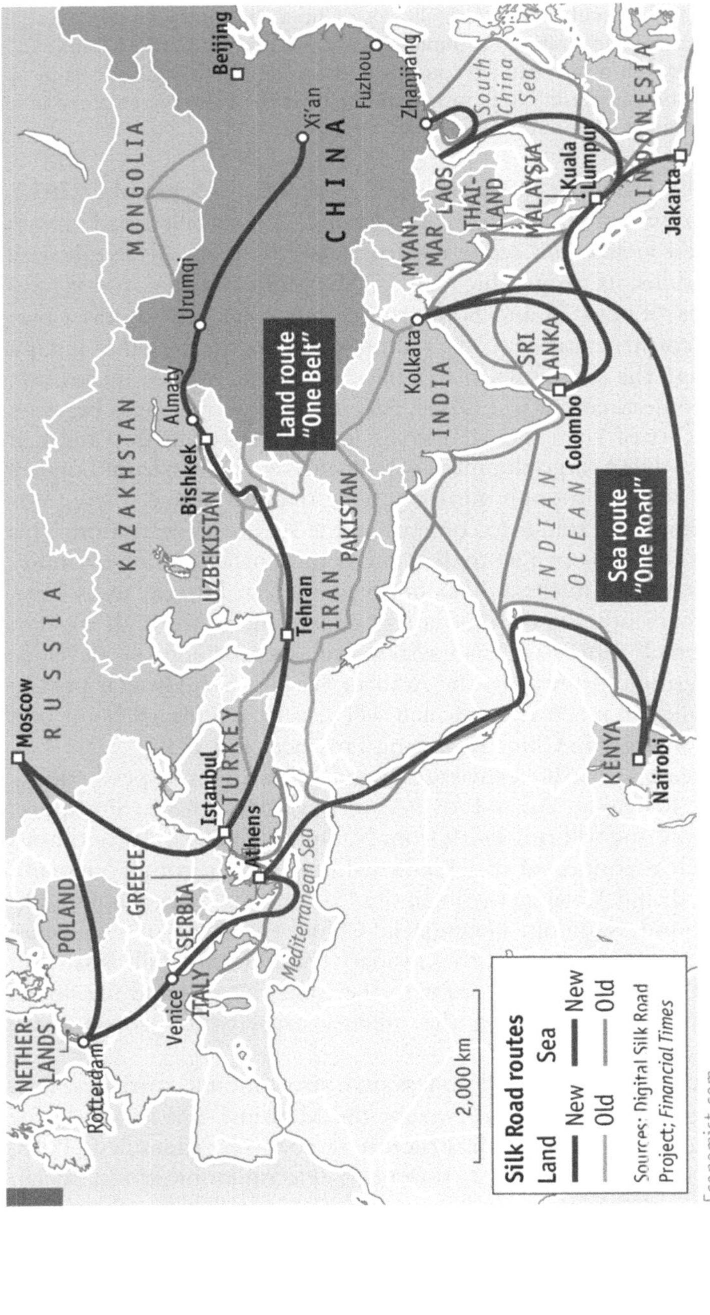

Fig. 6.1 The Belt and Road, 2016. Source: The Economist (2016). Our bulldozers our rules. June 2. Retrieved from https://www.economist.com/news/china/21701505-chinas-foreign-policy-could-reshape-good-part-world-economy-our-bulldozers-our-rules

construction, energy, and environment of which a third of were in China and the rest in BRI participant countries.

An initiative of this scale inevitably draws criticisms that range from the capability to deliver, competition from other powers like Japan, and political changes with so many countries involved.[19] There can be little doubt that in an initiative of such breadth and complexity, these challenges, and obstacles yet unidentified, will need to be confronted and overcome. That not every piece of the BRI jigsaw has to be built from scratch—some infrastructure needed to bring the network to fruition already exists while others, like the Beibu Gulf Economic Zone, predate the launch and are under implementation—would help ease somewhat the burden of project planning and execution. Even more important, even if BRI ends up being only partially successful, its impact on the existing economic order will still have been substantial. This impact will have been in enhancing China's international reputation and inspiring emerging economies with similar development aspirations (Crabtree & Ming, 2017). That, rather than the "global commercial empire", desirable as it is, is clearly China's preeminent objective.

6.6.3 The Role of State Enterprises

Given the size and complexity of the BRI, it should be no surprise that it is many things to many people. As Joshi (2017) observed,

> The problem with trying to understand what it is all about is that it is a combination of many things: an economic plan for taking the Chinese economy on to the path of sustainable growth, a scheme for market development and dominance, an effort to export of excess capacity in key infrastructure industries, all adding up to a geopolitical assertion of China's major power status.

Whatever perceptions of China's motivation behind the BRI, there is little dispute that it signals the advance of China's state enterprises in that more and better opportunities should arise for their internationalization—more because of the coverage of the BRI and better because they come with state support. In noting this development, the Economist (2017) saw it as "bad for China and the world". A less cynical view saw the major role played by state enterprises as the consequence of the BRI being just the next phase of "Going Out", which was led by state enterprises. A similar conclusion was reached by those focused more narrowly on short-term challenges who believed that the BRI represented the means by which China exports its excess capacity.

Looking beyond these specifics, the logic of state enterprise leadership in the BRI is clear. First, as already noted, although not the only factor, the state's overarching strategic imperatives driving this initiative requires state enterprises, as key institutional instruments of the state, to take the lead in planning and executing these projects. The use of state enterprises would ensure not only that state priorities would be adhered to but also, by not focusing on profit maximization, help to strengthen the reputation of the Chinese state and bolster its soft power. Second, the BRI could also enhance the control of the economy by the Communist Party under President Xi through "Top-level design" of economic development and "incessantly strengthen the vitality, control and influence of the state economy" (Lam, 2015: 3). This control extends to provinces, many of which have been approved for participation in BRI projects.

Third, state enterprises themselves have strong credentials for participation in BRI projects. Years of honing their competitive skills through domestic reforms, fierce competition in the domestic economy, and extensive experience with projects passed along by the state have produce state enterprises that can compete with the best international firms for projects. Indeed, supported by Chinese financial institutions like the China Development and Export-Import Banks, these enterprises will not find it hard to beat their international competition even under open bidding for contracts. Fourth, most of the BRI projects have been in infrastructure construction including transport and energy, areas in which state enterprises have had extensive experience in domestic projects.

The dominance of state enterprises is shown in the list of enterprises that appeared in the official Belt and Road Portal (https://eng.yidaiyilu.gov.cn/index.htm). Of the 84 enterprises listed, all were state enterprises, and most were central (classified as strategic) state enterprises (Table 6.4). Of the 84 enterprises, most (16) were in transportation, mining was next (14) while 12 were in power. These attest to the importance of connectivity and the securing of energy sources. Another six were in construction, reflecting the physical infrastructure construction phase of the BRI. Telecommunications and electronics enterprises and engineering enterprises also fit well into this phase. In addition to these, there were manufacturing enterprises producing steel, automobiles, and textiles. Of the 84 enterprises, all but 6 were central state enterprises.

Table 6.4 List of Chinese enterprises in the Belt and Road Initiative

Main activity	*Number*
Power, including nuclear	12
Transportation, including shipping, aviation	16
Construction	6
Mining	14
Industry, including steel	6
Engineering	6
Telecommunications and electronics	7
Others	17

Source: Belt and Road Portal, at https://eng.yidaiyilu.gov.cn/info/iList.jsp?cat_id=10080&cur_page=3

What has been the extent of state enterprise involvement in the BRI? Xinhua Finance (2017) reported that over the most recent three years, 47 centrally administered state enterprises participated in 1676 projects in countries and regions along the Belt and Road covering energy, infrastructure, and industrial cooperation. Infrastructure projects allowed these enterprises to plat to their competitive advantage in railway and highway construction. Companies under the state-owned China Communications Construction Company (CCCC) alone were reported to have built some 10,320 km of highways, 95 deep-water wharves, 10 airports, 152 bridges, and 2080 km of railways in Belt and Road countries (Xinhua Finance, 2017). Lam (2015: 4) cited the China State Construction Engineering Corporation (CSCEC), a multinational real estate and civil-engineering conglomerate, and China CAMC Engineering Co. Ltd. (CAMCE), one of the world's largest engineering and construction contractors, as BRI participants.

In the energy sector, central SOEs were also reported to have constructed more than 60 energy projects and oil and gas cooperation projects in over 20 countries along the Belt and Road, and to have constructed energy transportation projects and thermal power stations, hydropower stations, and nuclear power stations (Xinhua Finance, 2017). And in the development of industrial zones, China had, as of May 2017, established 56 economic and trade cooperative zones in 25 countries along the Belt and Road route, with total investment exceeding US$ 18.5 billion.

Central state enterprises are of course not the only state enterprises in the BRI. Provincial and local enterprises also have a role to play. Given President Shi's desire to include every province in the endeavor, all provinces will, over time, be included even if they have not at present (Beauchamp-Mustafaga, 2015: 1). Also, cities that are end-points of transcontinental railways, such as Yiwu, Chengdu, and eventually Nanning will of necessity be participants of the BRI. Provincial governments and their enterprises are also involved. For instance, The Guangxi Autonomous Region, through the Guangxi Beibu and Qinzhou Investment Development Co. Ltd., is upgrading Malaysia's Kuantan port, while the development of the deep sea Malacca Gateway Port was supported by the Guangdong provincial government (Mok, 2016).

The heavy involvement of state enterprises in the BRI should not be interpreted to mean non-state enterprises are excluded. Just as with China's forays into Latin America and Africa, non-state enterprises considered leaders in their respective fields like Alibaba and Huawei have been offered their fair share of projects by the state. A good example is Malaysia, where telecommunications giants Huawei and state-controlled ZTE were both awarded projects (Li & Cheong, 2017). In the official BRI portal, non-state enterprises like the China Fortune Land Development Co. Ltd., Wintime Energy Company Ltd., China Minsheng Investment, and Sany Group were also reported to be working on or collaborating with state enterprises to work on BRI projects. In viewing the role of non-state enterprises, it is well to remember that the state-private sector divide is nowhere as sharp in China as envisaged in mainstream Western economic literature. What matters more is whether the head of the enterprise has close connections to the state and/or party leadership. Lam (2015: 4) singled out the case of the Sany Group as being likely to benefit considerably from BRI infrastructure projects. Sany's founder, Liang Wengen was a faithful party member and a strong candidate for the Central Committee of the 18th Communist Party Congress.

6.7 Conclusion

"Going Out" and the much more expansive BRI mark two important phases of China's development trajectory. Much to the dismay of critics of China's state enterprises, these enterprises have been at the center of each initiative. Hence, there should be no doubt that efforts by the state to streamline its state enterprise sector through downsizing should not be interpreted as efforts to shrink the sector's role. In fact, the opposite is true. State enterprise reform, together with these initiatives, is to hone the competitive skills of these enterprises to match the best of the rest of the world's global enterprises. In doing so, they remain key instruments of state policy, a role that is ignored by many "mainstream" assessments of these enterprises' worth.

In comparing these two strategies, several common features can be identified. First, as with prior state enterprise reform, both strategies involve a gradualist approach. The "Going Out" strategy first saw state enterprises engaged primarily in extractive industries, but then rapidly diversified to seek both markets and technology. In pursuing the latter, the use of M&A represents a uniquely Chinese method of technology catchup. Foreign technology acquisition complemented a program promoting indigenous innovation and an aggressive technology transfer-policy stance for foreign firms. Similarly, the rollout of the BRI began with infrastructure construction, but will likely evolve to forms of cooperation that utilize this enhanced connectivity.

This gradualist approach embodies a process of learning. As Chinese state enterprises venture out, they learn that host government perceptions of their ties to the Chinese government matter. While emerging and developing economies' governments tend to have a positive impression, governments of advanced countries are generally suspicious of the Chinese government's hidden hand. With the BRI, the importance of diplomacy based on in-depth knowledge of host governments' political economy is slowly being learned as obstacles to implementation emerge.

A third commonality is the lead taken by state enterprises. This is hardly surprising, given both initiatives exemplify government strategies and state enterprises are instruments of state policy. As the experience of "Going Out" has demonstrated, however, the initial phase of state enterprise involvement would be followed by participation by the non-state sector especially with the greater role technology embodied in Chinese enterprises. In a sense, state enterprises also played a useful role in shouldering early risks associated with learning. With the BRI too, articulation of the state's strategy required implementation by state enterprises. As the initiative develops, however, the role of state enterprises should diminish.

There are also differences between the two strategies. First, as already indicated, while "Going Out" aimed to groom state and non-state enterprises to compete with the best of the foreign rival, it does so within the frame of the existing economic order. With BRI, China is moving to reshape the existing order into one that serves China's best interests. The challenge in achieving the latter will be considerably greater. For instance, coordination among enterprises is a major task for those engaged in the BRI; it is not an issue with "Going Out".

Second, state enterprises possess different strengths as they participate in these initiatives. Those going out have to compete on a more or less level playing field in the international market. For them, strength comes from their ability to innovate, to deploy new technology. With China now at the cutting edge in technologies like green technology, specific areas of ICT and automation, this is beginning to occur. On the other hand, BRI, with the full backing of the Chinese state, state enterprises have a much stronger hand. However, this strength has to be tempered by the fact that their counterparts are most likely government entities of participating governments. Diplomacy will be essential to such interface and may make or break projects. Chinese state enterprises, used to conditions in China, will have a steep learning curve.

As this chapter concludes, it is well to remember that the public and private sector divide is nowhere as sharp as assumed in mainstream market economics. As already explained, state enterprise reform has produced a continuum of enterprise ranging from 100% state-owned to those in which the state has only nominal control or none at all. That is why we have avoided the use of the word "private", preferring the term "non-state" instead. Indeed, the government has no qualms about giving non-state firms like Huawei the level of support it extends to state enterprises. Instead of ownership, the key is the extent to which enterprise leadership are close to the party or national leadership.

Led by its state enterprises, China has charted a development path, to quote Frost, "less traveled". Indeed, no other country has traveled down this path before. Whether this path leads to the desirable destination remains to be seen. But progressive learning through a step-wise approach will at least allow course correction to take place. Perhaps, quoting Frost again, "that has made all the difference."

Notes

1. As discussed later in this chapter, China should be in stage 2 of Dunning's (1981) Investment Development Path and a recipient of primarily inward foreign direct investment.
2. OFDI data for the BRICS countries other than China are from the OECD database at https://data.oecd.org/fdi/fdi-flows.htm.

3. The studies they reviewed referenced more than 12 different theories, with Dunning's OLI paradigm most common, followed by those based on the RBV, the IBV, and the Uppsala model (Berning & Holfbrugge, 2012: 174).
4. Scholars are divided as to how different Chin's OFDI is. See, for instance, Dunning and Lundan (2008) who argue for the applicability of existing theories, and Barney and Zhang (2009) for the opposite view.
5. Van Wyk (2009) estimated that the state enterprise share of OFDI flows was 73.5% in 2003, 82.3% in 2004, and 83.2% in 2005.
6. The plan calls for accelerating China's "Going Out" policy through, first, expanding outward investment; second, emphasizing the equal importance of FDI in China and Chinese outward investment; and, third, transformation of China's trade and outward investment models (Xu, 2011. 14).
7. The Sixth Forum on China-Africa Cooperation (FOCAC) was held in Johannesburg, South Africa, in 2015. In this forum, China committed to investing $60 billion in Africa (Sun, 2015).
8. These failed deals include CNOOC (China) and Unocal (US), Haier (China) and Maytag (US), Huawei (China) and 3Com (US), and Chinalco (China) and Rio Tinto (Australia).
9. As far back as 2009, Van Wyk (2009) predicted that "as Chinese firms become fully integrated into the global market, increasingly accountable to shareholders".
10. Swanson (2017) cited the examples of Huaxin buying 85% of French telecom company Alcatel-Lucent; Alibaba spending $220 million for a 20% stake in mobile video app Tango and joining in a $250 million fundraising round for car service Lyft; and Baidu investing in Uber.
11. See the websites for BOC Singapore (http://www.bankofchina.com/sg/aboutus/ab1/201001/t20100120_955880.html) and BOC Malaysia (http://www.bankofchina.com/malaysia/en/aboutus/ab1/201211/t20121109_2133238.html)
12. From ICBC's website http://www.icbc-ltd.com/ICBC/%e6%b5%b7%e5%a4%96%e5%88%86%e8%a1%8c/%e9%a9%ac%e6%9d%a5%e8%a5%bf%e4%ba%9a%e7%bd%91%e7%ab%99/en/AboutUs1/ICBCMalaysiaProfile/ and Xinhuanet (2016b).
13. For an example of how Chinese enterprises coexist in Malaysia, see Li and Cheong (2017).
14. This section draws heavily from the authors' published paper (Li & Cheong, 2017) in the Journal of Contemporary Asia. Permission by the Journal publisher Taylor and Francis to use content from this paper in this chapter under its Authors' Assignment of Copyright Agreement, clause 4(x), is gratefully acknowledged.

15. Examples of its homegrown technology are its multimode phones that work on several systems (including GSM/WCDMA and GSM/TDSCDMA) simultaneously, and its Gogo technology for mobile broadband internet, developed with Qualcomm, that is in use on most airlines today (Fan & Gao, 2016: 229).
16. Deng's (2015: 119) use of "responsible power" is with reference to President Clinton's 1995 remark that while the US welcomed China to the great power table, great powers had great responsibilities. These responsibilities were framed by the international system the US created after the Second World War.
17. Casarini (2015) argues that together with the benefits come the risks of difficulty to frame a common stand in dealing with Beijing, a popular backlash, and more difficult relations with Washington.
18. PwC (2017: 19–23) details six main economic corridors running through Eurasia and Southeast Asia.
19. Devonshire-Ellis (2017) has a listing of papers critical of the BRI.

References

Athreye, S., & Chen, W. (2009). Go west for fame and fortune? The role of internationalization in the growth of Chinese telecommunications firms. Paper presented at 3rd China Goes Global Conference, Harvard University, Cambridge, September 30–October 2.

Bank of China (2017). Outlet introduction. Retrieved from http://www.bankofchina.com/my/en/aboutus/ab1/201211/t20121109_2133238.html

Barney, J.B. (1991). Firm resources and sustainable competitive advantage. *Journal of Management, 17*(1), 99–120.

Barney, J.B., & Zhang, S. (2009). The future of Chinese management research: A theory of Chinese management versus A Chinese theory of management. *Management and Organization Review, 5*(1), 15–28.

Berning, S.C., & Holtbrugge, D. (2012). Chinese outward direct foreign investment: A challenge for traditional internationalization theories? *Journal Betriebswirtsch, 62*, 169–224.

Badkar, M. (2013). China stimulated its economy like crazy after the financial crisis... and now the nightmare is beginning. *Business Insider.* June 17. Retrieved from http://www.businessinsider.com/chinas-excess-capacity-problem-2013-6/?IR=T

Beauchamp-Mustafaga, N. (2015). Chinese provinces aim to find their place along new silk road. *China Brief, 15*(10), 1–3.

Calkins, J. (2013). Banking abroad: The globalization of Chinese banks. Retrieved from http://knowledge.ckgsb.edu.cn/2013/03/28/china/banking-abroad-the-globalization-of-chinese-banks/

Callahan, W.A. (2016). China's "Asia Dream": The Belt Road Initiative and the new regional order. *Asian Journal of Comparative Politics, 1*(3), 226–243.

Camacho, L. (2011). Challenges and opportunities for Chinese and Indian banks to emerge as global players. Speech at the 28th General Meeting and Conference of the Asian Bankers Association held in Colombo, Sri Lanka, October 4.

Cantwell, J. (1998). The globalization of technology: What remains of the product cycle model? In A.D. Chandler, P. Hagstrom, & O. Solvell (Eds.), *The dynamic firm: The role of technology, strategy, organizations and regions* (pp. 263–288). New York: Oxford University Press.

Casarini, N. (2015). Is Europe to benefit from China's Belt and Road Initiative? Working Paper 15/40, *Istituto Affari Internazionali.*

China.com (2011). Wen Jiabao: China did not exploit one single drop of oil or one single ton of minerals from Africa. September 15. Retrieved from http://www.china.com.cn/economic/txt/2011-09/15/content_23419056.htm

China Hands (2015). China 'Going Out' 2.0: Dawn of a new era for Chinese investment Abroad. Retrieved from https://www.huffingtonpost.com/china-hands/china-going-out-20-dawn-o_b_7046790.html

Crabtree, J., & Ming, C. (2017). Why soft power could be the real value of China's massive Belt and Road project. *CNBC,* May 22. Retrieved from http://www.cnbc.com/2017/05/22/one-belt-one-road-why-the-real-value-of-chinas-project-could-like-in-soft-power.html

Cui, J. (2012). State ownership effect on firms' FDI ownership decisions under institutional pressure: A study of Chinese outward-investing firms. *Journal of International Business Studies, 43,* 264–284.

Das, D.K. (2014). China's outbound foreign direct investment: Sources of growth and transformation. Working Paper # 35, Research Center for Chinese Politics and Business, Indiana University, Bloomington, IN.

Davies, K. (2013). China investment policy: An update. *OECD Working Papers on International Investment,* 2013/01, OECD Publishing. Retrieved from https://doi.org/10.1787/5k469l1hmvbt-en

Deng, Y. (2015). China: The post-responsible power. *The Washington Quarterly, 37*(4), 117–132.

Devonshire-Ellis, C. (2017). China faces OBOR criticism following the Belt and Road Forum. Dezan, Shira and Associates. Retrieved from https://www.silkroadbriefing.com/news/2017/05/26/china-faces-obor-criticism-following-belt-road-forum/

Drogendijk, R., & Blomkvist, K. (2013). Drivers and motives for Chinese outward foreign direct investments in Africa. *Journal of African Business, 14,* 75–84.

Dunning, J.H. (1980). Toward an eclectic theory of international production: Some empirical tests. *Journal of International Business Studies, 11*(1), 9–31.

Dunning, J.H. (1981). Explaining the international direct investment position of countries: Toward a dynamic and development approach. *Weltwirtschaftliches Archiv, 117*(5), 30–64.

Dunning, J. H. (1993). *Multinational enterprises and the global economy*. Boston, US: Addison-Wesley.

Dunning J.H., & Lundan S.M. (2008). Institutions and the OLI paradigm of the multinational enterprise. *Asia Pacific Journal of Management, 25*(4), 573–593.

The Economist (2017). China's state enterprises are not retreating but advancing. July 20. Retrieved from https://www.economist.com/news/leaders/21725295-bad-china-and-world-chinas-state-enterprises-are-not-retreating-advancing

The Economist (2016). Our bulldozers our rules. June 2. Retrieved from https://www.economist.com/news/china/21701505-chinas-foreign-policy-could-reshape-good-part-world-economy-our-bulldozers-our-rules

Fallows, J. (2007). China makes, the world takes. *The Atlantic*, July/August. Retrieved from http://www.theatlantic.com/magazine/archive/2007/07/china-makes-the-world-takes/305987/

Fan, P. & Gao, X. (2016). Catching up and developing innovation capabilities in China's telecommunication industry. In Y. Zhou, W. Lazonick, & Y. Sun (Eds.), *China as an innovation nation* (pp. 215–236). Oxford: Oxford University Press.

Fiala, Z. (2014). The role of government influence in Chinese outward foreign investment. Master's Thesis, School of International Business, Bremen University of Applied Sciences.

Forde, B. (2013). Xi's Chinese dream: collective strength for national rejuvenation. *East Asia Forum*, July 5. Retrieved from http://www.eastasiaforum.org/2013/07/05/xis-chinese-dream-collective-strength-for-national-rejuvenation/

Globerman S, & Shapiro D (2009). Economic and strategic considerations surrounding Chinese FDI in the United States. *Asia Pacific Journal of Management, 26*, 163–183.

Godehardt, N. (2016). No end of history: A Chinese alternative concept of international order. Research Paper 2, German Institute for International and Security Affairs, Berlin.

Gomez, E.T. (2017). *Ministry of Finance Incorporated: Ownership and control of corporate Malaysia*. Petaling Jaya: Strategic Information and Research Development Centre.

Hindustan Times (2017). BSNL to spend Rs 6,000 crore on expansion: Nokia, ZTE to get contracts. September 8. Retrieved from http://www.hindustantimes.com/tech/bsnl-to-spend-rs-6-000-crore-on-expansion-nokia-zte-to-get-contracts/story-JOcqODSjRqtfDMsx11SaFI.html

Ilheu, F. (2010). Chinese outward foreign direct investment: In search of a new theory. International *Journal of Asian Business and Information Management, 1*(4), 43–56.

Ivanovitch, M. (2016). China's Belt and Road project will ease SOE slowdown, as social welfare boosts incomes. *CNBC,* July 3. Retrieved from http://www.cnbc.com/2016/07/03/chinas-belt-and-road-project-will-ease-soe-slowdown-as-social-welfare-boosts-incomes.html

Joshi, M. (2017). China's One Belt One Road Project is paving its way into Europe. *The Wire,* May 13. Retrieved from https://thewire.in/135236/china-obor-europe/

Johanson, J., & Mattsson, L. (1987). Interorganizational relations in industrial systems: A network approach compared with the transaction-cost approach. *International Studies of Management & Organization, 17*(1), 34–48.

Johanson, J., & Vahlne, J.E. (1977). The internationalization process of the firm—A model of knowledge development and increasing foreign market commitments. *Journal of International Business Studies, 8*(1), 23–32.

Kumar, A. (2014). Telekom Malaysia and ZTE form research partnership in quest for higher bandwidth. *Computerworld Malaysia,* July 18. Retrieved from https://www.computerworld.com.my/print-article/62734/

Lam, W. (2015). "One Belt One Road" enhances Xi Jinping's control over the economy. *China Brief, 15*(10), 3–5.

Lee, Y.S. (2002). Business networks and suppliers' locational choice. *Environment and Planning A* 34(6), 1001–1020.

Lee, B.B., & Ghosh, A. (2012). The ASEAN chronicles of the Chinese Yuan. *Insights 2012,* Standard Chartered Bank, July.

Lee, Y.N. (2017). China's start-ups usher in new phase of "Going Out" movement. *CNBC,* April 16, 2017. Retrieved from https://www.cnbc.com/2017/04/16/chinas-start-ups-usher-in-new-phase-of-going-out-movement.html

Levine, S. (2015). China is building the most extensive global commercial-military empire in history. *Quartz,* June 9. Retrieved from https://qz.com/415649/china-is-building-the-most-extensive-global-commercial-military-empire-in-history/

Li, R., & Cheong, K.C. (2016). How much "state" is in China's state enterprises: A case study of ZTE Corporation in an era of reform. *International Journal of Chinese Studies, 7*(3), 245–270.

Li, R., & Cheong, K.C. (2017). Huawei and ZTE in Malaysia: The localisation of Chinese transnational enterprises. *Journal of Contemporary Asia, 47*(5), 752–773.

Madsen, T.K., & Servais, P. (1997). The internationalization of born globals: An evolutionary process? *International Business Review, 6*(6), 561–583.

Mak, L. (2016). Bank of China Hong Kong chief sees regional expansion as antidote to local slowdown. *South China Morning Post,* June 6. Retrieved from http://www.scmp.com/business/banking-finance/article/1967479/bank-china-hong-kong-chief-sees-regional-expansion-antidote

Malay Mail (2015). Najib launches Bank of China as Renminbi clearing bank. April 14. Retrieved from http://www.themalaymailonline.com/money/article/najib-launches-bank-of-china-as-renminbi-clearing-bank

Malaysian Insider (2014). China's ZTE Corp hopes to continue providing LTE solutions in Malaysia. January 30. Retrieved from http://www.themalaysianinsider.com/business/article/chinas-zte-corp-hopes-to-continue-providing-lte-solutions-in-malaysia

Mathews A.J. (2006). Dragon multinationals: new players in 21st century globalization. *Asia Pacific Journal of Management, 23*(1), 5–27.

McCoy, A. (2015). The geopolitics of American global decline. *TomDispatch*, June 7. Retrieved from http://www.tomdispatch.com/post/176007/tomgram%3A_alfred_mccoy,_washington%27s_great_game_and_why_it%27s_failing_/

Meyer, K.E. (2015). India's and China's new motives for foreign investment. *Forbes Asia*, February 24. Retrieved from https://www.forbes.com/sites/ceibs/2015/02/24/india-and-chinas-new-motives-for-foreign-investment/#73588c69798e

Mtigwe, B. (2006). Theoretical milestones in international business: The journey to international entrepreneurship theory. *Journal of International Entrepreneurship, 4*(1), 5–25.

Mok, O. (2016). Construction for Malacca Gateway Port to start next year. *Malay Mail*, November 8. Retrieved from http://www.themalaymailonline.com/malaysia/article/construction-for-malacca-gateway-port-to-start-next-year#pGsxCVaLb5VZZyBb.97

Morck, R., Yeung, B., & Zhao, M. (2008). Perspectives on China's outward foreign direct investment. *Journal of International Business Studies, 39*, 337–350.

Poncet, S. (2010). Inward and outward FDI in China. In D. Greenway, C. Milner, & S. Yao (Eds.), *China and the World Economy* (pp. 112–134). New York: Palgrave Macmillan.

Porter, M.E. (1980). *Competitive strategy.* New York: Free Press.

PwC (2017). Repaving the ancient silk routes. Singapore.

The Organization for Economic Cooperation and Development (OECD) (2008). *Investment policy reviews China. China Outward Direct Investment.* Paris: OECD.

Oviatt, B.M., & McDougall, P.P. (1994). Toward a theory of international new ventures. *Journal of international Business Studies, 25*(1), 45–64.

Peng, M.W., Wang, D.Y.L., & Jiang, Y. (2008). An institution-based view of international business strategy: A focus on emerging economies. *Journal of International Business Studies, 39*(5), 920–936.

Que, L. (2015). An analysis of EMNEs' internationalization strategies: The case of Chinese enterprises in the telecommunications equipment industry. Master Thesis, Fribourg University, Fribourg.

Salidjanova, N. (2011). Going Out: A review of China's outward foreign direct investment. Staff Research Report, US-China Economic and Security Review Commission, March 30.

Sarkar, S. (2012). ZTE offers tech and partnership. *China Daily Asia*, September 25. Retrieved from http://www.chinadailyasia.com/business/2012-09/25/content_75925.html

Shrader, R., Oviatt, B., & McDougall, P. (2000). How new ventures exploit trade-offs among international risk factors: Lessons for the accelerated internationalization of the 21st Century. *Academy of Management Journal, 43*(6), 1227–1247.

Sauvant, K.P. (2011). China: inward and outward foreign direct investment. *Transnational Corporations Review, 3*(1), i–iii.

Shane, D. (2015). Beware Bank of China Hong Kong's foray into Southeast Asia. *Barron's*, August 13. Retrieved from http://www.barrons.com/articles/beware-bank-of-china-hong-kongs-foray-into-southeast-asia-1439437541

Si, Y., Liefner I., & Wang, T. (2013). Foreign direct investment with Chinese characteristics: A middle path between Ownership-Location-Internalization model and Linkage-Leverage-Learning model. *Chinese Geographical Science, 23*(5), 594–606.

Stratfor (2015). China's outward push in high-tech investment and innovation. *Stratfor Worldview*, June 12. Retrieved from https://worldview.stratfor.com/article/chinas-outward-push-high-tech-investment-and-innovation

Sun, Y. (2015). Xi and the Sixth Forum on China Africa Cooperation: Major commitments but with questions. *Brookings*, December 7. Retrieved from https://www.brookings.edu/blog/africa-in-focus/2015/12/07/xi-and-the-6th-forum-on-china-africa-cooperation-major-commitments-but-with-questions/

Swanson, A. (2017). Gold rush: Chinese tech companies invest overseas. *South China Morning Post*, March 29. Retrieved from http://www.scmp.com/tech/enterprises/article/1800746/gold-rush-chinese-tech-companies-invest-overseas

Timokhina, O. (2014). Chinese foreign direct investment in Africa in corporate social responsibility context. Working Paper No. 2014/29, Maastricht School of Management, Maastricht, Netherlands.

Van Wyk, B. (2009). Why, who and where? Chinese OFDI on the world stage. INSEAD Knowledge, October 12. Retrieved from https://knowledge.insead.edu/economics-politics/why-who-and-where-chinese-ofdi-on-the-world-stage-1421

Vernon, R. (1966). International investment and international trade in the product cycle. *Quarterly Journal of Economics, 80*(2), 190–207.

Wang, G. (2015b). China's Eurasia strategy to counter US naval power. *Straits Times*, August 1. Retrieved from http://www.straitstimes.com/opinion/chinas-eurasia-strategy-to-counter-us-naval-power

Wang, H. (2016). A deeper look at China's "Going Out" policy. Commentary, Center for International Governance Innovation, Waterloo, Canada, March.

Wang, Y. (2015a). Outward direct foreign investment of Chinese enterprises: review and analysis. *Industrial Engineering and Management*, *4*(4), 1–4.

Wei, Z. (2010). The literature on Chinese outward FDI. *Multinational Business Review*, *18*(3), 73–112.

Wong, J., & Chan, S. (2003). China's outward direct investment: Expanding worldwide. *China: An International Journal*, *1*(2), 273–301.

Xinhua Finance (2017). OBOR countries become major investment destinations for Chinese central SOEs. May 26. Retrieved from http://en.xfafinance.com/html/Economies/Investment/2017/334212.shtml

Xinhuanet (2016a). Bank of China celebrates 15th anniversary of reopening in Malaysia. Retrieve from http://www.xinhuanet.com/english/2016-02/24/c_135124364.htm

Xinhuanet (2016b). China Construction Bank acquires commercial banking license in Malaysia. Retrieved from http://www.xinhuanet.com/english/2016-11/01/c_135797392.htm

Xu, T. (2011). Destination Unknown: Investment in China's "Go Out" Policy. *China Brief* 11(17), 13–17.

Yang, Z. (2015). Outward foreign direct investment, market segmentation and eradication of excess capacity. *Journal of International Trade, 11*. Retrieved from http://en.cnki.com.cn/Article_en/CJFDTOTAL-GJMW201511011.htm

Yin, W. (2015). Motivations of Chinese outward foreign direct investment: An organizing framework and empirical investigation. *Journal of International Business and Economy*, *16*(1), 82–106.

Yiu, D. (2010). Multinational advantages of Chinese business groups: A theoretical exploration. *Management and Organization Review*, *7*(2), 249–277.

Yong, Y. (2016). Bank of China sees Malaysia as a regional hub. *The Edge Financial Daily*, November 7. Retrieved from http://www.theedgemarkets.com/my/article/bank-china-sees-malaysia-regional-hub

Zhang, F., Yu, M., Yu, J., & Jin, Y. (2017). The effect on RMB internationalization on Belt and Road Initiative: Evidence from bilateral swap agreements. *Emerging Markets Finance and Trade*, *53*(12), 2845–2857.

Zhong, W. (2017). 19th Party Congress to be a monument to Xi Jinping. *Asia Times*, September 29. Retrieved from http://www.atimes.com/article/19th-party-congress-monument-xi-jinping/

Zhou, J., Hallding, K., & Han, G. (2015). The trouble with China's One Belt One Road strategy. *The Diplomat*, June 26. Retrieved from http://thediplomat.com/2015/06/the-trouble-with-the-chinese-marshall-plan-strategy/

ZTE Corporation (2004). What is next for ZTE's "Going Out" strategy? Retrieved from http://www.zte.com.cn/global/about/press-center/press-clipping/200402/351349

CHAPTER 7

Conclusion

7.1 Prevailing Views of China's State Enterprises

Just four decades after opening up its economy, China's rise to contest the global leadership of the US has sparked much debate in the West about a China "model" characterized as authoritarian. That this model not only continues to survive but thrives, with strong domestic support, represents, to commentators in the West, a direct challenge to the democratic model they consider to be universally the ideal. This belief in the superiority of the democratic model of governance has spawned predictions of doom for the Chinese system.

Criticism of the Chinese system with its heavy state involvement naturally extends to its key institutions. State enterprises, which dominated the economy when it was centrally planned, and continued to exercise a much larger influence even after economic liberalization, would appear to be a perfect target. For, do not Western public enterprise theory argue that these are less efficient than private enterprises? And evidence of such inefficiency and misallocation of resources abound in China. Acknowledging such inefficiencies, the Chinese government itself had launched a sequential program of state enterprise reform. Hopes that China was dismantling its state enterprise sector rose when in 1992 then Premier Zhu Rongji initiated reforms that led to massive layoffs and state enterprises privatized or liquidated. These hopes were dashed when China's reforms resulted in fewer but much larger state enterprises. Also, thus strengthened, state enterprises were at the forefront of China's "Going Out" strategy

R. Li, K. C. Cheong, *China's State Enterprises*,
https://doi.org/10.1007/978-981-13-0176-6_7

encouraging Chinese enterprises to compete in global markets. When the new century dawned, Chinese state enterprises have become transnationals able to compete globally. And with the BRI launched in 2013, state enterprises have really taken center stage in the Chinese government's long-term strategy.

With Chinese state enterprises becoming more, not less, important, they have been viewed with greater alarm by many commentators, with criticisms ranging from the same old inefficiencies bolstered by the state (the latest name being "zombie enterprises")—as if decades of state enterprise reform have produced nothing by way of improving these enterprises' performance—to engaging in unfair competition—grudging acceptance of their competitiveness but disparaging the source of this competence.

This book has argued that such criticism is misplaced, not because these allegations are baseless but because of a fundamental misconception about the Chinese state and its enterprises. And that is that the prevailing discourse on these is dominated by the application of Western political and economic concepts which ignore China's cultural and political history where the state has played a major role and is "embedded", to use Polanyi's term, in Chinese society. This misconception may have stemmed from seeing China absorbing and apparently applying foreign ideas and concepts. The reality though is that China has always adapted foreign ideas to fit its own circumstances, a fact long known by historians and to seasoned "China hands".[1] Thus, the state's role in numerous innovative reform experiments during China's economic transition from a command to a socialist market economy is indicative of the application of Western ideas. Yet the retention of a strong state sector is very much home-grown.

Relying mainly on these ideas, most assessments of Chinese state enterprises are unbalanced. The preoccupation with a state-private dichotomy has led to the failure to recognize the emergence of a distinct corporate entity. In fact, Chinese state enterprises are distinguished from those defined by stereotypical Western public economics theories by the manner in which they are owned and controlled. There is a need to reframe the analysis of China's state enterprises to recognize how its particular cultural and political history has shaped these institutions. Central to this analysis are the reforms that have been put in place by the government to consolidate and strengthen this sector, and not, as many believe, to diminish their role.

To better understand China's state enterprises, several specific questions require at least a tentative response. First, after state enterprise reform, what is the dynamic role of the Chinese state in relation to its state enterprises in terms of ownership structure and governance structure, and how different is it from what Western public enterprise theory argues? Second, what is the role of state enterprises for the Chinese state in the economy? Third, do different ownership-governance combinations affect performance outcomes? Finally, with better understanding of the role state enterprises play in China, what future role is expected of these enterprises as China moves progressively to superpower status.

Deep understanding requires the use of qualitative research methods. These, supported with descriptive secondary data analysis, are the main methods to explore these research questions here. The methods are historical narrative, case study, ethnography, and phenomenology. Of these, historical narrative and case study are the primary methodologies utilized while the other two are supporting methodologies. These methods are more appropriate than the quantitative methods used in most studies because of the need to gain deep insights into the construction of the state enterprise sector and its relationship with government.

In the next section, we summarize our findings on three key dimensions of the state enterprise sector—ownership and governance, meeting state objectives, and enterprise performance. While the first dimension is at the heart of understanding what constitutes a state enterprise in the Chinese context. The second and third dimensions relate to the role they perform as institutions of the state.

7.2 Understanding Chinese State Enterprises

A proper understanding of China's state enterprise system does not require a rejection of Western economic concepts. It does require that whatever concepts applied to the Chinese situation be founded the Chinese context, a context that is shaped by millennia of history that has seen little Western influence until recent times. Kuhn's characterization that China's system is "endogenously evolved" is most apt. This needs to be borne in mind in the following sections.

7.2.1 Ownership and Governance and the State–Non-State Dichotomy

The state enterprise sector has been officially classified as consisting of three types of enterprises. The first type consists of enterprises wholly owned by the state only—referred to as "state-owned enterprises"—that refers to wholly state-owned enterprises, wholly state-owned companies, and state joint-run enterprises. The second type, referred to as "state-holding enterprises", are those enterprises in which the state has majority ownership (more than 50%), or has the highest ownership among stock holders even if it is a minority stockholder (less than 50%), or not the highest but where the state exercises control through the agreement to make sure the state has de facto control. The third type, referred to as "state joint-stock enterprises", consists of those in which the state has minority ownership and exercises no control.

The issue of state ownership has been complicated by state enterprise reform that produced various corporate structures and types. State ownership ranges from 100% through majority ownership to minority ownership, the last of which does not appear in government statistics. Apart from national-level enterprises, sub-national enterprises belonging to provincial and local governments also exist in large numbers and function alongside, often compete with, national enterprises. There are also enterprises for which ownership is ambiguous, including quasi-state entities, non-state enterprises, urban collectives, and local government-owned township and village enterprises.

The government's role may well be larger than what the official statistics suggest because parts of government (minority) ownership are undocumented and/or under multiple layers of indirect ownership that may indicate the government has an important say if not exercising strong control. However, there is no way of knowing what role the government plays in these enterprises that do not come under the banner of state enterprises.

State control is exercised through the administrative body, the SASAC, which functions at various levels of government. Control channels are through governance, such as top management appointments. Furthermore, some state enterprises are managed and run as private firms in terms of rewards for performance, such as executive compensation linked to corporate performance, talent attracted through listings internationally, foreign investors represented on the Boards of Directors, and private sector top managers and executives hired with high compensation in the open labor market. Efforts had been made to use attractive employment terms to target better corporate governance to achieve competitively domestically and internationally.

For strategic state enterprises in what the state considers sectors vital to the economy or national security, the state retains a controlling position in terms of ownership and governance even after innovative reform. In addition, the state exercises control through governance by Party Committees as a part of enterprise management. Such control is needed to ensure the government's strategies are followed. Thus, state strategies can be and are executed through state enterprises. In return for compliance with state strategies which this control mandates, state enterprises are favored by explicit state support including preferential credit access. This role of state enterprises does not exist in Western public enterprise theories.

For "commercial" state enterprises, such control has been made on commercial rather than political grounds. Reform experiments have produced progressive reductions in state ownership without commensurate diminution of state control. There is de facto separation between ownership and control, with the former declining and the latter in the hands of professionalism management. Thus, this control is only lightly exercised through ensuring compliance with state strategies rather than through day-to-day management. As shown in Chap. 5, ZTE Corporation has good relations with the state and in the presence of state support receives preferential treatment from it with state funding.

Given the many types of enterprises linked to the state at various levels, the distinction between state and non-state enterprises is nowhere as sharp as Western theories postulate. What matters is not ownership but the relationship between the founders or heads of the enterprises and the leadership of the state. Enterprises such as Alibaba, Huawei, and Tencent are officially non-state enterprises, but are no less favorably treated by the state than state enterprises. In China's relationship-based environment, the state versus private dichotomy does not mean all that much, and the argument that more state means less private, an argument made even by some Chinese commentators, does not necessarily carry much weight.

7.2.2 Meeting State Objectives

Since state enterprises are key players in China's economy, they should have a material impact on growth and distribution. Since this century started, negative findings on the relationship between state enterprises and economic growth were replaced by increasing positive analysis. However, little empirical research existed that could make the direct link associating loss-making state enterprises with damaging state enterprise performance and China's economic growth. The emergence of globally competitive state enterprises like China Petrochemical Corporation (Sinopec Group) is one of the major manifestations of their economic revival. Productivity growth in the state sector has also been reported.

The central state enterprises from "pillar industries" were selected as national champions and have been driven to achieve global competitiveness in terms of scale and technology. They were consolidated into conglomerates supported by incentives to act as key players in China's economy. China's state enterprises are viewed by the state as engines of growth to promote innovation that facilitates the technological catchup to the West.

On the negative side, reforms have led to worker layoffs and have freed state enterprises from social responsibility, even to the workforce that was retained. Despite its many shortcomings, the end of the social role these enterprises originally played has left a void in the social safety net that has not been filled even today. Social security experiments to take over this redistributive role, from the rehiring of some laid-off workers and compensation packages for those laid off to the establishment of the National Social Security Fund have helped relieve some of the hardships caused by the layoffs but have yet to come near anything resembling a national social security system.

Reform has also changed the role of enterprises in income distribution. Spatial income distribution has also been affected by a shift in industrial production to coastal regions. State enterprises, whose original mandate included construction and provision of housing for their employees, began to undertake the construction of residential (and commercial) units for profit on land owned or acquired from profits amassed through profit retention. To be fair, state enterprises have continued to support the government in such activities as disaster relief and diplomatic confidence building. Also, national champions and enterprises in strategic sectors with powerful corporate interests distribute part of their earnings as dividends to the government.

For strategic state enterprises, they exercised government functions on the government's behalf. Historically, the Chinese banking sector's role was transformed from being a government department to supporting other state enterprises as government entities. However, after China's financial liberalization, this role has diminished. Instead, under China's opening-up policy, the banking sector is considered to be the key institution executing state strategies. This is evidenced during China's entry to

WTO. Even after China's entry to the WTO, this sector continued to assist the government's "Going Out" strategy. This role notwithstanding, the government has made efforts to liberalize the banking sector. However, the GFC was a wake-up call to Chinese leaders of the excesses of financial liberalization. Hence, a major impact of the Crisis would have been to slow down the pace of China's financial liberalization.

Even "commercial" state enterprises may be designated as part of "pillar industries" as long as they actively support government strategies. An example is ZTE Corporation, one of the largest firms in the integrated communications manufacturing industry. From the government's perspective, ZTE Corporation spearheads the country's drive to upgrade national technological capability. It cooperates with China's leading state-holding telecommunications services operators such as China Telecom to provide telecommunications products and assists other state enterprises in other industries such as Railway ICT construction. ZTE Corporation has put forth effort in support of the state's global strategy and delivered products and services internationally on a large scale. Moreover, as a state instrument, it has provided assistance to third-world countries. Notably, in terms of state support, there is not much difference between state and non-state enterprises in national pillar industries. ZTE and Huawei benefited almost equally from the country's policies to support the development of national communication industry. Additionally, state and non-state enterprises have to undertake almost the equal role in the national pillar industries' going out process. Again, when ZTE and Huawei contributed to China's economic diplomacy, both of them got the priority to gain the state's support.

7.2.3 State Enterprise Performance

During the early stages of state enterprise reform, state enterprises were criticized for their economic inefficiency and poor profitability, the result of bureaucratic management, monopoly positions, and fulfilling state objectives at any cost. However, as reforms progressed, this poor performance was progressively reversed. Recent studies have reported positive economic performance. Nevertheless, state favor plays an important role in making this happen. In addition, some Chinese state enterprises have made great efforts in technology catchup with the West in line with the state policies and national strategies in the presence of research and development (R&D) funding from the state. As a result, some were even in the forefront of innovation and comparable to firms in developed countries. At the same time, because of the large numbers of state enterprises that exist at various levels of government, non-strategic state enterprises were facing intense competition created as much by other state enterprises as by non-state sectors and foreign firms. The competitive conditions facing state and non-state enterprises were thus converging, a development invariably ignored by critics of China's state enterprises. Thus, government preferential treatment comes with intense competition. With the government's "Going Out" strategy, state enterprises have also gone international and faced even more fierce competition.

In the reform process, different routines have resulted in different corporate entities. As a result, some were successful while some were not. Successful entities might be criticized for being the subjects of state favoritism. The number of successful entities is not known and may be a small proportion of the total, but in terms of size and share of industrial output, they are likely to be significant. The reason for this is that they are typically listed companies and national champions. The results may not permit categorization of the Chinese state enterprise sector as profitable, innovative, and competitive, but the argument that the state sector is inefficient can be decisively rejected. Also, as already indicated, the notion that there is a clear distinction between private and state enterprise also cannot be applied.

For strategic state enterprises, the overall performance was considered good. Nevertheless, it had to be linked to the government policies such as for the banking sector which is to a great extent attributable to transfers of bad assets to Assets Management Companies, loan growth, recapitalization, write-offs, and China's strong economy. Listings on stock exchanges and international competition have mandated these banks to conform to international corporate governance benchmarks. Moreover, the GFC that decimated banks in the West had propelled them up the global rankings. While unfavorable comparisons of these institutions with fully private financial institutions continue to be made and have some merit, the sub-optimal performance of these Chinese banks could be a matter of conscious choice made by the Chinese state, which is prepared to bear the costs to have these banks continue to be instruments of state policies. Efforts to strengthen efficiency of banks represent the state's efforts to minimize these costs. These statements are likely to be true of state enterprises in general, given they are vital instruments of the model of state capitalism that China has embraced.

ZTE Corporation, as a representative of the group of "commercial" state-holding enterprises, has sustained profitability thanks to its ability to take advantage of the government's drive for indigenous innovation. Its record of accomplishment for innovation is reflected by the number of patent applications as well as by its leading role in various products and services technology innovations. By innovating domestically and introducing international technologies, it was recognized and rewarded by the Chinese government and other countries. Facing a domestic competitive environment, the enterprise has used a combination of "insiders" who are familiar with the enterprise and the employment of professional management that has ensured acceptable governance standards. In addition to professionalism in management, links with the state have brought the Corporation a range of benefits from preferential access to business opportunities that have also played an important role in improving its efficiency.

7.3 Into the Future

From the discussion in earlier chapters of this book, summarized in the previous section, it is clear that rather than a piecemeal half-hearted attempt at reform, the government has embarked upon a gradual but systematic process to strengthen state enterprises. This process began with allowing greater managerial responsibility with incentives to reward performance to improve enterprise efficiency, and continued with disposing of loss-making enterprises through sale, privatization, or closure to consolidate the sector. The decision to "grasp the large, releasing the small" then represented further consolidation to ensure state enterprises achieve sufficient scale to compete in the market. Thus reformed, state enterprises would be able to stand on their own feet, but supported no doubt by state contracts directed their way. And when the GFC struck, it was primarily the state enterprise sector that was the beneficiary of the fiscal stimulus.

As China's domestic market competition intensified and corporate margins squeezed, the announcement of the "Going Out" strategy facilitated the internalization of state enterprises to compete in global markets and acquire technology through mergers and acquisitions (M&A). Although not meant for state enterprises alone, these enterprises are more ready to respond to the government's strategy because the support of the state is guaranteed.

This major move has significance far beyond giving state enterprises a leg up in competition. First, it represents the emergence of globally competitive Chinese enterprises that can also match Western and Asian advanced economies' (Japan and Korea) transnational corporations in size. And this is occurring within an international economic order created by the US after World War Two. Indeed, with Chinese state (and non-state) enterprises working in tandem with state banks, they are able to offer terms advanced countries' transnational corporations cannot match. Second, the more projects these enterprises are able to snare, the greater their expertise and competitiveness. Third, because Chinese overseas FDI is frequently bundled with official development assistance, state enterprises have also become the Chinese government's instruments of soft power projection.

State enterprise internationalization is taken a step further with the launch of the BRI in 2013. As already indicated, the BRI, if and when it comes to fruition, has the potential to change the international economic order to China's advantage. This engagement with countries in Eurasia and South and Southeast Asia will mean even greater projection of soft power through Chinese state enterprises. The fact that the bulk of the projects under the BRI consists of infrastructure and construction means Chinese enterprises will not only strengthen their already formidable competitiveness but also earn additional revenues for themselves and the government. And to be implemented over decades, the BRI will entrench the role of state enterprises for years to come.

7.4 Final Thoughts

This book's revisionist narrative has raised questions about the applicability of Western theories to the Chinese context. In this final section, we revisit this issue. The specificity of the Chinese context also raises questions as to whether the Chinese system has relevance for the rest of the world. This is the second issue we take up.

7.4.1 The Applicability of Extant Theories

The specific context of China means that even if partially valid, Western theories of public enterprise must be modified to consider the unique nature of the Chinese state and society. This means many arguments based on prevailing theories must be revisited and judgments revised. For instance, the assumption that state enterprises are run by bureaucrats is invalid because many Chinese state enterprises, especially those listed on stock exchanges, are not run differently from private enterprises, and actually pay better and attract the best talent.

The assumption that state enterprises are monopolies is also invalid. In China, many state enterprises compete fiercely among themselves and with the non-state sector. The result has been management professionalism and innovation capabilities for an increasing number of state enterprises, which contradicts the stereotype perception of uncompetitive state enterprises.

Even more fundamental has been the assumption that the state and private sectors are distinct. For China, the boundaries are not distinct. The non-state sector is not all private, and includes Town and Village Enterprises (TVEs) and collectives. The state sector has ownership interests in enterprises to different degrees, and also been given large doses of private sector management. To make things even more opaque is the de facto separation between ownership and control, with the former declining and the latter in the hands of professional management for the most important enterprises. This is producing, in effect, a system, many characteristics of which are not that different from Western models.

This lack of a clear partition between public and private enterprises has produced apparent paradoxes that Western economic theories, such as agency, public choice, property rights, have been unable to explain. However, while alternative theories, such as economic embeddedness, market socialism, and developmental state, have relevance, they are also not wholly applicable. This is likely because these alternative theories have also been developed to explain situations at variance with what exists in China. The most obvious example is that of the developmental state. Applied initially to Japan and then to Korea, it envisages extensive state intervention to shape the competitiveness of the private sector, which is envisaged to be the driver of economic growth. In China's case, despite expectations by many for a greater private sector role, it remains the state that is in the driver's seat. More fundamentally, none of these theories has accommodated a situation in which the state is at the apex of an orderly hierarchy in which layers of society make up the rest of the pyramid. Nor do any of these models envisage a role of the state as expansive as that of the Chinese state throughout its history.

However, what is indisputable is that with its millennia of history providing lessons for the state's decision-making processes in general and state enterprises in particular, total reliance on economic arguments can provide only partial explanations of the behavior of the Chinese state and its enterprises. For instance, decisions made to keep the banks under state control have as many historical antecedents and strategic priorities as any economic considerations of rationality and efficiency. It may well be that with this complexity, with a wide span of state control though ownership and governance, developing a theoretical framework for all Chinese state enterprises is a herculean task. It is even unclear if such an endeavor is a meaningful pursuit, given the limited applicability of such a framework outside China. A more meaningful academic pursuit may be to seek greater in-depth understanding of key sectors like telecommunications or key areas like innovation that are likely to impact economies well beyond China's shores.

Finally, with Chinese state enterprises given an ever-growing role, any assessment of their role must take into account all dimensions of their role. These would include supporting state strategy, advancing soft power, all non-economic factors. Assessment based on purely economic considerations of efficiency would be totally inadequate.

7.4.2 Lessons for Other Countries

Even if China's historical trajectory cannot be emulated, China's experience has implications for other countries. The Chinese state is still the key agent that cares for the macro economy and its institutions and has a vital role to play in this regard. This is also the case in developing countries where information and other asymmetries create all manner of negative externalities that the state must overcome. However, the China experience shows that the emphasis on ownership may be misplaced The essence of the state's role is control. In this sense, the importance attached to privatization may be exaggerated on the one hand while resistance to its implementation may likewise be overdone on the other.

Second, a number of ways exist to improve performance of state enterprises of all shapes and sizes. One way adopted by China is listing on foreign stock markets. This imposes market discipline on the listed enterprises, while the fact that listing is done overseas removes the ability of the state to interfere in the enterprises' governance. Another is to emulate the Korean example of setting mandatory performance benchmarks as conditions for state favor. Like the Korean model but unlike the Japanese, the state, through its 100% ownership of the largest banks, controls the sources of finance for its state enterprises. While some of the largest state enterprises have put this to good use, in the many breaches of this rule that have been widely reported lies also a negative lesson for other countries, suggesting the difficulty of adopting this model in a relationship-based corporate environment.

Third, the Chinese experience offers lessons on how state enterprises can share if not take the lead in technological innovation. Detailed planning for technological upgrading with a specific role for the state is accompanied by implementation in accordance with these plans. Within this planning framework, Chinese enterprises that innovate are rewarded by various benefits. Although outside the scope of this book, that ability rests on the growing depth of China's human resource pool. Emulating China would require considerable effort toward augmenting human resources.

Finally, lessons from China cannot be learned as long as there is denial that the Chinese model, with state enterprises at its core, represents a viable alternative, at least for China, to the Western democratic, market-driven model. Such denial is rooted in quite extensive contemporary writing on China, especially with the country's ascendancy which is increasingly viewed with alarm.[2] The Chinese state and its enterprises has its own flaws, but just like the liberal order of the West, has lessons for the rest of the world. Those who deny this reality should be reminded of the fact that not too long ago, the Chinese kingdom considered itself superior to and refused to learn from the "barbaric West". The result was "a hundred years of shame" for China. China has moved on since, absorbing from the West what it believed to be beneficial to its own development. But for those in denial, Churchill's admonition: "Those who fail to learn from history are doomed to repeat it" is no less salient today.

Notes

1. Among historians who expressed this view is Cambridge University's Philip Kuhn, while economists who argued for differences between the Chinese and Western economies include Nicholas Lardy and Yukon Huang. Huang's latest book, *Cracking the China Conundrum* (2017), takes a contrarian view of China's growth. Lardy has also dismissed predictions of doom for China that were premised on the country's rapid growth (Woetzel, 2015).

2. A good example is the Leader in the November 9, 2017, The Economist (2017) which lamented the dwindling of America's global influence under Trump. "America", it says, "has long been the greatest force for good in the world, upholding the liberal order and offering an example of how democracy works". This has made it "more tempting for other countries to copy China's autocratic model".

References

The Economist (2017). America's global influence has dwindled under Donald Trump. Retrieved from https://www.economist.com/news/leaders/21731132-presidential-tour-asia-cannot-hide-fact-america-has-turned-inward-hurting-itself?cid1=cust/ednew/n/bl/n/2017119n/owned/n/n/nwl/n/n/ap/79430/n

Huang, Y. (2017). *Cracking the China conundrum: Why conventional economic wisdom is often wrong*. Oxford: Oxford University Press.

Woetzel, J. (2015). 5 reasons why China's economy won't collapse. China Point Blog, McKinsey & Co China. October 14. Retrieved from http://mckinseychina.com/5-reasons-why-chinas-economy-wont-collapse/

Index[1]

[1] Note: Page numbers followed by 'n' refer to notes.

R. Li, K. C. Cheong, *China's State Enterprises*,
https://doi.org/10.1007/978-981-13-0176-6

The manufacturer's authorised representative in the EU is Springer Nature Customer Service Centre GmbH, Europaplatz 3, 69115 Heidelberg, Germany. If you have any concerns regarding our products, please contact ProductSafety@springernature.com

Printed and bound by CPI Group (UK) Ltd, Croydon, CR0 4YY

30/09/2026

02225443-0002